Becoming Interculturally Competent through Education and Training

LANGUAGES FOR INTERCULTURAL COMMUNICATION AND EDUCATION
Series Editors: Michael Byram, *University of Durham, UK* and Alison Phipps, *University of Glasgow, UK*

The overall aim of this series is to publish books which will ultimately inform learning and teaching, but whose primary focus is on the analysis of intercultural relationships, whether in textual form or in people's experience. There will also be books which deal directly with pedagogy, with the relationships between language learning and cultural learning, between processes inside the classroom and beyond. They will all have in common a concern with the relationship between language and culture, and the development of intercultural communicative competence.

Full details of all the books in this series and of all our other publications can be found on http://www.multilingual-matters.com, or by writing to Multilingual Matters, St Nicholas House, 31-34 High Street, Bristol BS1 2AW, UK.

LANGUAGES FOR INTERCULTURAL COMMUNICATION AND EDUCATION
Series Editors: Michael Byram and Alison Phipps

Becoming Interculturally Competent through Education and Training

Edited by
Anwei Feng, Mike Byram and
Mike Fleming

MULTILINGUAL MATTERS
Bristol • Buffalo • Toronto

Library of Congress Cataloging in Publication Data
A catalog record for this book is available from the Library of Congress.
Becoming Interculturally Competent Through Education and Training
Edited by Anwei Feng, Mike Byram and Mike Fleming
Languages for Intercultural Communication and Education: 18
Includes bibliographical references.
1. Multicultural education--Case studies. 2. Intercultural communication--Economic
aspects--Case studies. 3. Diversity in the workplace--Case studies. I. Feng, Anwei.
II. Byram, Michael. III. Fleming, Michael
LC1099.B44 2009
370.117--dc22 2009009452

British Library Cataloguing in Publication Data
A catalogue entry for this book is available from the British Library.

ISBN-13: 978-1-84769-163-7 (hbk)
ISBN-13: 978-1-84769-162-0 (pbk)

Multilingual Matters
UK: St Nicholas House, 31-34 High Street, Bristol BS1 2AW, UK.
USA: UTP, 2250 Military Road, Tonawanda, NY 14150, USA.
Canada: UTP, 5201 Dufferin Street, North York, Ontario M3H 5T8, Canada.

The policy of Multilingual Matters/Channel View Publications is to use papers that are natural, renewable and recyclable products, made from wood grown in sustainable forests. In the manufacturing process of our books, and to further support our policy, preference is given to printers that have FSC and PEFC Chain of Custody certification. The FSC and/or PEFC logos will appear on those books where full certification has been granted to the printer concerned.

Typeset by Techset Composition Ltd., Salisbury, UK
Printed and bound in Great Britain by the Cromwell Press Group

Contents

About the Authors

Catharine Arakelian works as an intercultural educational consultant. She provides courses for the support of international staff in the National Health Service. She is currently developing programmes for non-English speaking staff working with people with dementia in the social care sector. She has a research degree in Migration Studies from Oxford University.

Mike Byram taught French and German in secondary school and adult education. At Durham University since 1980, he has researched the education of linguistic minorities and foreign language education. He is also an Adviser to the Council of Europe Language Policy Division. His most recent book is *From Foreign Language Education to Education for Intercultural Citizenship* (2008).

Anwei Feng is Reader in Education in the College of Education, University of Wales at Bangor. His research interests include intercultural studies, international education and bilingualism and bilingual education. He has recently edited *Living and Studying Abroad* (2006, with M. Byram) and *Bilingual Education in China* (2007).

Claudia Finkbeiner is Professor in the School of Modern Languages, at the University of Kassel, Germany. She is the president of the Association for Language Awareness. Her field is in applied linguistics with a special focus on literacy and culture. She has published widely and her latest publication is (edited with Patricia Schmidt) *The ABC's of Cultural Understanding and Communication: National and International Adaptations* (2006).

Mike Fleming is Professor of Education at the School of Education, Durham University. His research interests include: drama in education, particularly drama as a method in the classroom; art and aesthetic education and intercultural education. He is a member of working group at the Council of Europe developing a policy for languages of education.

Evelyne Glaser is Director of the Centre for Business Languages and Intercultural Communication at Johannes Kepler University Linz, Austria.

She coordinates the department as well as exchange programmes with 55 partner universities. Her teaching and research focus is on intercultural communication and applied business languages.

Manuela Guilherme is a researcher in the fields of Intercultural Education and Intercultural Communication for the Centre for Social Studies, University of Coimbra for whom she planned and coordinated two European projects, namely the INTERACT – Intercultural Active Citizenship Education (2004–2007) and the ICOPROMO – Intercultural Competence for Professional Mobility (2003–2006). She is the author of *Critical Citizens for an Intercultural World: Foreign Language Education as Cultural Politics* (2002) and co-editor of *Critical Pedagogy: Political Approaches to Language and Intercultural Communication* (2004).

Gavin Jack is Reader in Culture and Consumption at the School of Management, University of Leicester, UK. His research interests include: international, cross-cultural and diversity management; postcolonial organisational analysis; communication, language(s) and power in organisations; anthropological and cultural studies of consumption.

Ulla Lundgren is Senior Lecturer in Education at School of Education and Communication, Jönköping University, Sweden. She has a research interest in the intercultural dimension of foreign language education and has taught in teacher education for many years where among other things she has developed and worked in interdisciplinary international courses of Intercultural Encounters.

María del Carmen Méndez García is lecturer in the Departamento de Filología Inglesa, Universidad de Jaén. She researches in areas including cultural dimensions in EFL and intercultural communication. She is the author of *Los aspectos socioculturales en los libros de inglés de Bachillerato* and coauthor of *Foreign Language Teachers and Intercultural Competence*.

Terry Mughan is Professor of International Management at Anglia Ruskin University and has been working in the field of intercultural communication for 15 years. He was the Founding President of the UK section of SIETAR, the leading world professional society for interculturalists. His current research interests centre on the role of culture in knowledge transfer.

Celia Roberts is Professor of Applied Linguistics at King's College London. Her research interests are in intercultural communication, institutional discourse and ethnographic method. Her publications include *Language and Discrimination: A Study of Communication in Mutliethnic Workplaces* (1992), *Achieving Understanding* with Bremer *et al.* (1996), *Talk,*

Work and Institutional Order with Sarangi (1999) and *Language Learners as Ethnographers* with Byram *et al.* (2001).

Barry Tomalin is Director of Cultural Training at International House London, Director of the International House Business Cultural Trainers Certificate and visiting lecturer at the University of Westminster. He is co-author of *The World's Business Cultures and How to Unlock Them* (2007) and *Cultural Awareness* (1995).

Foreword

ADRIAN HOLLIDAY

This new edited collection comes at a time of change which is also reflected in the content of the chapters, which represents a full range of activity, through universities, business and the public sector. The differences and potential tensions between education and training are not new, but the way in which they are addressed here is informed by the need for new thinking and the reassessment of established knowledge about the nature of culture and what happens between people from different backgrounds. Several of the authors refer to the new complexities of interculturality created by globalization and massive movements of people within and from outside Europe and the West. An increased awareness of the possibility of postcolonial and other political factors underlying the cultural realities which divide us is another theme that emerges. There is reference to the connection between cultural misunderstanding and race after the Stephen Lawrence case. It becomes clear in all of the studies in this collection that in every walk of life, in schools, hospitals, small and large businesses, organizations, universities and schools, it has become more than simply a point of efficiency, but a moral imperative to understand and address cultural difference – because the cultural realities of people who are strange to us underpin the very essence of who they are.

The change may be in the complexity of cultural interaction and the moral and political stakes which underlie it. It may not, however, be a change in the nature of culture. There are those who argue that cosmopolitanism has been with us for longer than we have imagined, and that the recent forces of globalization have simply forced us to rediscover the intercultural qualities that have always been there. Recent events such as 9/11 have simply shaken us into new understandings of who we have always been. We have all always been culturally complex; but we are only recently beginning to revisit the broader implications of this possibility. The most important change is therefore in the way in which we look at things.

In almost every chapter in this collection there is therefore a reassessment of the models and methodologies for educating, training and describing, and whether or not we need to have them at all. There has been much discussion in recent times concerning the problems with stereotypes and essentialist models of culture. While varying degrees of cultural fixity are still projected in current thinking there seems to be a strong movement in the direction of seeing them as only starting points from which to explore complexity. Several of the chapters address this and argue either that novices need the security of safe descriptions from which to venture out, or that the participants in courses take agendas into their own hands and overturn them. Is intercultural awareness something new that needs to be introduced to us gradually by means of a carefully staged programme taking us from the known to the unknown, or is it something already deep inside us which needs to be found, expressed and explored?

There is a tendency in the book to move towards the latter view. Indeed, prevalent throughout the book are the accounts of participants, through interviews, logs, blogs, chats, evaluations and acts of resistance – oral, written and observed – which, on the whole seem stronger, richer and more complex than the models and theories given to them. Ironically it is the previously uncharted, the people who come from what has been considered the margins, who have had to struggle most with unrecognized identities, who take more easily to radical exploration, who are perhaps the most competent at cultural exploration and negotiation. The ethnographic turn has done much to influence this liberation of voice; but some distance still has to be travelled before means can be found to unleash it from leading questions and established vocabularies. The need to teach, structure and secure, whether in education or training may inhibit us from allowing ethnographies really to speak for themselves.

It is here that the crux of the conflict between education and training becomes apparent. In some educational settings there is the freedom to allow people to explore and perhaps grow beyond the starting models, theories and questions. On the other side there are an increasing number of instrumentalities which need to be met. It used to be considered that only the business world was the victim of the need to model, predict and secure outcomes. Since Stephen Lawrence and developed sensitivities regarding equality and diversity, public institutions recognise a moral, rather than a business imperative, to ensure not just fair treatment, but fair labelling. Labelling itself has become a difficult and dangerous matter. What some consider the failures of multiculturalism have taught us that placing people within cultural categories or suggesting types of cultural behaviour can result in not the intended celebration of difference but neo-racism. Hence the near impossible dilemma of how to educate (imply-ing open, expansive reflection) while ensuring a tightly ethical and disci-plined outcomes – how to refrain from Othering while defining precisely what it takes to recognise and treat well and efficiently with the foreign and the unfamiliar. The dilemma is caught in the sheer complexity of orga-nizational settings themselves. Several chapters give space to the cultural complexity of locations, where any notion of the 'foreign' culture is sharply mediated by cultures of organizations, cultures of departments, cultures of training, cultures of interviewing, cultures of analysis, cultures of the Other and cultures of politics. At the same time it is very evident in other chapters that training and business needs to be informed by the broader explorations gained in education. Indeed, there is little evidence in this collection of education or training which is not talking to each other.

Canterbury Christ Church University, 2008

Foreword

ANNE DAVIDSON-LUND

In the year 2000 I had a conversation with one of the editors of this anthology, my former doctoral supervisor, Mike Byram, about an international applied research project. Its aim was to develop a framework to measure intercultural competence. Why? In education in the 21st century, for reasons which some authors here address, learning or achievement which cannot be measured, assessed, charted, scaled, is frequently regarded as peripheral. Yet in this same 21st century, the need to foster intercultural understanding has seemingly never been more acute and efforts are being encouraged to foster such understanding throughout the education sector, from the youngest age. The European Union acknowledged the significance of intercultural understanding in declaring 2008 the Year of Intercultural Dialogue. Intercultural dialogue also features extensively in the 2008 policy statement on Multilingualism published by the Commission of the European Communities.

In the Council of Europe *Common European Framework*[1] it was acknowledged that 'all aspects of sociocultural competence are ... very difficult to scale for a number of reasons. ... This is not to say that a scale for sociocultural competence cannot be produced, but that its production is likely to be most successful if it is undertaken in a separate project set up for that purpose'. With funding from the European Commission's Leonardo da Vinci programme, 'INCA' (Intercultural Competence Assessment) was that project. (www.incaproject.org).

The INCA project deliberately transgressed a number of traditional boundaries. From across the European continent it brought together engineering professionals and trainers working in engineering with experts in intercultural competence, in diagnostic testing and assessment, and academics from a range of disciplines: education, behavioural psychology, linguistics, management science and more. Taking among our starting points the Common European Framework and Byram's 'savoirs', we created a draft framework for the assessment of intercultural competence, a linked bank of tests – a rudimentary diagnostic tool – and a portfolio-style record of competence developed for use with the framework and the diagnostic tool, to capture the individual's reflections during the iterative learning and assessment cycle, and to chart any discernible progress.

Many were the conversations at the outset around apparently polarised concepts: 'education' v. 'training'; 'academic' v. 'vocational', 'pure' v. 'applied', 'university' v. 'workplace', 'summative assessment' v. 'formative assessment', 'theoretical learning' v. 'experiential learning', 'deep learning' v. 'surface learning', 'norm referenced' v. 'criterion referenced', 'essentialist' v. 'interpretative', 'bicultural' v. 'generic', 'absolutism' v. 'relativism', and so on. Over the three years of work together we learned that these concepts were in all instances points on a continuous spectrum. Just as in intercultural interaction a third space is created, so we discovered the third spaces which allowed for solutions offering pragmatic compromise between the binary extremes.

Since INCA thinking has moved on. We worked with an exceptionally spartan empirical database. This anthology draws on some of the now rapidly multiplying databases born out of real and researched experience. This is balanced by further developmental theorising, the two richly complementing one another.

We struggled with the means to record and systematise what are inevitably unique individual experiences in such a way that they might offer a third party insight into an individual's past, present and possible future capacities. We tussled with the unwritten rules of power discourse. And at every turn, we looked for means of promoting and recognising the centrality of self-reflection and criticality, the crucial step beyond 'mere' cognitive, affective and behavioural learning.

Each chapter in this anthology seems to take an aspect of this work further. The authors demonstrate clearly the complexity of deriving reliable models for theorising and for applications in education and training, then go on to set out replicable exercises where it has been possible to draw theory and practice together and observe or record altered behaviours, even altered schemata, among learners.

All aspects of the field of intercultural competence development are dynamic. The external world offers a context of unprecedented global mobility and population diversity, the discipline's terminology is evolving still, the parameters for 'intercultural' as a discipline are fluid: one glance at the wide range of bibliographical references for this anthology makes this breadth and dynamism clear. Yet each author here puts down a marker, a record of tangible activity which can help others make progress in developing intercultural competence theory and practice in education and training.

The eclectic mix of articles drawn from a range of disciplines and settings is in the spirit of the original INCA work, refusing to be bound by supposed limits, but rather, offering the reader a range of theoretical, teaching and learning models, described and analysed so as to encourage replication in yet further different circumstances. The 'nation state' element, so prevalent in early work in this field, is here largely relegated at last to its rightful place as one potential factor among many.

Teachers, trainers and course designers from any discipline and fostering learning in any context will find here practical examples to adopt and adapt. Those seeking to engage further with the theory of intercultural competence development will also find much food for thought. Yet the relevance of this anthology is not limited to the arena of formal schooling. For intercultural learning to be effective, Arakelian's chapter illustrates the necessity not only for the 'targeted' learner to engage, but also for all those around to engage as well. Vast as it seems, one might posit that intercultural education offers a framework for every individual to develop the depth and breadth of their understanding and relationships with everyone with whom they interact.

By the end of the INCA project we had realised, and had demonstrated at least for ourselves, that all assessment is formative, whatever its explicitly stated intention. It was also clear to us that intercultural learning is messy, it does not proceed in a neat linear sequence, and may over time deteriorate as well as improve. In this anthology Jack comes closest to describing the inherent conundrum we faced: how does one identify an identity change in the individual, as opposed to a false assessment outcome? One might ask 'does it matter?', provided the learned behaviours, applied consistently, are those of an interculturally competent person.

Bhabha (1990b, in Feng, this volume) states that 'all forms of culture are continually in a process of hybridity'. Could intercultural education then really be about learning to deal positively with constant change in the turbulent world we all inhabit?

Introduction
Education and Training: Becoming Interculturally Competent

MIKE FLEMING

'Becoming interculturally competent: how does it happen?' was the starting point for this book and the chapters it contains, evolving from two symposia in Durham. When we planned the two symposia we wanted to bring together two groups, one from the world of commercial training and the other from academia, in particular from higher and further education. In practice these are not completely discrete sectors but we were aware that a difference of aims, methods and discourse had developed between two approaches largely identified with the two groups, even though both are concerned with the development of intercultural competence. This disparity could be described at the very least as a difference in emphasis but in many cases had led to what seemed to be an unbridgeable chasm. One explanation for the difference is that two groups occupy different worlds, particularly in terms of how they are financed. For example, cross-cultural training when funded by the business sector is likely to have very specific short-term goals and performance indicators. Higher education is funded differently and is not driven in the same way by specific economic imperatives. It is important to acknowledge this difference but our intention was to focus on more conceptual and methodological considerations; the implications of the way the sectors are financed, therefore, have not been the main focus of this book. Given that both groups have similar broad aims – to help people become more interculturally competent – the question 'how does it happen' seemed to be an appropriate starting point for exploring differences.

One possible answer to this question is to claim that people acquire intercultural competence purely through experience, through living abroad, travel, meeting new people and being in different situations. It might be further claimed that to assume that it is possible to acquire intercultural competence in any other way, through for example more formalised learning, amounts to mere self-deception. At the other extreme it may be claimed that intercultural competence is acquired only through participation in systematic programmes of instruction in which objectives are clear and learning is not left to chance. These positions are of course extremes and not in themselves tenable. It is difficult for example to isolate 'pure' experience from experience plus reflection and it may well need contexts of formalised learning to promote that reflection. Similarly, the argument that intercultural competence is only acquired through systematic instruction is self-defeating because it isolates the competence from its application in real situations. These polar positions are extreme formulations but they may be useful as caricatures to highlight some of the arguments that underpin differences in approach. They can also serve to reveal weaknesses in arguments. It is not uncommon, when disputes lend themselves to polarities, for people to position themselves on a more moderate part of the continuum but argue against a more extreme version of the opposing view.

A less extreme account of different approaches to the question 'how does it happen?' is embodied in the contrast between 'education' and 'training'. As indicated, in the intercultural field there has been a perceived gap between those who study the relationships among cultures in universities as an academic discipline, and those who work (either in universities or elsewhere) to prepare people to discharge specific, often vocational tasks in different cultural contexts. Does the gap represent a real difference in either ends, for example, helping people to become interculturally competent, or means, for example, a process of education or training? It is easy to be locked into preconceptions and polar positions induced by the terms 'education' and 'training'. Rather than start with definitions, it is helpful to look at different ways of conceptualising the relationship between the two terms and exploring the consequences of making distinctions in particular ways. For language can trap us prematurely into false choices and narrow preconceptions.

It could be argued that one aspect of being able to decentre is to be able to step outside the confines that language imposes through the terms and concepts to which we have become accustomed. The etymological origin of the two words 'education' and 'training' provides some insight into the way they are often distinguished. According to the Oxford English Dictionary 'education' derives from the Latin word 'educare', meaning to bring up or nurture which in turn is related to 'educere' meaning to lead or bring out. 'Training' is thought to have its origins in the Latin 'trahere', meaning to drag. The contrast between direct and more subtle approaches to achieving learning goals is conveyed in the origins of the words. Education is sometimes conceived as 'a process of acquiring knowledge and understanding', while training is seen as 'a process of bringing someone to an agreed standard of proficiency by practice and instruction'. However, a more comprehensive examination of the relationship between the two concepts other than just considering contrasting definitions reveals a more complex picture.

The Relationship between 'Education' and 'Training'

The relationship between 'training' and 'education' can be conceptualised in different ways. A traditional view, one often found in analytic philosophy of education in the United Kingdom in the 1970s and 1980s and still common among some academics, is to polarise the two concepts and see 'training' in a negative light. As Winch (1995: 315) has said, 'training has a very bad press amongst educators' and is often thought of as the 'antithesis of education'. Likewise, Barrow (1981: 171) referred to the 'widespread feeling that training is something to be embarrassed about' and suggested that education is almost universally thought of as a good thing, while 'training is seen as inherently unattractive, belonging more to the Victorian era than to today'. Training in this formulation is seen as a very authoritarian process involving unquestioning acceptance of instruction with very limited goals, often in the form of the 'master' training his 'apprentice'. It was thought to take place through fairly mindless, repetitive action. In the United Kingdom, for example, there is still some reluctance in universities to employ the term 'training' to describe the pre-service preparation of teachers. The cliché that 'training is something you do to animals not people' is not uncommon.

Within this fairly extreme view, 'training' is a term used to describe mastery of a particular narrow performance, as for example in vocational training for a trade, in which practice is seen as an essential component (Peters, 1966). There is little emphasis on theory, underlying rationale or understanding of principles. Education is in contrast not harnessed to utilitarian purposes but seeks to develop freedom and independence of thought, involving 'the notion of understanding rather than the mere acquisition of specific skills or limited bodies of knowledge' (Magee, 1971: 58). It embodies the goal of developing rational, autonomous individuals and celebrates the intrinsic value of knowledge and understanding. Just as training is seen in a negative light as a reductive concept, so too the acquisition of skills is seen as somewhat inferior to higher more cognitive pursuits. Training has as its goals low-level pursuits, whereas education aims towards more sophisticated taxonomies such as knowledge, comprehension, application, analysis, synthesis and evaluation (Bloom, 1956).

Winch (1995) locates the origin of hostility to the idea of training in Rousseau's *Emile* and the progressive movement. The education that Rousseau envisages for Emile is based as far as possible on nature: 'Childhood has its own methods of seeing, thinking, and feeling. Nothing shows less sense than to try to substitute our own methods for these' (Rousseau, 1911: 54). Rather than subscribe to a doctrine of original sin, it is based on a positive view of human beings who are corrupted by society 'Coming from the hand of the Author (God) of all things everything is good; in the hands of man, everything degenerates' (Rousseau, 1911: 58). Education is therefore seen as a process of natural unfolding rather than as inculcation from outside. Freedom and autonomy were central to Rousseau's view of education and of course that view was taken up by the romantics and later by the child-centred movement. The pedagogic emphasis on discovery and the creation of a genuine desire to learn can be found in *Emile* and is also reflected in later progressive theorists. Education was thus traditionally distinguished from training both on the basis of ends (independent, thinking human beings) and means (student-centred, discovery methods).

However, the view that sets education and training apart as polar opposites in such an extreme way can be seen as flawed because it mistakes training for conditioning and authority for power (Winch, 1995). To dismiss training as mere rule-following, as the mindless acquisition of skills through repetitive practice (which is more appropriately called conditioning) does not do justice to the way the term 'training' is actually used. For example we speak quite comfortably of training in professional contexts (counsellors, lawyers, doctors, surgeons), as well as with reference to other occupations, without in any way diminishing the level of theoretical understanding needed to discharge the role.

An alternative, less extreme and probably more contemporary view does not polarise the concepts but sees training as a necessary and significant part of a broader process of education. It is therefore less hostile to the concept and recognises that an element of training is involved in all sorts of educative processes: learning a language, developing knowledge of mathematics and acquiring understanding of philosophy may involve some training. The concept of training in 'key skills' as part of university studies is a recognition that learners need to be able to communicate, argue, defend a position, use a computer as important facets of what it means to be educated.

In this formulation the relationship between 'training' and 'education' is seen in a hierarchical way: the notions of range and depth tend to apply to the concept of education, whereas training is a narrower concept. Winch (1995: 316) reflects this more balanced position when he suggests that 'it is not part of my aim to argue that training should be a substitute for education, but that it should be recognised as having an important role to play in education'. It is worth noting than many organisations and official publications, for example those produced by the Office for Standards in Education (Ofsted) in the United Kingdom, use both terms 'education' and 'training' in tandem. This could either be mere political expediency or a tacit recognition that to omit one or the other term is to leave out something that is important.

To summarise, a traditional view sees 'education' and 'training' as polar opposites. A second, more moderate, view recognises the value of 'training' but as a sub-component of a wider conception of education. Thus, instead of seeing the concepts as being entirely separate there is a tendency to blur the distinction in the interest of avoiding what is perceived as an unhelpful dualism. This approach is, in part, the aim of this introduction as a means of presenting a vision of the chapters which follow. However, following Carr (1995: 3) in his discussion of the contrast between a liberal and vocational education, highlighting conceptual differences rather than opting immediately for a pragmatic reconciliation may help in the pursuit of a more 'fine-grained picture' of the relationship between the two concepts. In the more general discussions of education and training in analytic philosophy of education it was always 'training' that was subject to critical scrutiny and rarely the concept of 'education' that was questioned. It may be helpful to examine whether there are any formulations of the concept of education that can be criticised or cases in which training ought to take precedence over education. The distinction between the two terms may be further illuminated by focusing on a specific context (in this case the development of intercultural competence) rather than conducting the conceptual discussion in purely general terms.

The Limitations of 'Education'

Peters (1966: 46) saw education as 'initiation into worthwhile activities'. Reference to the limitations of education therefore may be thought to be a contradiction in terms because education is invariably seen as an intrinsic and necessary good. However, such arguments rest on an analytic distinction that is uninformative (in the way the statement that a bachelor is unmarried says very little). Wilson (2002) has challenged the view that education is necessarily a good thing, questioning the assumption that this can be taken for granted on purely logical or conceptual terms. It is worth asking therefore whether certain formulations of the term 'education' have limitations that may go unrecognised because of the normally accepted positive connotations of the term. A liberal education, aiming as it does at knowledge and understanding for its own sake, autonomy and independence of thought has largely positive associations. However, some of the criticisms levelled at liberalism in political philosophy advanced by advocates of communitarianism may also apply to this view of education (Callan & White, 2003). The emphasis on the value of intrinsic knowledge, personal autonomy and individuality may distract from the importance of social purpose, communal learning and culture. Hand (2006) has questioned the appropriateness of autonomy as a general aim of education, largely on the basis of the incoherence of the arguments advanced in its favour: sometimes it is appropriate to act autonomously in society but many times it is not. Of course much here depends on how the term 'autonomy' is being used but it may be that an emphasis on autonomy is less important than the development of social responsibility, the ability to act with others and take part in communal decisions. Cuypers (1992: 15) has also questioned autonomy as a fundamental principle of education arguing the need for children who are 'devoted and sociable people instead of detached observers or cool manipulators'.

A liberal conception of education, it can be argued, is too romantic and optimistic, and insufficiently focused on praxis or theoretically informed 'action in the world'. Intercultural competence in its various conceptions and models implies a commitment not just to knowledge and understanding for its own sake but crucially to forms of behaviour, ideas that are more central to certain conceptions of training. It is of no surprise that writers on interculturalism have adopted the word 'competence' and been drawn to critical pedagogy and criticality.

Of course there are dangers in the kind of view that privileges action over cognition and dismisses liberal education too readily. A liberal approach to education arose in part as a protest against narrow, functional views of education and certain of its tenets associated with independent thinking are clearly desirable. An argument in favour of 'training' can appear suspiciously close to a reactionary call to a return to utility rather than a plea for a more action-orientated, communal and culturally based view of education. It is important therefore to explore some of the limitations of 'training'.

The Limitations of 'Training'

As already demonstrated, many of the limitations of training rest on a particularly narrow view of what is meant by the term. Training in most modern contexts does not mean the mindless acquisition of skills but embraces knowledge, understanding of principles and the ability to adapt to different circumstances. However one feature of training that distinguishes it from education is the specificity of the ends. This is, of course, one of its strengths; faced with the prospect of being operated on by a surgeon who is either well educated or well trained one might well be inclined towards the latter option. However, it is precisely the need for specificity that can make training problematic in intercultural contexts. Weber (2003: 197) has summarised some of the limitations of intercultural training within business, pointing to the fact that many such programmes betray ethnocentric intentions and neglect the dynamic nature of culture and interactions. Jack (this volume) highlights the dangers of presenting national characteristics in fixed categories in ways that essentialise culture, a view also taken up by Feng. A dynamic rather than static view of culture is a theme that runs through several of the chapters. The question of how far culture should be conceived in terms of national characteristics is a contested area. Tomalin's view is that despite the dangers of stereotyping, assigning cultural characteristics (such as high/low context, formal/informal, concise/expressive) provides a concrete basis for business people who plan to work in other countries.

Traditional intercultural training guides or programmes that are largely based on 'what to do' and 'what not to do abroad' are often presented as one-way encounters. They implicitly present the unlikely spectre of a highly critical receiving host, ready to take offence at any deviation in normal behaviour. There is little consideration in such approaches to the possibility of a social encounter based on openness and healthy curiosity aimed at mutual understanding. Of course there is much to be said for finding out about local custom and practice but the snippets of information acquired in formal training are sometimes viewed as a superficial passport to success rather than emanating from a deeper moral basis of respect and consideration.

Such training programmes are often predicated on a misleading view of how human behaviour and cultural practises have meaning. Reducing even fairly simple social encounters to causal explanations in rationalistic, scientific terms is to underestimate their symbolic and expressive import. Understanding meaning relies on intuitive sensitivity in specific contexts not just on generalised, formulaic explanations. Wittgenstein's criticism of

The Golden Bough was precisely because he thought that its author Fraser misunderstood primitive rituals, interpreting them as scientific errors.

> The fundamental reason why Wittgenstein condemns Frazer's explanations is not simply that they are false or at any rate highly contestable. It is simply that they are explanations, and that explanation serves to prevent us seeing what should really attract our attention. (Bouveresse, 2008: 5)

Bouveresse goes on to quote Wittgenstein's (1998) remark, recorded in 1941, that people who are constantly asking 'why?' are like tourists standing in front of a building reading a guide book and failing to see what is there in front of them. Even simple social actions such as greeting someone, buying someone a drink or giving a present are diminished if they are explained in generalised terms. To claim that 'it is part of X culture to give gifts in Y circumstances' may be true but that formula is in danger of stripping away the human warmth and generosity in the act itself. There is a danger in such training approaches of promoting the habit of looking for surface explanations of actions rather than attending to their contextual richness and depth.

Paradoxically it is the inculcation of habit or disposition that is missing from some formulations of what education entails. Placing an emphasis on rational explanation and decision making detracts attention from the need to see intercultural competence displayed in instinctive, automatic reactions to people and situations. Some of the chapters in this volume that place emphasis on identity, affective dimensions and attitudinal change seek a balance to an exclusive emphasis on rational explanation. The use of critical incidents makes some of these points evident in practice. They have developed as a tool both in intercultural training and assessment. However, many of them are formulated on the basis of an implicit erroneous assumption that people always think things through before acting. What is needed is a balance between the superficial formulation embodied in the way training is sometimes conceived and the narrow conception of education that emphasises scientific rationality at the expense of other important aspects of being human.

Surface and Depth

It is for that reason that the position represented by the concepts of 'education' and 'training' as more usefully seen in a dialectical relationship rather than in oppositional or hierarchical terms. It is important not to dispense with 'depth' concepts embodied in the notion of 'education' such as understanding and meaning but it is also important to retain 'surface' notions of action and experiential immediacy. Education's concern with individual autonomy and the value of intrinsic knowledge should not result in a lack of specificity that loses sight of its purpose in making the world a better place.

The terms 'education' and 'training', 'surface' and 'depth' need to be seen in relation to each other to reflect the complex blend of understanding, experience, reflection, involvement and action that is involved in becoming intercultural. Making space for the less appealing concepts of 'surface' and 'training' may appear to be embracing superficiality but that is to miss the point; the point is rather to avoid rarefied and separatist notions of what education involves.

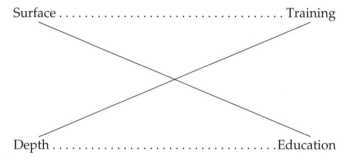

Shusterman highlights the importance of concepts of surface and depth in relation to aesthetic experience:

> Aesthetics surely gains in knowledge the more it digs beneath the sensory surface, yet this metaphoric trajectory of ever increasing depth presents a paradoxical image. On our round earth, the deepest soundings should eventually bring us back to the surface again. (Shusterman, 2002: 2)

This metaphor can be usefully applied to the process of education and training for intercultural competence. Understanding of principles and deep reflection must lead 'back to the surface'.

The concepts of education and training are of course relevant to contrasting views of means as well as ends. A process of education tends to be associated with exposure to academic debate and logical argument. Training in contrast is often seen as more goal, task and behaviour orientated. However, the subtle blend of experience and reflection, instruction, propositional learning, procedural learning, affective engagement, inducements to 'notice' and to 'see things in particular ways' that learning involves, particularly in the process of becoming intercultural, is hardly captured by such crude polarities.

In the context of intercultural understanding the tension and differences between advocates of 'education' and 'training' have not been helpful. This is amply illustrated when attention turns from the universal to the particular when intercultural competence is being developed for specific purposes. The different chapters here illustrate that a polarised conception of the concepts of 'education' and training' does not do justice to the complexity of what is involved in becoming intercultural.

The authors seek in different ways to advance understanding of how it is that people become interculturally competent. The intention is not to pursue the question of definitions and debates but to present reflections on the process and specific realisations of education/training. The chapters also explore ways in which it is possible to conceptualise what is happening. The first three chapters present investigations of intercultural encounters and learning, providing general insights into key ingredients and conceptual frameworks that inform that learning. The remaining chapters present reflections on teaching and learning programmes; the diversity of contexts and purposes (e.g. hospitals, business training, diversity management, teacher education, higher education) makes for a rich collection. It is hoped that the details of course design and concrete, practical teaching activities will be valuable reading for teachers/lecturers/trainers facing similar challenges but equally important is the description of the underlying theoretical rationale that seeks to inform the practice.

Roberts' chapter draws attention to the need to relate two perspectives on culture in the workplace. The organisational culture of an institution needs to be examined alongside perspectives on culture based on ethnicity. As the data from vocational interviews demonstrates, individuals who do not know the rules of the 'game' in the organisational sense may be disadvantaged if culture is conceived too narrowly. The process of becoming interculturally competent needs to be seen in broader terms.

Mughan's chapter draws on data from an empirical project to examine factors that make small and medium businesses successful in international markets. Such factors as prior education, personal attitudes and language skills are antecedents to the development of the necessary intercultural competence. Unlike larger companies such businesses are unlikely to have access to formal training programmes, but the development of intercultural competence can take place through a combination of other factors that the chapter elucidates.

Ryan draws attention to the development of cultural competence as a process of evolving cultural identity. She maps the experience of five women studying on an academic student exchange programme as their cultural awareness and identities developed. The data and analysis highlight the complexity and subtlety of that process; for example an element of stress is seen as a positive ingredient and self-reflection is a key.

Feng continues the theme of challenging binary opposites drawing on and extending theories of 'thirdness' (third space and third place) to explain intercultural development. He presents empirical data to show how students from Confucian heritage cultures studying at British universities develop intercultural competence and negotiate identity. Although they begin with specific views of learning and teaching based on Confucian and Socratic preconceptions, these positions provide a basis for more mediated perceptions.

Jack's account of teaching for critical intercultural learning in a management school in a higher education context illustrates the challenges involved in meeting that goal. Drawing on poststructuralist and postcolonial theories that underpin the course, he emphasises the importance of the highly contextualised, subjective experiences of individuals rather than a form of broad cosmopolitanism. He thus challenges more essentialist approaches to training based on narrow concepts of national culture.

Lundgren's chapter presents details of a pilot course aimed at developing teachers' intercultural understanding as part of a teacher education programme in Sweden. The analysis of the course demonstrates how the deliberate use of self-reflection supported the students' process of developing intercultural competence, helping them to decentre and reflect critically on their own reactions.

Finkbeiner uses the metaphor of a human global positioning system to represent and unravel some of the ingredients necessary for intercultural competence. For example the need to process information from different 'satellites' and to position the self at the centre of the process is highlighted through the analogy. She presents a variety of exercises and concrete examples (such as the use of mind maps, critical incidents and autobiographies) designed to promote meta-cognitive language awareness and cultural awareness.

Arakelian's chapter describes an intercultural skills programme delivered in hospitals in the United Kingdom, consisting of two complementary courses, for new international staff and for their supervisors, team leader and managers. The different tools used (e.g. reflective diaries, role plays using scenarios from real life encounters) are described and explained. As the chapter makes clear, although the course is aimed at developing specific skills and competences, it is conceived in broad holistic educative terms, aimed at both reflection and change in behaviour.

The course described by Guilherme, Glaser and Mendez-Garcia, has been designed to develop intercultural content in the context of diversity management as part of a larger European project. The chapter describes some of the concrete activities, how these were implemented in different countries and the responses from both consultants and participants. For example the initial expectation in one context that the course would offer more concrete guidelines is a challenge likely to face many such course designers. Detailed consideration is given to the underlying learning theories based on experiential and transformative approaches.

Tomalin provides an account of a range of specific experiential activities used for intercultural business training, including card games, simulations and other exercises. As the author himself says in the chapter some of the activities that are based on an assumption of national cultural characteristics might be viewed as simplistic and edging towards stereotyping but his argument is that business trainees need a platform and starting point on which to base further reflective discussion.

References

Barrow, R. (1981) *The Philosophy of Schooling*. Sussex: Wheatsheaf Books.

Bloom, B. (1956) *Taxonomy of Educational Objectives*. London: Longman.

Bouveresse, J. (2008) Wittgenstien's critique of Frazer. In J. Preston (ed.) *Wittgenstein and Reason* (pp. 1–20). Oxford: Blackwell.

Callan, E. and White, J. (2003) Liberalism and communitarianism. In N. Blake, P. Smeyers, R. Smith and P. Standish (eds) *The Blackwell Guide to Philosophy of Education* (pp. 95–109). Oxford: Blackwell.

Carr, D. (1995) The dichotomy of liberal versus vocational education: Some basic conceptual geography. United States *Philosophy of Education Year Book*. On WWW at http://onlinebooks.library.upenn.edu/webbin/serial?id=pes.

Cuypers, S. (1992) Is personal autonomy the first principle of education? *Journal of Philosophy of Education* 26 (1), 5–17.

Hand, M. (2006) Against autonomy as an educational aim. *Oxford Review of Education* 32 (4), 535–550.

Magee, J. (1971) *Philosophical Analysis in Education*. London: Harper and Row.

Peters, R. (1966) *Ethics and Education*. London: Allen and Unwin.

Rousseau, J. (1911) *Emile* (B. Foxley, trans.). London: Dent.

Shusterman, R. (2002) *Surface and Depth*. Ithaca: Cornell University Press.

Weber, S. (2003) A framework for teaching 'intercultural competence'. In G. Alred, M. Byram and M. Fleming (eds) *Intercultural Experience and Education* (pp. 196–212). Clevedon: Mutlilingual Matters.

Wilson, J. (2002) Is education a good thing? *British Journal of Educational Studies* 50 (3), 327–338.

Winch, C. (1995) Education needs training. *Oxford Review of Education* 21 (3), 315–325.

Wittgenstein, L. (1998) *Culture and Value* (2nd edn). Oxford: Blackwell.

Part 1
Investigations of Intercultural Encounters and Learning

Chapter 1

Cultures of Organisations Meet Ethno-linguistic Cultures: Narratives in Job Interviews

CELIA ROBERTS

> *What power, what interests wrap this local world so tight*
> *that it feels like the natural order of things to its inhabitants?*
> Agar, 2000

Introduction

Traditionally, 'culture' has been understood in terms of belonging and otherness as if people felt part of one group and so separate from another. The global flows of people into increasingly multilingual cities have been matched by a critique of this cultural absolutism. In cities such as London 'hyper-diversity' (Kyambi, 2005) requires groups to work and interact together – to find ways of being intercultural, simply to get things done. In these settings, interculturality is not an ideal to be worked towards but a 'muddling through', shot through, often, with stresses and misunderstandings. Besides ethno-linguistic cultural practices there are organisational ones. Recent studies of the discourses of organisations have shown that this 'culture' is changing as the interests of organisations change. This chapter looks at how the British job interview is a prime site for seeing this cultural change at work and its impact on migrants to the UK who are caught between togetherness and otherness as they become more settled in this country. In particular, I focus on narratives in the job interview since they are so central to identity construction. Examples from real job interviews will illustrate narratives at work.

15

Theoretical Backdrop

Interculturality in the context of institutional encounters will be looked at from three perspectives.

(1) Language and cultural processes

Talk cannot be unpicked from cultural processes. As Agar says 'language and culture are wired in together' (Agar, 1991) in what we can call communicative style. Ethnographic evidence suggests how difficult it is for individuals who move to new linguistic/cultural environments to transform some aspects of how they interact, however fluent they become in the new language. Those features of communicative style that are hardest to shift usually have to do with self and stance – how to present yourself to others and how to align with them. Indeed, whether people should try to make these changes is questionable. Sociolinguistic work on how culture enters into talk-in-interaction (Gumperz, 1982, 1996; House *et al.*, 2003) looks at how rhetoric, pragmatics and metapragmatics and politeness convey intention and speaker stance. When speakers take a longer turn to tell a story, give an explanation or make a request, the persuadability of talk depends crucially upon the presentation of self in performance and how information is conveyed to make it processable.

Judgements of speakers by listeners in potentially intercultural situations (not all encounters where people are from different cultural backgrounds are intercultural, Auer (1998)) depend on what linguistic ideologies are brought to the interaction. Whether these are conscious or not (Silverstein, 1992), they legitimate social domination (Bourdieu, 1991) through a process of 'symbolic valorisation' whereby certain languages (or types of language) index a certain moral worth (Blommaert, 2003; Irvine & Gal, 2000; Woolard & Schieffelin, 1994). This 'often makes discrimination on linguistic grounds publicly acceptable whereas corresponding ethnic or racial discrimination is not' (Woolard & Schieffelin, 1994: 62). In gatekeeping settings such as the job interview, the asymmetrical relationship between the interviewer and candidate means that marked cultural differences in communicative style and misunderstandings feed into linguistic ideologies and so shape the context of the interaction.

(2) Institutional and organisational cultures

The interview demands certain modes of speaking and certain ways of being from the candidate. It is governed by institutional discourses that control how the interviewer and candidate can speak (Bourdieu, 1991; Thornborrow, 2002), and which, according to Iedema (2003), have in recent years become increasingly 'textualised' and 'normalised' in the post-bureaucratic organisation. As Auer and Kern (2000) point out, the interview is not solely concerned with the reaching of mutual understanding through communication; it is also the site of the production and maintenance of institutional and social order (Makitalo & Saljo, 2002; Mumby, 1988), where the boundary between those who belong in the organisation and those who do not is repeatedly demarcated. In some cases, the task of communication can become overridden by the task of producing and maintaining institutionality.

In most organisations, control over the interaction and validation of its outcomes is achieved by templates for narrative structure and follow-on questions, and a written record of the interview that is converted into marks out of 10 for each question, and so a mathematically quantifiable result. This type of homogenised, replicable interviewing practice requires the candidate to be *bureaucratically processable* (Iedema, 1999: 63), to construct a simplified, coherent narrative 'version' of themselves (Heydon, 2005; Linde, 1993) which the interviewer can evaluate, score on a scale of 1–10, and note down on a pre-structured form. To meet this requirement may be a particularly difficult task for those candidates 'born abroad' who must 'manipulate their experience – inevitably messy, complicated and confusing – to provide a straight, simple narrative reality' (Jacquemet, 2005: 200; see also Maryns, 2005).

The rules of interview interaction, as with other institutional discourses, are unwritten, and conveyed through subtle *contextualisation cues* and tacit markers of changes in footing and discursive mode (Goffman, 1974; Gumperz, 1982; Scheuer, 2001). As Bourdieu writes, to understand these institutional rules 'also means to understand without having to be told, to read between the lines' (Bourdieu, 1991: 158). In order to overcome this barrier, candidates need *linguistic capital* (Bourdieu, 1991). This capital consists of resources, developed over time, to both present oneself and make appropriate inferences from other speakers in particular institutional settings. It is a process of socialisation rather than something that can be taught. In the context of the job interview, linguistic capital includes the ability to synthesise more institutional modes of discourse – more analytic, discreet and euphemised ways of talking – with more personal modes where the candidate engages with the interviewer as a social being and reveals aspects of their 'real personality'.

As well as the wider institutional discourses that constitute job interviews, there are the cultural imperatives of the 'new work order'

(Gee *et al.*, 1996). Organisations are now flatter, with less hierarchical management and more responsibility given to relatively low-level workers who are expected to manage themselves in self-organising teams. They are also expected to be flexible and manage the kind of organisational change that is now routine in many sectors of industry and public services. This new work order has affected the job interview. It is now organised around 'competency frameworks' and candidates are expected to talk about their team working competence and their capacity to be flexible and so on. In low-level jobs these competencies are assessed through asking candidates to give narratives of their experience.

(3)   Narratives and narrative structure in the job interview

As Makitalo and Saljo (2002) argue, genre-based activities such as interviews invoke specific traditions of argumentation, reasoning and categorisation in order to accomplish interaction and construct certain kinds of subject positions. Over time they form patterns that are sedimented into fixed and obligatory communicative means that become central to the official interview in different organisations, the knowledge it transmits, and the social reality that it constructs. As has been demonstrated by Maryns (2005), Jacquemet (2005) and Kerekes (2003), when an interviewee's narrative responses do not conform to institutional expectations, they are often dismissed as incorrect, untrustworthy or irrelevant.

In one of our major research sites, interviewers were trained to elicit a generic pattern or narrative structure that corresponded closely to the classic narrative structure as set out by Labov (1972: 363). The six-part structure proposed by Labov, and often cited by narrative theorists since, consists of an abstract and orientation, followed by complicating action, evaluation, result or resolution and finally a coda. The extract on 'questioning techniques' shown below is taken from guidelines given to interviewers in one of our research sites, and outlines how a form of Labovian narrative should be elicited by interviewers. It advises that the type of answer interviewers are looking for should, first, lay out the situation described (or the Labovian 'abstract'), then the task that the candidate has to do (orientation), followed by their action (complication), and then the result of the events (resolution, conclusion and evaluation).

In this document, the Labovian narrative structure, which is unconsciously reproduced, is conflated with a deductive argumentative structure – which flags up the main points to be made at the outset of the turn at talk, and follows this with evidence, and then a conclusion that links the claims and evidence. In this model, and in the document quoted

---

Questioning Techniques

Funnelling

The concept of funnelling is that through a series of questions you initially broadly identify a situation and some of the background, and then subsequently drill down into the finer detail. This technique will help you to establish the full story and get better evidence on which to make your decision. Once you have established the situation, you should then try to pin down the details of the candidate's task, including things like the objective, why the task was necessary, who else was involved and so on. It is important to find out what actions **they** took to complete the task; we are interested in their contribution, before asking about the end result. The following diagram illustrates the funnelling concept:

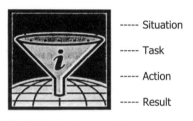

----- Situation

----- Task

----- Action

----- Result

---

above, 'good evidence' is acquired by 'broadly identifying a situation' and then 'drilling down to the finer detail'. Indeed, 'the funnel' image stands in an iconic relationship to the 'standard' narrative and deductive linear rhetorical style. The funnelling model also places a strong emphasis on the need for action and personalisation in narratives – so that the 'task' and 'action', or complication, of the narrative are identified for the interviewer by reference to what that candidate's task and action were. The underlying assumptions evident in the statement that the elicitation of a pre-existing 'full story' provides the best evidence of the candidate's attitudes and suitability have their origins in the field of psychology where, as Bamberg argues, 'interviews are considered to be "disclosures" of the inner world of the interviewee, granting entrance for the trained clinician into mind, soul or emotional interiors of the interviewee' (Bamburg, 2006: 139).

This rhetorical model is presented as culturally normal, universally rational. However, rhetorical features such as deductive argumentation, levels of personalisation and the amount and position of action and contextual information in narrative are culturally specific (Auer, 1998; Chafe,

1980; Fitzgerald, 2003; Tannen, 1989). These factors may mean that even if candidates *are* conforming to the required structure, this may not be recognised by the interviewer. So, there are two potential problems for interviewers' processing of candidates' narratives. First, that the candidates may be employing a 'non-standard' narrative structure. (The extent to which there is a western narrative structure has been challenged but there is no space to discuss this here.) Second, candidates may produce narratives that fit into the Labovian paradigm, but these are misread by interviewers because they are masked by unexpected rhetorical styles.

The conflation of narrative structure and rhetorical features (such as personalisation and deductive argumentation) in the above training diagram may mean that interviewers' prompts and readings of candidate responses could confuse these different requirements. For example, they might not recognise a candidate's description of a complicating action as such, because it is not sufficiently personalised. For example, in our data there were two candidates from former communist states (Poland and Kerala), who repeatedly framed their answers in terms of what 'we' did or what a good worker 'should' do, rather structuring their answer around personal agency. This led to repeated misunderstandings, failure of interviewers to take up their narratives, frequent interruptions of their narratives and rephrasing of questions. These more impersonal discourses are also found in the job interviews with candidates from former East Germany (Auer & Kerns, 2000; Birkner, 2004) and are a good example of ethno-linguistic differences resulting from wider socio-political influences.

Data

The costs to the candidate of (perceived) failure to adhere to the narratological and rhetorical requirements of the interview are illustrated in the extract below, taken from an interview between a Filipino candidate, Luis, and his Nigerian interviewer, Abeni, for a manual delivery post.

Extract One: Luis: Unsuccessful

1	I:	my first question is erm working with people
2	C:	yeah
3	I:	(.) could you give me an {[dc] experie:nce (.) you've had (.) in the past (.)

4		or present (.) where you have worked with a group of different people to
5		achie:ve something (.)}
6	C:	[mhm
7	I:	I] need to know (.)
8	C:	((coughs))
9	I:	the name of the company (.)
10	C:	mhm
11	I:	How many people were involved (.) and your main responsibility
12		[15 seconds of talk deleted]
13	C:	okay (.) g- ah- here my p-ah I have a part-time work as a bar staff as a bar
14		tender? (.) ((sniffs)) in (XXXXXX)
15	I:	mhm
16	C:	i-it's a in a restaurant ba- yeah then (.) ((coughs)) in ah I'm [working
17	I:	what is the] name of the bar?
18	C:	the bar- name of the bar
19	I:	mhm
20	C:	is it's ah the (XXXX) chargrill in-on (XXXXX) (.)
21	I:	(XXXXX) =
22	C:	= (XXXXXX) [yes ma'am
23	I:	(spell that for me)] please? (2) ((looks through application for reference))
24	C:	[that's it
25		[10 seconds of talk deleted]
26	I:	okay (.) now tell me about (XXXXX)
27	C:	oh [yeah
28	I:	how] many people were there?
29	C:	ah we a- I think we are (.) we only eh nine [staff
30	I:	mhm]
31	C:	and two managers (.)
32	I:	okay [and wh-
33	C:	and] working in a restaurant is er- really busy [really
34	I:	what w-] what was your main role your responsibility what did you [do
35		there
36	C:	er- I am a] bar staff as i-

37	I:	bar staff
38	C:	yeah serv[ing-
39	I:	you] sell drinks
40	C:	drinks, cocktails, beverages
41	I:	mhm
42	C:	er at first they said I'm going- just going to serve th- some spirits and
43		some wine, but when eh I-I start the work
44	I:	mhm
45	C:	they just added some addition job to me er- er they giving me th- er
46		serving the cocktail, serving the beverages mm [serving some-
47	I:	serving] what?
48	C:	some-some soda, beverages some coke some (.) coca-cola [and fruit
49	I:	coke] see
50	C:	and some coffee as in cappuccino an-
51	I:	cappuccino coffee [mm
52	C:	yeah] an er an it was er you're gonna say its gonna be a physically
53		demanding because you have to be alert, you have to be always on motivated
54		because [you're in
55	I:	but could you] tell me er what do you like most about working with a team

The preconceptions that the interviewer has about the candidate's ability to provide the requisite narrative structure in this first question of the interview are evident in her slow speech and segmented and stretched vowels (L3–11), and the way in which she specifically demarcates the opening structure and content required. Here, she identifies the name of the company and number of teammates as details, which provide a suitable description of the 'situation', and the candidate's role as the opening of a complication, or 'task-action' section. The interviewer was not so specific in outlining a required response with other interview candidates, who were White British or shared her ethnicity. Abeni also does not tolerate any pauses from Luis, for example his pause after her question in line 5 occasions her further explanations, and when Luis pauses at line 31, she immediately attempts to intervene with a further question. This evidence that Abeni's lack of confidence in Luis leads to the repeated rephrasing of questions is here corroborated by her comment to the researchers that she quickly judged Luis's communication skills to be poor, that she frequently saw Filipino candidates whom she perceived as having poor communication skills and failed them on these grounds. However, the interviewer could not specify much beyond this about what the sources of these communication issues were. This chapter argues that, in this case at least, they could be partly the result of the repeated hyperexplanation (Erickson & Shultz, 1982), hypercueing, closed questions and interruption, which were employed by the interviewer as strategies to encourage the candidate to conform to specific rhetorical requirements.

Abeni repeatedly cuts into Luis' responses in an attempt to make his speech conform to the narrative style she has been trained to look for (L7, L17, L28, L32, L34, L39, L47, L55). She uses interruption, closed questions concerning trivial details and statements summarising his speech; or 'formulations' (Heydon, 2005) as strategies of control and containment. Throughout the interview, the interviewer 'translates' Luis' answers with summary statements before writing them down – thus enacting the process of translating a non-member of the organisation's speech into bureaucratically processable language. Many of these interventions are specifically related to stages in the narrative structure that she has been trained to elicit, and that has become, through routinisation, linked to specific content, and therefore more rigidly demarcated. For example, her prompts at lines 17 and 28 seek to elicit contextual information that establishes the 'situation' – in particular, the name of the employer and the number of people in the team. The prompts at lines 34, 39 and 47 seek to elicit 'task'- or 'action'-related information that demonstrates his particular role and achievements. By line 55, the interviewer is already seeking a 'result' or conclusion in terms of the favoured points of this work, before a narrative about team work has even been elicited. This question cuts into an attempted introduction of a new topic by Luis (L52–54) concerning his understanding of the physical and motivational demands of the job, which the interviewer does not sanction. Luis' contribution here is in fact a recycling of a topic which the interviewer introduced just before the extract shown above, in a segment in which she described the physical demands of the job and asked Luis if he understood these, before cutting into his response. Luis' return to this topic was, however, described by the interviewer as 'irrelevant' in post-interview feedback, as it came in the context of the new topic of team working.

Although Luis' opportunity to contribute here is fairly limited, the effect that the interviewer's interactional behaviour has upon his responses can to some extent be gauged by looking at the answers he does give in the above extract, and comparing this to his talk in other parts of the interview. The narrative opening that he attempts in line 33, 'working in a restaurant is really busy', before being interrupted appears to be a form of orientation, not recognised by the interviewer, which is inductive, depersonalised and non-temporally located – it does not immediately demonstrate how Luis will answer the question of what *his* role was, and begins with detail rather than key points. This opening is interrupted by Abeni in the next line. However, it may be an attempt to introduce the interviewer to an emic perspective on the felt reality for Luis of the restaurant, while subtly suggesting that he has the skills required to cope with a very busy environment.

The suggestion that Luis may be employing a different rhetorical style to that expected by the interviewer is supported by several studies that have found that Chinese and other Asian language speakers narratives tend to use an inductive style in which 'definitive summary statements of main arguments are delayed till the end', as are personal evaluations (Young, 1982: 75), whereas English narratives often use a deductive style (Fitzgerald, 2003). Young also notes that the rhetorical style of the Chinese businessmen's contributions to meetings often does not use preview statements (1982: 80), but rather seeks to establish shared context by giving contextual information. This finding seems to match the evidence from Luis' opener 'working in a restaurant is really busy', and suggests that an abstract that sets one's argument and establishes relevance about one's skills may not be an integral part of the narrative structure that Luis is employing here. Luis' apparent unawareness of the requirements for a particular kind of abstract and orientation, and his hesitation at lines 18 and 29, and new topic introduction at line 52 may indicate a lack of understanding as to why he is being asked for this specific contextual information. The closed questions that Luis is given (for example, 'serving what?' in line 47), sudden topic shifts and interruptions of his talk mean that it is difficult for him to structure responses of more than a few words. In the post-interview, Luis commented that he felt under 'time pressure' in the interview, and was unsure of the purpose of some of the questions.

Feedback from the interviewer to researchers indicated that Luis' hesitations and perceived digressions were taken by the interviewer as not a lack of understanding of rhetorical or narratological requirements, but a lack of general understanding and ability in English – which was given as a reason for his failing the interview. Indeed, the hypercueing shown above does appear to have a detrimental impact on Luis' fluency in English. The interruption by both participants, as they struggle for turns (L33–39), means that focus of energy for both participants comes to be on this interactional work rather than establishing what skills Luis has. Luis is much more fluent in later segments of the interview – where the interviewer does not prompt him. In these segments, he does not hesitate, interrupt himself or struggle for words so much, and is able to structure long and relevant turns at talk without prompting (Roberts & Campbell, 2006). Despite this, the initial interactionally constructed disfluency shown above is viewed by the interviewer as evidence of an internalised, reified and fixed 'level' of English ability which he has (and which is insufficient for the job interview and by implication for the job). When giving feedback to us on the interview, Abeni commented that within the first two minutes of the interview she had judged this level as 'insufficient' and given up on the candidate.

Luis' 'failure' to produce the narrative form expected by the interviewer in this early stage of the interview contributes to negative judgments of both his linguistic ability and personal aptitudes, and his eventual failure. This sequence of talk also has a negative impact on the ensuing interaction – for example, the next question is repeated five times in quick succession due to 'inadequate' responses. The interview's task of justifying and enacting institutional discourse is also evident here in the focus on maintaining institutionalised discourse patterns, which are prioritised over communication, with failed candidates in particular. The closed questions, cut offs and formulations that are used to make Luis' talk processable also prevent him from giving any substantive evidence of his suitability for the job.

A revealing contrast to the extract from Luis' unsuccessful interview given above is provided by a mini-narrative from a successful interview with a White British candidate, Duncan, for the same position. This interview was carried out by a different interviewer, Toby, whose parents were from South Asia, but who was born in the United Kingdom. Duncan produces the correct narrative form, and this is vital to his positioning himself as a potential member of the organisation holding the interview. He successfully displays the kind of tacit knowledge which Linde describes as 'Individual social knowledge [which] includes knowledge about what the identity of the group is, what it means to be a member, and how to be a member', and which, Linde argues, 'is the kind of knowledge which is most frequently and best conveyed through narrative' (2001: 2).

Extract Two: Duncan: A successful candidate and narrative structure

1   **I:**   yeah so (.) what I'm looking for here is an example where you have done a

2   similar kind of like routine (.) repetitive work o- over a period of time

3   **C:**   well one specific agency contract I got it was only four months but it was

4   (.) the complete mind numbingly same repetitive stuff

5   **I:**   okay

6   **C:**   I was working for (XXXXXXXXXX) in Harrow and we were building

7   headsets for helicopter pilots and my specific task was to get this tiny little

8   ear piece and get a little drill and glue that and that was all I had to do (.) all

9   day everyday (.) I didn't have problem with that because I was sat round a

10   table with half a dozen other blokes and you know you don't really need to

11   turn your brain on to do something like that you can just chat and get the job

12   done and it's you got to keep yourself amused for boring jobs it's as simple

13   as that and I absolutely love working outdoors (.) I've got no problem

14   at all with (.) doing the same round day in day out (.) I could quite easily do

15   that

Here, Duncan concisely sets out his narrative in terms of the situation, task, action and result paradigm. He immediately establishes the content, purpose and relevance of his narrative in an abstract (L3 and L4) and gains the interviewer's agreement with this (L5). He then quickly lays out the situation or orientation (L6 and L7), before moving on to 'my specific task' (L7) so directly moving into the 'task' and 'action' sections of the narrative. He sets out his actions in terms of his strategies for dealing with the boredom. Finally, he begins his evaluation and resolution in lines 12–13, moving onto the general, extractable moral of the story 'keeping oneself amused' and 'I've got no problem' – bringing the narrative into the present interaction by relating this experience to the job applied for. As Duncan conforms to both the structural and rhetorical requirements of the interview, his answers are easy for the interview to process and fit into the boxes on his assessment sheet (see Roberts & Campbell, 2005 for a more detailed discussion).

The interviewer's behaviour here contrasts sharply with that of Luis' interviewer. Duncan is allowed the freedom to construct his narrative as he wishes, and is not interrupted or prompted either for particular pieces of information (such as how many people there were in his team), or to move on to a new part of the narrative structure. Duncan's introduction of the new topic of his enjoyment of working outdoors (L13) is sanctioned implicitly by the interviewer's lack of interruption, and was explicitly praised by the interviewer when watching the recording. This contrasts with the dismissal of Luis' introduction of a new topic seen above. This discrepancy may in part be explained by the fact that Duncan is free to structure his own response and is therefore able to explicitly link this new topic to that of repetitive work (in his references to 'doing the same round' 'day in day out', and the fact that he will have no problem keeping himself amused because he 'loves' working outdoors). This ability to 'glide' between topics (Adelsward, 1988) is partly a result of the greater freedom that Duncan has to structure his narrative as he wishes, and the conversational tone of his interview. So, one can see how the relaxation of the institutional requirements and the favouring of a particular narrative style benefits successful candidates such as Duncan, who are able to control their narrative structure, and gain extra credit by turning the talk to their advantage in introductions of new topics such as this.

Duncan uses the opportunity that the narrativisation of his experience offers him to give subtle evaluations of his behaviour which rely on the separation between the narrating self and the narrated self (Linde, 1993). Duncan's 'narrating self' is the self as a storyteller in the present of the interview; the 'narrated self' is the character in the past whom he describes working in a factory and not 'really [having] a problem with that'. By carefully balancing these assessments of the narrated self with narrative 'evidence' and contextual information, Duncan produces a persona that is convincing to the interviewer. The interviewer's assessments of Duncan demonstrate again how stylistic features come to be equated with features of the candidate's personality, which is viewed as fixed, continuous and measurable by the internal logic of the interview. So, Duncan's concise and dynamic response was reflected in the interviewer's assessment of him as efficient, enthusiastic and a man of action. By contrast, Luis' (enforced) hesitance is taken to indicate dithering incompetence and a lack of ability in English.

Conclusions

In interviews with successful candidates, the institutional control and requirements are often relaxed, while in interviews with unsuccessful candidates, these requirements are tightened and made stricter. For example, successful candidates are more often permitted to negotiate questions, and are better able to do so once given the chance. They are allowed to introduce new topics, digress, and to move between more and less formal registers. In short, they are permitted to 'play with the rules of the cultural game', an ability that Bourdieu (1991) cites as the ultimate privilege of successful candidates who are 'sure of [their] cultural identity' and accepted as 'members' of the institution.

By contrast, institutional demands and regulations are made stricter for those who are less successful (Roberts & Campbell, 2006). This is in part because the need for accountability and defensibility is more pressing with candidates who fail, and who therefore may challenge the interview decision, and partly because it is those candidates who transgress the rules of expected behaviour that the interviewer feels the need to control so that a certain level of institutional order is maintained.

The cultural norms of the British job interview are realised in the taken for granted assumptions about what is acceptable narrative structure. How the self should be presented in a gatekeeping encounter relates both to new organisational cultures of the 'entrepreneurial self' and to the wider institutional discourses that control how 'to be' in formal encounters. Ethno-linguistic differences are brought into sharp relief by these organisational and institutional cultures. But the management of differences and difficulties is dealt with largely implicitly. And these problems of communicating feed into linguistic ideologies and unreflected-upon notions of 'poor English'.

'Culture' in the world of work tends to be viewed from two perspectives that are rarely related. When ethnicity and diversity are in focus, 'culture' is taken to be an ethnicised culture of difference and strangeness. The agenda here is about 'fitting in', 'integrating', 'understanding cultural differences' and 'respect'. The other perspective is of organisational culture. This is seen as universal and normative – about similarities not differences. This culture, of which the job interview is a concentrated example, is not seen as an ethnicised culture, fabricated from difference and culturally specific. Rather it is the taken for granted way of doing things, and those who cannot read between the lines are evaluated negatively in terms of poor skills or personality. Becoming intercultural in the workplace, requires a blending of these two perspectives and a realisation that organisational culture is as much an ethnic phenomenon as the 'diversity' culture ascribed to those who are not part of the white majority group.

Implications for Educational Interventions

Putting the microscope on detailed interactions and developing an analytic language for discussing them can raise awareness of issues that are usually not analysed. Training programmes for interviewers, on fair interviewing in a diverse society, and for job seekers from all ethno-linguistic groups, are routine but they rarely examine the detailed discourse processes of the job interview. Rather they focus on generalisations or, in the case of interviewer training, look at individual performance rather than habitual conduct and its cultural base.

Research of the kind described in this chapter, based on real video recordings of job interviews, can be used for educational interventions. Training DVDs, using these data, produce a different genre of training material. Most DVDs are made from simulations or humorous caricatures that exaggerate poor performance and produce a laugh. But DVDs based on real interviews illuminate the complexity of interaction and the subtle ways in which cultural assumptions enter into the interaction. Two such DVDs: *Successful at Selection* (Roberts *et al.*, 2007a) for interviewers and *FAQs: Frequently Asked Questions* (Roberts *et al.*, 2007b) for job seekers have been widely disseminated within the United Kingdom. These DVDs are best used with other 'action learning' type of events or they can be part of more academic courses on intercultural communication.

Transcription conventions

(.)   short pause
(2)   longer pause in seconds
[ ]   overlapping speech
-          cut off word or self-interruption
= =   latching turns
(word)   possible speech but not entirely clear
(xxxx)   unclear word or words or anonymised names
[dc]   slow speech

{ }   indicates the stretch of talk over which a particular feature is
             evident
(( ))   non-verbal communication or action

References

Adelsward, V. (1988) Styles of success: On impression management as a collabora-
tive action in job interviews. *Linkoping Studies in Arts and Science* 23. Linkoping:
University of Linkoping.
Agar, M. (1991) The biculture in bilingual. *Language in Society* 20, 167–181.
Agar M. (2000) *The Professional Stranger*. New York: Academic Press.
Auer, P. (1998) Learning how to play the game: An investigation of role-played job
interviews in East Germany. *Text* 18, 17–38.
Auer, P. and Kern, F. (2000) Three ways of analysing communication between East
and West Germans as intercultural communication. In Di Luzio and S. Günthner
(eds) *Culture in Communication: Analysis of Intercultural Situations*. Amsterdam:
John Benjamins.
Bamburg, M. (2006) Stories: Big or small: Why do we care? *Narrative Inquiry* 16 (1),
139–147.
Birkner, K. (2004) Hegemonic struggles or transfer of knowledge? East and West
Germans in job interviews. *Journal of Language and Politics* 3 (2), 293–322.
Blommaert, J. (2003) A sociolinguistcs of globalisation. *Journal of Sociolinguistics*
7 (4), 607–623.
Bourdieu, P. (1991) *Language & Symbolic Power* (John Thompson, ed.; Gino Raymond
and Matthew Adamson, trans.). Cambridge: Harvard University Press.
Chafe, W. (1980) *The Pear Stories: Vol III Advances in Discourse Analysis*. Norwood
NJ: Ablex.
Erickson, F. and Shultz, J. (1982) *The Counsellor as Gatekeeper*. New York: Ablex.
Fitzgerald, H. (2003) *How Different Are We?* Clevedon: Multilingual Matters.
Gee, J., Hull, G. and Lankshear, C. (1996) *The New Work Order: Behind the Language
of the New Capitalism*. St. Leonards: Allen & Unwin.
Goffman, E. (1974) *Frame Analysis: An Essay on the Organization of Experience*.
Boston, MA: Northeastern University Press.
Gumperz, J. (1982) *Discourse Strategies*. Cambridge: Cambridge University Press.
Gumperz, J. (1996) The linguistic and cultural relativity of conversational infer-
ence. In G. Gumperz and S. Levinson (eds) *Rethinking Linguistic Relativity*.
Cambridge: Cambridge University Press.
Heydon, G. (2005) *The Language of Police Interviewing*. Basingstoke: Palgrave.
House, J., Kasper, G. and Ross, S. (eds) (2003) *Misunderstanding in Social Life:
Discourse Approaches to Problematic Talk* (pp. 227–257). London: Longman.
Iedema, R. (1999) Formalising organizational meaning. *Discourse and Society Special
Issue: Discourse in Organisations* 10 (1).
Iedema, R. (2003) *Discourses of Post-Bureaucratic Organisation*. Amsterdam:
Benjamins.
Irvine, J. and Gal, S. (2000) Language, ideology and linguistic differentiation. In
P. Kroskrity (ed.) *Regimes of Language: Discursive constructions of Authority,
Identity and Power*. New Mexico: School of American Research.

Jacquemet, M. (2005) The registration interview: Restricting refugees' narrative performances. In M. Baynham and A. de Fina (eds) *Dislocations/Relocations: Narratives of Displacement* (pp. 194–216). Manchester: St Jerome.

Kerekes, J. (2003) Distrust: A determining factor in the outcomes of gatekeeping encounters. In J. House, G. Kasper and S. Ross (eds) *Misunderstanding in Social Life: Discourse Approaches to Problematic Talk*. London: Longman.

Kyambi, S. (2005) *Beyond Black and White: Mapping New Immigrant Communities*. IPPR: London.

Labov, W. (1972) *Language in the Inner City*. Philadelphia: University of Pennsylvania Press.

Linde, C. (1993) *Life Stories: The Creation of Coherence*. New York: Oxford University Press.

Makitalo, A. and Saljo, R. (2002) Talk in institutional context and institutional context in talk: Catagories and situational practices. *Text* 22, 57–82.

Maryns K. (2005) Displacement in asylum seekers' narratives. In M. Baynham and A. de Fina (eds) *Dislocations/Relocations: Narratives of Displacement (Encounters)* (pp. 174–193). Manchester: St Jerome Publishing.

Mumby D. (1988) *Communication and Power in Organisations: Discourse, Ideology and Domination*. Norwood, NJ: Ablex.

Roberts, C. and Campbell, S. (2005) Fitting stories into boxes: Rhetorical and textual constraints on candidate's performances in British job interviews. *Journal of Applied Linguistics* 2 (1), 45–73.

Roberts, C. and Campbell, S. (2006) *Talk on Trial: Job Interviews, language and ethnicity*. DWP Report 344. On WWW at http://www.dwp.gov.uk/asd/asd5/rrs2006.asp#talkontrial.

Roberts, C., Campbell, S., Channell, J, Twitchin, J. and Lailey, C, (2007a) *Successful at Selection*. Sheffield: DWP and King's College London.

Roberts, C., Campbell, S., Cooke, M. and Stenhouse, J. (2007b) *FAQs: Frequently Asked Questions*. Leicester: JobCentre Plus and King's College London.

Scheuer, J. (2001) Recontextualisation and communicative styles in job interviews. *Discourse Studies* 3, 223–248.

Silverstein, M. (1992) The uses and utility of ideology: Issues and approaches. *Pragmatics* 2, 311–324.

Tannen, D. (1989) *Repetition, Dialogue and Imagery in Conversational Discourse*. Cambridge: Cambridge University Press.

Thornborrow, J. (2002) *Power Talk: Language and Interaction in Institutional Discourse*. Longman: London.

Woolard, K. and Schieffelin, B. (1994) Language ideology. *American Review of Anthropology* 23, 55–82.

Young, L. (1982) Inscrutability revisited. In J. Gumperz (ed.) *Language and Social Identity* (pp. 72–84). Cambridge University Press.

Chapter 2

Exporting the Multiple Market Experience and the SME Intercultural Paradigm

TERRY MUGHAN

The purpose of this chapter is to examine factors that make small and medium businesses successful in international markets. Unlike larger companies, such businesses are unlikely to have access to formal training programmes, so how is it that intercultural competence develops and what are the influential factors? The chapter draws on an empirical study to provide some answers to that question.

'Learning by doing' is a commonly used term in the business world, particularly among small- and medium-sized enterprises (SMEs) who are typically under-resourced and unable to solve problems by hiring better qualified staff or training up existing ones. How, then, do these companies overcome the many challenges they face when they expand their business operations into international markets whose languages and cultures are unfamiliar?

SMEs are the object of considerable investment in skills and knowledge development for exporting, in the United Kingdom and elsewhere (OECD, 2006). It might be expected, in the global era, that increased and more diverse patterns of trading would lead to significant interest in the ability of SMEs to communicate effectively with an increasingly large range of international clients and partners simultaneously. There has, however, been little progress in the intercultural experience of the SME as most investment in international skills analysis and development has continued to focus on the foreign language needs of the first-time exporter and largely ignores the intercultural dimension. While interest in the intercultural strategies of large firms has increased, our knowledge of SME behaviour and experience remains limited and is currently drawn from two separate schools: one focusing on foreign language acquisition (Hagen, 1999) and the other on international orientation (Manolova & Manev, 2004). This chapter will review the relevant literature and attempt to identify some key characteristics and determinates of intercultural competence in SMEs.

When it comes to assessing the capabilities and competences of SMEs, the figure of the owner-manager (or decision-maker) is key (Knowles *et al.*, 2006). What we know about the small-business intercultural experience can be narrowed down to our knowledge of this role. The process by which firms tend to pursue international opportunities wherever they may be depends on this person. All resource-dependent decisions within the firm are made by him/her and this includes how the firm enters and behaves in foreign markets. This gives rise to a complex, socially constructed picture of foreign cultures perceived through the lens of the decision-maker.

The key factors in determining the exposure of the firm to foreign cultures are the readiness of the owner-manager to explore international opportunities, the availability of resources and the capacity to respond to business opportunities (Ibeh, 2000). Research has shown that as the firm embeds itself in international business, exposure to an increasing number of national markets comes about in an almost random and occasionally hectic fashion (Lloyd-Reason & Mughan, 2003). A firm that has been helped to prepare for a venture into a specific national market (and has undergone language training for that purpose) is subsequently pulled or pushed into other markets with little preparation or planning as a result of opportunity or necessity (what we will call the *multiple market experience*). If the opportunity offers the prospect of increased revenue or an improved market position, most firms will pursue it even if the country concerned, notably its language and culture, is not known to them. In some cases, the owner-manager and the company may find themselves responding to business opportunities in several countries at once, with all that is involved in terms of communication challenges. This may happen while they are undergoing language training for their first foreign market and are just beginning to build their competences and confidence in that market.

At this stage, the company moves from the specific to the generic in its experience and exposure to the *SME intercultural paradigm*. Having begun to explore matters of cultural difference on a bilateral level between the native culture and that of the first target market, they now are exposed to a number of different cultures and need to develop understanding and strategies to communicate and operate multilaterally. A process of learning about cultural differences and intercultural processes takes place here in a non-linear fashion within a tightly constrained framework of business resource and opportunity. It is accompanied by issues of language competence but not limited by them. It embraces the entire personal and business experience of the owner-manager. It may be formal, that is, assisted by training or consulting processes and will almost certainly be experiential and contingent too. The owner-manager will approach and encounter intercultural situations and challenges with a plethora of questions and uncertainties in mind, relating not just to the concepts of difference and communication but also, and probably firstly, to the business opportunity, its financial, logistical, legal and commercial dimensions.

Using qualitative and quantitative data from a study of exporting companies in the east of England, this chapter will endeavour to model the international business development process for the SME and some of the ensuing features of the intercultural learning that takes place. What do exporters experience of foreign cultures and how does their learning about them take place? Is there a relationship between language learning and intercultural adaptability and, on a further level, exporting success?

What Do We Know About Communication Patterns of Exporting Companies?

There is a substantial body of knowledge about the foreign language needs and capabilities of exporting SMEs. This has come about to a large extent because of the investment by governments in language skills as part of the drive to increase exports. It is often asserted, explicitly or implicitly, that success in international trade is dependent on such skills (Knowles *et al.*, 2006). Language training has therefore been a prominent element of government policy in the United Kingdom aimed at increasing international trade (CILT, 2003; Hagen, 1999; Morgan, 1997; Wright & Wright, 1994). Studies have been carried out that attempted to measure the financial consequences to the company and to the economy of the inability to communicate verbally in the target market language (CILT, 2006). Misunderstandings, inability to handle documentation properly, failure to appreciate the importance of good communication with the market and poor relationship management can lead directly and indirectly to lost opportunities and revenue.

In a multilingual European community, other work has sought to establish the respective importance of individual European languages (Hagen, 1993) to inform policy-makers and educational planners. What is the importance of English vis-à-vis French, for example, and how does this map out geographically and across sectors?

The same research has also sought to provide data on a micro-level. What kind of skills, speaking, listening, reading and writing are required by particular companies and employees? Audit tools have been developed to identify the most appropriate learning targets for individual companies and the best way of meeting these needs. The SME language-learning community faces some daunting challenges, however, when one considers some elements of the complexity of global language use (British Chambers of Commerce, 2003). Not least of these is the matter of language selection. The time needed to acquire skills that make a significant difference to one's ability to communicate and build relationships is considerable and can suddenly appear wasted if market opportunities in that location dry up or the firm is attracted to better ones elsewhere. This leads some SMEs (anglocentrics) to focus their exports on the 'old British Empire countries' where English is spoken.

One aspect of the global use of English, which has been described by Wright and Wright (1994) and a number of the interviewees in this study, is that native speakers of other languages learn the English language with great enthusiasm because they see it as a gateway to global business, whereas native English speakers are often at a loss to choose a foreign language that will improve their communication with a large number of their trade partners. Holden (1989) shows that the 4500 (or so) languages in the world may be reduced to six European languages, which are used as official languages in sovereign states throughout the world, these are English: 143 states, French: 49 states, Spanish: 21 states, Portuguese and German: 6 states each and Russian: 5 states (Holden, 1989: 4). He also offers 23 'key languages of marketing value', which may be used as business linguae francae in different parts of the world. These categorisations serve further to confuse the would-be business language-learner, especially as they give no indication as to the size of each language community's population or their respective attractiveness as trading locations.

All these data have a national competitive dimension too. If, say, UK SMEs are less multilingual than their French or German counterparts, the UK government will be urged to invest more in language learning to redress the disadvantage. The data are therefore used to influence government policy at every level from primary to higher education and to justify on-going investment in subsidised language training and associated services for employees of SMEs (Nuffield Foundation, 1998).

Most though not all of this training is offered as part of a broader package including other elements of support for skills and knowledge development in areas such as market research, market visits and export planning (Sear *et al.*, 2001). In the United Kingdom (www.uktradeinvest.gov.uk) and in many other countries, this package is targeted primarily at companies that are seeking to export for the first time, that is, entering their first foreign market. Governments are particularly keen to increase the total number of exporting firms by easing their initial steps into the business process and reducing the psychic distance between home and foreign markets by providing information and skills to communicate where a different language is spoken. Some 'second-market' training and associated support may be offered but it follows from this policy tradition that much of our understanding of the communication patterns of SMEs based on language training is largely derived from companies that are operating in a single foreign market. Our knowledge of established exporters is much more limited because government services are so strongly focused on the first-time exporter (Mughan & Lloyd-Reason, 2006).

This level of understanding of SME operations is therefore primarily defined by the bilateral level of business development. Language learning has in this context been championed on both commercial and political levels as a tool to help companies do business and the nation-state balance its payments. The international success of British businesses is often said to be limited by low levels of skill in the particular languages of trade partners, which has led to a perception that it is necessary for decision-makers to be aware of the languages of all their trade partners (CILT, 2003; Hagen, 1999) and to develop language management strategies (use of translators, interpreters and other intermediaries) to deal with them accordingly.

At the same time, a case is often made that language skills make a contribution to the development of a broader mindset and to better decision-making in the international environment (CILT, 2007). Some consider linguistic ability to be more important as a 'bridge to culture' than as a tool for verbal or written communication (Morgan, 1997; Mughan, 1990; Naor, 1983, cited by Morgan, 1997: 77; Wright & Wright, 1994). There is a lack of consensus as to whether the linguistic skills of export managers lead to international success, but there is a recognition that proficiency in foreign languages may facilitate a 'more general cultural sensitivity' and a reduction in psychological distance from trade partners (Williams & Chaston, 2004: 464).

Clarke (1999) reports on the results of research on export managers who had taken part in an intensive one-week language course in either French or German six months previously. Many of them claimed that their language proficiency had improved and that they were now using these skills while on business abroad. However, they all still rated their skills as 'poor' or 'very poor'. The disadvantages of this type of training were found to be its short duration, in which it was felt not to be possible to become fluent enough to conduct business, and the lack of industry-focused vocabulary that was taught. Participants drew particular attention to the need for a cultural content in these courses as they required a familiarity with the acceptable behaviour during business dealings rather than merely the lexical tools. While these findings may not reflect the full range of results obtainable from professional language providers, they do illustrate some of the key shortcomings of the training model.

The training implications of foreign language use among the decision-makers of successfully internationalised SMEs appear to be bound within competing concerns. The global use of English as a business linguae francae forms an attractive basis for native anglophone decision-makers to disassociate themselves from the necessity of learning foreign languages at all; on the other hand, it is felt to be essential to learn the languages of trade partners in order to succeed in international business. Where language learning is favoured, there is a further split between the use to which linguistic skills should be put: Are decision-makers expected to communicate fluently with overseas trade partners in their own languages (in which case, which language should they learn?) or is the true value of language learning in the intercultural competences that it teaches (Mughan, 1993)? While policy and educational institutions, for example CILT and UKTI, have navigated a route through this dilemma which hinges on the informed management of skills and business channels, the aforementioned resource shortcomings of many SMEs prevent them from exploring or adopting such strategies. These debates are set within the British context of a reluctance to learn languages and widely experienced underachievement when this is attempted.

In summary, therefore, the global (multiple market) business environment presents SMEs and policy-makers with some very tough choices in the area of foreign language acquisition. The multiplicity of languages and cultures that can be encountered simultaneously can never be adequately addressed by companies with such limited resources. A firm exporting to, say, Italy, Dubai and China is rarely going to possess or acquire the language skills or market-specific knowledge necessary to approach all those markets and clients in their own language. While it is acceptable for a German firm to approach those companies in English, it is generally held that for a British firm to do so smacks of complacency and even laziness, particularly if they use English in 'native-speaker mode', that is, with liberal use of idiom and with an unmodified regional accent.

So foreign language skills appear to have both a specific and a generic dimension to them. They both enable direct communication with native speakers of specific countries and promote a mindset that is sensitive to language as a concept and thereby helps communication with others whose language we do not understand. Is it, however, just foreign language awareness that helps successful businesspeople adapt to second and third foreign markets successfully? The languages-based literature on intercultural competence, while rich in methodological discussion (Byram & Fleming, 1998), has a weak empirical base regarding SMEs and suffers from a systemic difficulty in separating intercultural issues from language ones (Hagen, 1998). There is another well-established branch of literature focusing on the SME, one we will call International Orientation, which might help us identify some further critical concepts and processes.

The literature on the influence of personal characteristics of decision-makers on the successful internationalisation of SMEs (Lloyd-Reason & Mughan, 2002; Manolova & Manev, 2004) has its roots in the business and management community and the resource-based school of business theory. It incorporates elements of personal characteristics and resource management practices that can add some value to the language-based perspectives. Personal characteristics of decision-makers include the demographic (such as age, level of education and length of service in the firm), international experience or orientation (such as language skills, periods spent living/working/studying abroad and personal foreign networks) and psychological (such as uncertainty avoidance). Dichtl *et al.* (1990) combined these types in their six-country, cross-cultural study of export success compared with decision-maker characteristics. They found that, generally decision-makers are 'not foreign market-oriented' if they are older, less well educated with lower levels of skill in foreign languages, and if they display a number of psychological barriers to exporting. Morgan (1997) categorised decision-maker characteristics as objective (language skills, experience of having lived abroad, education, previous experience of international trade) and subjective (perceptions of the risks, profitability and costs of internationalisation). He found from the literature that the differences between successful and less successful exporters were often insignificant – for example, there was little difference between in their respective educational attainments and that the greatest differences occurred between exporters (or decision-makers with an interest in exporting) and non-exporters. The former often had superior foreign language skills, had had more experience of living and travelling abroad, had higher levels of education, had more previous exporting experience and were more risk averse. As several review articles demonstrate, there is a considerable lack of consensus as to which of these characteristics really make the difference between successful and less successful attempts to internationalise or indeed between international and non-international firms (Ibeh, 2000).

Manolova and Manev (2004: 51) differentiate at firm level between internally 'controllable' factors (including the psychological management attitudes and perceptions) and internally 'uncontrollable' factors (including the demographic management characteristics) although it seems relevant to argue that 'controllable' attitudes and perceptions might occur as the result of 'uncontrollable' characteristics. These authors find from their survey of the literature that overall it is the internally controllable factors that have greater effect on success than the internally uncontrollable ones.

The work on International Orientation interestingly makes little of foreign language competence and places much more store on knowledge (of people, markets, technical, legal and industrial factors). It thereby embraces a number of concepts and processes that can be equally associated with intercultural competence. Interaction with other cultures, attitudes and psychological adaptability all sit easily with intercultural theory and may indeed form an interdisciplinary bridge between the two.

An attempt to synthesise the two schools of literature was made by Lloyd-Reason and Mughan (2002: 127). The decision-maker in the form of the owner-manager is at the centre of the 'internationalisation web'. This model demonstrates the interlinkages between the psychological and demographic decision-maker characteristics. It shows that 'cultural orientation', derived from a mixture of demographic and psychological characteristics including language skills and education, knowledge of overseas competitors, experience of foreign cultures, foreign networks of friends and colleagues, attitudes to visits abroad and willingness to welcome foreign visitors, influences the behaviour, which leads to successful internationalisation. This model was integrated into a large-scale study that provides evidence of the learning patterns of SME owner-managers involved in international operations.

The Study

Methodology

The Competing Effectively in International Markets (CEIM) study (Lloyd-Reason & Mughan, 2003) investigated the processes of internationalisation of SMEs (defined as companies with up to 249 employees) in the east of England. The aim of the project as a whole was to identify successful aspects of international business planning, resource management, international networking, market intelligence gathering and global skills and knowledge development that could be made transferable across business sectors via training, educational development and recruitment programmes. The distinctive feature of these data is therefore that although most previous studies focused on languages (and/or intercultural awareness) as isolated elements in the performance of decision-makers and business, this one located them as just one part of a portfolio of competences required to undertake international business successfully.

Both qualitative and quantitative data were collected in two phases over a 12-month period from mid-2002 to mid-2003. The first phase consisted of telephone interviews with the decision-makers of 1200 businesses in the east of England. These organisations were mainly SMEs but also included a small 'control group' of much larger companies. The largely qualitative element of the face-to-face interviews with the decision-makers of 74 SMEs in the second phase of this study contributes to a growing trend of qualitative research on the internationalisation of SMEs, which enriches the quantitative techniques that have predominated in previous studies (Bell *et al.*, 2004: 30; Regional Languages Network, n.d., believed 2003; Fillis, 2001).

The respondent firms were categorised into five types according to the levels of international business activity and expertise evident in the first phase of the study (see Lloyd-Reason & Mughan, 2003). This chapter concentrates on the findings from the qualitative study and compares the characteristics of the decision-makers of the firms in the 'successful' group with those in the other four less successful groups.

In phase two of the project, 80 companies were interviewed face-to-face on their own premises between December 2002 and June 2003. The interviews were semi-scripted and were recorded. In all cases the person interviewed was the strategic decision-maker for international activity (usually the owner-manager). Each interview lasted for about one hour.

Building on the findings from the telephone survey, the purpose of the interviews was to obtain detailed data about company behaviour in international markets including managerial traits, skills and knowledge needs, problem-solving and their views of support services. The interview schedule included a mix of open questions where the interviewee was encouraged to talk about their motivations and experiences in their international activities, and closed questions concerning specific problem areas, where they looked for support, and their opinion on the effectiveness of support provided.

The sample of 74 companies was selected from the larger sample on the basis of experience of international trade, skills and knowledge and the application of these to their international activities. The key consideration was not the volume of international activity, but rather how effective the application of their experiential learning had been in contributing to turnover generated from international activities. In this respect, mode of activity, geographical location and sector were regarded as secondary considerations.

General Findings

On the basis of the immediate results from the quantitative study, the interviewed companies could be classified into five bands:

(1) The *Curious* have considered international activity, but have not yet taken action. Little awareness of available support.
(2) The *Frustrated* have previously been, or are occasionally involved in, international activity, but are no longer actively pursuing this, often due to negative experiences. Little awareness of available support.
(3) The *Tentative* have limited experience of international activity, have developed some skills but have some major problems looking for solutions. Some experience of available support.
(4) The *Enthusiastic* have considerable experience of international activity and are keen to grow this side of their business but are experiencing barriers to that growth. Have developed a range of skills but suspect that these need to be developed. Largely aware of available support with some experience, often positive.
(5) The *Successful* have extensive experience of international activity with some major successes. Very high skills and knowledge development, highly aware of available support with a high degree of usage. Often aware of skills and knowledge gaps and very keen to improve effectiveness in international activity.

Findings from the qualitative study included the following:

- Planning (the way in which the firm plans its involvement in foreign markets), manning (the way in which the firm organises or develops its resources to service foreign markets) and scanning (the way in which the firm informs itself about those markets) are the areas of skills and knowledge required by all firms active in international markets.
- The configuration of these skills, and the support designed to improve them, varies according to experience, sector and size.
- All firms benefit from strategic planning and management development.
- All firms benefit from the development of international skills (foreign languages and/or intercultural awareness). It is the development of

these skills within successful firms that facilitates the transfer of business acumen from domestic to international markets.

- Firms new to international activity (the Curious and the Frustrated) are very receptive to, and appreciative of, current support provision.
- Successful firms have specific skills and knowledge needs that are not all met by current provision.
- An intermediate set of firms exists (the Tentative) whose international activity is static, who have lost the initial enthusiasm for international activity and who need tailored support that is not currently available.
- Demand transformation: there is a need to distinguish between what companies want and what they need. They want information, money and solutions to precise, small problems. They need to learn to plan, to broaden their management mindset and build better manning and scanning skills.
- Skills and knowledge development for international trade takes place via the processes of exporting, importing, inward investment and international partnership/alliance arrangements.
- Best practice in firms often emanates from patterns of trading involving one or more of these elements (a multi-modal approach).

Skills and Knowledge

The method adopted was to observe and record the behaviour of companies. We did not seek to squeeze these companies into a pre-conceived analytical framework but attempted to identify the variables in their composition, culture and context which played a significant part in their progress, or otherwise. It was not our aim to locate the companies or their personnel on a scale of educational achievement, although we are able to make some general estimates of the relationship between performance and educational qualification of key personnel.

Our analysis, therefore, focuses on the skills and knowledge required by companies, in normal circumstances, to sustain successful performance in a competitive international trading environment. Some of these skills (general management) may apply equally to the domestic trading environment. Others (foreign language skills) may be specific to the international environment. Very importantly, and this is something to which we will return, we were interested in the nature of the transition from domestic trading to international trading, from a skills and knowledge perspective. Do all companies make this transition successfully, or is there something about the make-up of some that helps them do it better? If there is, could it be language skills or the benefits they convey, in one way or another? What is the inter-relationship between language skills and general management skills? To explore this matter, we will describe the broad skills and knowledge sets we identified among successful decision-makers under the headings of *Planning, Manning* and *Scanning*. We will simultaneously discuss the place of language skills within them.

The Specific Findings on International orientation

Impact of educational experience

Firstly, comparison of the educational experience of the decision-makers shows that the successful group was far more academically qualified. Sixty-four per cent of the successful group had post-compulsory educational qualifications (A levels, and graduate and post-graduate degrees) compared with 37% of the less successful groups. They also had more professional qualifications (16% compared with 6%). The less successful groups had more trade qualifications such as apprenticeships and City & Guilds certificates, at 14% (4% of the successful group), and they were also more likely to have no qualifications at all (12% compared with 4% of the successful group) (Table 2.1).

Table 2.1   Educational qualifications of the decision-makers in the successful and less successful groups

Qualifications	Successful groups (%)	Less successful groups (%)
Graduate/post-graduate qualifications (including BA, BSc, MA, MBA, PhD, etc.)	44	33
All post-compulsory-education academic qualifications (including above qualifications plus A levels)	64	37
Professional qualifications (including 'professional post-graduate', chartered accountant, etc.)	16	6
Trade qualifications (including apprenticeship, City & Guilds, etc.)	4	14
No qualifications	4	12
	N = 25	N = 49

The varied educational experience seen in this study is worthy of attention not only as a differentiating decision-maker characteristic in its own right, but because it also seems to have a large bearing on proficiency in foreign languages (see below).

Objective characteristics

With regard to the objective characteristics, which are considered more indicative of an international orientation, the successful group was found to be more likely to have experience in all the measures used – except that of likelihood to holiday abroad, which was almost equal in the successful and less successful groups. They were four times more likely to have trained abroad, more than twice as likely to have trained foreigners in the United Kingdom and nearly 50% more likely to have worked abroad (Table 2.2).

Decision-makers in the 'successful' group who had worked in a variety of countries in Europe, North America and Asia often also spoke of overseas training experience, whereas those in the less successful groups had rarely trained abroad. A member of the successful group (a software manufacturer), who held a PhD, had worked in Norway and had both worked and trained in the United States. Another member of this group (manufacturer of outdoor lighting equipment) had performed a training function in India and had worked and trained others in Singapore for five years.

These differences in education and international experience of the two groupings of decision-makers demonstrate very clearly the significance of objective characteristics in international success in contradistinction with findings from earlier research (Manolova & Manev, 2004; Morgan, 1997).

Table 2.2 'Objective' international characteristics of the decision-makers in the 'successful' and less successful groups

Characteristics	*'Successful' groups with such experience (%)*	*Less successful groups with such experience (%)*
Holidays abroad	88	90
Trained abroad	32	8
Worked abroad	52	37
Trained foreigners in the UK	56	27
	N = 25	*N = 49*

International attitudes and perceptions

International attitudes and perceptions were tested in the interviews with a number of elements of which the respondents were asked to rate the usefulness in international trade. In this chapter, we compare those in the successful and less successful groups who rate the usefulness of those elements which relate specifically to foreign languages and cultures. While language learning by key staff members is similarly valued by both groups, experience of other aspects of foreign cultures are rated highly by up to and beyond twice as large proportions of the successful group as the less successful (Table 2.3).

The differences in the usefulness in international activity placed on the international activities shows that these subjective, 'controllable' decision-maker characteristics are, like the objective ones, found to be significant in

Table 2.3 'Subjective' international attitudes and perceptions of the decision-makers in the 'successful' and less successful groups

Activity	'Successful' groups rating activity as very useful/ extremely useful (%)	Less successful groups rating activity as very useful/extremely useful (%)
Language learning by key staff members	36	33
Information about foreign markets	80	41
Foreign visits (to clients, potential clients, trade fairs, etc.)	80	51
Knowledge of foreign competitors	64	39
Links to international networks	40	18
Networks of foreign friends and colleagues	56	37
Foreign visitors to the firm	76	47
Experience of other aspects of foreign cultures	52	31
	$N = 25$	$N = 49$

international success in this study. This finding concurs with what has often been observed in previous research (Manolova & Manev, 2004; Morgan, 1997).

Language proficiency levels

Among the interviewed sample of 74, 41 (55%) of the decision-makers were found to have self-reported proficiency at a level of 'poor', 'moderate' or 'very good' in one or more of six languages.[1] The languages cited were all European and had usually been learned at school, with some having been learned at evening classes and a very small number from native-speaking parents (including those decision-makers who were bilingual). French was the most commonly cited language, with German as the second most common. Spanish and Italian were the third and fourth most common with Dutch and Norwegian accounting for one response each (Table 2.4).

The ordering of the languages accords with that found by Hagen (1999). It was addressed by one decision-maker in the less successful groups, who questioned the advisability of this choice:

> In my schooldays we were taught French ... but French was not the ideal language ... it was not a worldwide recognised language .... Possibly Spanish or German would have been better.' (Electronics Manufacturer)

Table 2.4 Language skills by language among this sample

Languages	Number citing	Percentage of whole sample	Percentage of those with language skills
French	34	46	83
German	17	23	41
Spanish	7	10	17
Italian	5	7	12
Dutch	1	1	2
Norwegian	1	1	2
		N = 74	N = 41

Table 2.5 Overall language skills in the 'successful' and less successful groups

Language skills	Successful groups (%)	Less successful groups (%)
Yes	72	47
No	28	49
Unknown	0	4
	$N = 25$	$N = 49$

The decision-makers of the successful group were more likely to have foreign language skills than those in the other groups (Table 2.5).

The successful decision-makers were not only more likely to have language skills, but it was also the only group to be distanced from the CILT (2003, see above) dismissal of school-acquired language skills as being of a low standard by the inclusion of self-reported skills at the 'very good' level. A more academic and professional education such as that received by the decision-makers in the successful group is very clearly associated with increased language skills. However, it would be over-simplistic to assert that the dimension of language skills should therefore be subsumed within that of educational attainment as this association was not the same in all cases. For example, the single decision-maker in the successful group to have undertaken an apprenticeship had language skills, whereas those who were similarly qualified in the less successful groups did not have such skills.

The aggregated data presented above were complemented by full transcripts of interviews. These were conducted on a semi-scripted basis, although each event was unique as an insight into a business organisation with its own history, activity and culture. Some further quotations from the interviews add a rich stream of authenticity to the tables above.

With regard to foreign languages, the awareness of the owner-managers of the complex role they play is evident. While they do not necessarily use them frequently, they realise how their use influences relationships and power. This power may be associated with economic and industrial position and forces that are sometimes not very forward-looking.

> I think it's important to learn languages, however it's not really needed because UK is the centre of world motor sport and everybody speaks English. It's a very bad attitude to have but it's a very British attitude. (An automotive engineering company)

While speaking English is seen generally as an advantage, actual experience indicates that speaking (or even being) English is not an end in itself. Difficulties of all kinds in international business have to be attributed to real causes.

> We had a problem in the United States where the person who set the company up and was appointed Chief Executive was English. No language problem. But he turned out to be a major problem. (A biotech company)

Intercultural competence is manifest in the process of learning to get jobs done. Encountering problems naturally generates forms of creative and schematic thinking. Harnessing this and placing it some kind of intellectual framework represent a challenge to educationalists involved with SMEs.

> More important than currency and exchange rates, probably invoicing and paperwork, less in Western Europe but to Eastern Europe, the Middle East and sub-continent, it is a nightmare. (A packaging company)

The logistics of international business are demanding and companies use all means at their disposal to reduce distance and maintain relationships. Good habits are often in place but need support and refinement.

> Obviously, in Europe it is easier because you can just go for a day if you want to. But Asia is a 2 week trip really. Really you have to trust them to say when they want help. You've got to talk to them regularly once a week. You've got to maintain that kind of relationship. E-mail is very useful too. (A musical equipment company)

As the company becomes more ambitious, it has to bring in the best resources it can afford. Good habits can be encouraged by new blood.

> We were fortunate that the guy who came in and became Managing Director had travelled widely. He was very experienced in travelling most parts of the world. The first thing we decided was where we were going to go and that was the Americas. There were only three of us so we decided to leave Europe for the time being and to fill in the gaps in Africa and South-East Asia too. (A biotech company)

The uniqueness of each company comes out more clearly from the quotations than from the data, as does the special way all the ingredients of international business activity manifest themselves in each case. The ability to identify and draw on resources and to learn from one situation to the next is critical. This ability involves awareness and use of foreign languages, market knowledge and networks across multiple national environments. Intercultural skills of a sort are often in place in SMEs and need shaping, and embedding and show-casing. Where this has been attempted by the author (Mughan & Lloyd-Reason, 2006), the results were very positive.

One firm, which was having difficulty converting an existing but small-scale sales-based relationship into a joint sales and marketing project with a French competitor, uncovered significant knowledge and attitude-based obstacles to French society at large among its workforce. A three-day training programme spread over two months and a programme of business interactions with the French partner uncovered both positive and negative predispositions among the UK team. A mixture of verbal exploration of attitudes, cognitive development of the team and job-based application of key principles led to a more inquiry-based approach towards the French partner based on knowledge of French social and organisational phenomena. Improved tolerance of uncertainty, better sense-making and real business progress ensued, all accompanied by more readiness to verbalise attitudes and adjust them when faced with conflicting data about the behaviour of the French as the cultural framework influencing these was now more comprehensible to the UK team.

Conclusion

We asked at the beginning of this chapter whether we could ascertain what exporters experience of foreign cultures, how their learning about them takes place and whether there is a relationship between language learning and intercultural adaptability and, on a further level, exporting success. Our study identified a group of companies that succeeded in building their business across multiple markets and cultures. This group of companies gives us some answers. They are more likely than not to be led by owner-managers with a formal qualification at a higher education level. They were also likely to have foreign language skills than the less successful companies (although not necessarily using them). Their knowledge of other cultures or business environments is nourished by prior professional experience, trips to other countries and frequent interaction with members of other cultures at home and abroad.

A hybrid, adaptive model of intercultural learning in SMEs emerges from this, one that embraces education, training and experience. The successful owner-managers tend to have a graduate-level educational background and welcome challenges encountered in international operations. At the same time, they lack the organisational resources needed to combat these challenges proactively by means of training, consulting or recruitment.

Using their personal resources, such as personal networks based on prior professional experience and language awareness as a key to relationship-building, they seek to leverage resources inside and outside the firm to achieve outstanding business results in terms of sales, contracts, partnerships and learning. Rather than follow a structured trajectory like the one familiar to a large company, an expatriate manager or the foreign language undergraduate, the SME intercultural paradigm is driven by the business and market imperative. The owner-manager's first duty is to generate the business (sales and contracts) required to sustain profitability and improve productivity. To understand how intercultural learning takes place, we have to acknowledge the primacy of this function and its place in the sequence of action and learning. Few owner-managers will articulate their learning in terms that correspond to or resemble the language of intercultural theory but, when analysed more closely, we see many of the elements of that theory manifested in their behaviour, attitudes and values. There is, however, evidence that this form of experience-based learning is not incompatible with formal, conceptually based intercultural learning.

Acknowledgement

Acknowledgement is made to Deborah Knowles for the data analysis and production of the tables in this chapter.

Note

1. Self-reported levels must be treated with extreme caution. Hagen (1999) concludes that the self-reported skill level of 'can communicate' probably means that respondents can 'put a few sentences together' and 'fluent' means A level standard (Hagen, 1999: 42). However, within a sample the modest may underplay and the confident overplay their actual proficiency (Wright & Wright, 1994). The validity of the findings of this study is enhanced by the possibility of triangulation within individual interviews in qualitative research.

References

Bell, J., Crick, D. and Young, S. (2004) Small firm internationalization and business strategy, an exploratory study of 'knowledge intensive' and 'traditional' manufacturing firms in the UK. *International Small Business Journal* 22 (1), 23–56.

Brinton, S. (2003) Foreword, in CILT, *East of England Language Skills Capacity Audit*. London: CILT the National Centre for Languages, Unnumbered first page.

Byram, M. (1998) *Language Learning in Intercultural Perspective*. Cambridge: Cambridge University Press.

CILT, The National Centre for Languages (2003) *East of England Language Skills Capacity Skills Audit*. London: CILT.

CILT, The National Centre for Languages (2006) *ELAN: Effects on the European Economy of Shortages of Foreign Language Skills in Enterprise*. London: CILT.

CILT, The National Centre for Languages (2007) On WWW at http://www.cilt.org.uk/employment/economic.htm. Accessed 13.12.2007.

Clarke, W.M. (1999) An assessment of foreign language training for English-speaking exporters. *Journal of European Industrial Training* 23 (1), 9–15.

Dana, L-P., Etemad, H. and Wright, R.W. (2004) Back to the future: International entrepreneurship in the new economy. In M.V. Jones and P. Dimitratos (eds) *Emerging Paradigms in International Entrepreneurship* (pp. 19–34). Cheltenham: Edward Elgar.

Dichtl, E., Koeglmayr, H-G. and Mueller, S. (1990) International orientation as a precondition for export success. *Journal of International Business Studies* 21 (1), 23–40.

Fillis, I (2001) Small firm internationalisation: An investigative survey and future research directions. *Management Decision* 39 (9), 767–783.

Hagen, S. (ed.) (1993) Language Skills in European Business. A Regional Survey of Small and Medium-Sized Companies. London: CILT.

Hagen, S. (1998) What does global trade mean for UK languages? In: Where are we going with Languages? London: Nuffield Foundation.

Hagen, S. (ed.) (1999) *Business Communication Across Borders*. London: Languages National Training Organisation in association with Centre for Information on Language Teaching and Research.

Holden, N. (1989) Toward a functional typology of languages of international business. *Language Problems and Language Planning* 13 (1), 1–8.

Ibeh, K. (2000) Internationalisation and the small firm. In S. Carter and D. Jones-Evans (eds) *Enterprise and Small Business, Principles, Practice and Policy* (pp. 435–455). Harlow: Pearson Education.

Knowles, D., Mughan, T. and Lloyd-Reason, L. (2006) Decision-maker characteristics and performance of internationalised SMEs. *Journal of Small Business and Enterprise Development* 13 (4), 620–641.

Lloyd-Reason, L. and Mughan, T. (2002) Strategies for internationalisation within SMEs: The key role of the owner-manager. *Journal of Small Business and Enterprise Development* 9 (2), 120–129.

Lloyd-Reason, L. and Mughan, T. (2003) Competing effectively in international markets: Identifying need, sharing best practice and adding value to the eastern region through skills and knowledge transfer. Final Report. On WWW at www.anglia.ac.uk/cib.

Manolova, T.S. and Manev, I.M. (2004) Internationalization and the performance of the small firm: A review of the empirical literature between 1996 and 2001. In M.V. Jones and P. Dimitratos (eds) *Emerging Paradigms in International Entrepreneurship* (pp. 37–63). Cheltenham: Edward Elgar.

Morgan, R.E. (1997) Decision-making for export strategy. *Small Business and Enterprise Development* 4, 73–85.

Mughan, T. (1990) 1992 – Is languages for export enough? *International Business Communication* 2 (3).

Mughan T. (1993) Culture and management: Crossing the linguistic Rubicon. *Language and Intercultural Training* 13 (1 Spring), pp.19–25.

Mughan, T. and Lloyd-Reason, L. (2006) H.I.G.H.E.R. Final Report (High International Growth and the Higher Education Resource). Project funded by i10. On WWW at www.anglia.ac.uk/cib.

Naor, J. (1983) International orientation of exporters: Some north–south trade implications. In M.R. Czinkota, J.L. Colaiácovo and E.M. Chant (eds) *Export Promotion: The Public and Private Sector Interaction* (pp. 24–261). New York: Praeger. (Cited in Morgan, 1997.)

Nuffield Foundation (1998) Where are we going with languages? Consultative Report of the Nuffield Languages Inquiry London, The Nuffield Foundation.

OECD (2006) Removing barriers to access to international markets. Final Report.

Sear Leigh, Dodd M. and Doole I. (2001) An audit of export services in England: Developing business focus support. The Small Business and Enterprise Development Conference, University of Leicester.

The British Chambers of Commerce (2003) BCC Language Survey - The impact of Foreign Languages on British Business - Part 1: The Qualitative Results, London, The British Chambers of Commerce.

Williams, J. and Chaston, I. (2004) Links between the linguistic ability an international experience of export managers and their export marketing intelligence behaviour. *International Small Business Journal* 22 (5), 463–486.

Wright, C. and Wright, S. (1994) Do languages really matter? The relationship between international business success and a commitment to foreign language use. *Journal of Industrial Affairs* 3 (1), 3–14.

Chapter 3
Evolving Intercultural Identity During Living and Studying Abroad: Five Mexican Women Graduate Students

PHYLLIS RYAN

Introduction

Studying abroad at a university in another country gives graduate students the opportunity to experience many forms of cultural differences in their daily lives. Exchange students are challenged as soon as they arrive in another country to respond to the newness of the environment they find and the differences they will continue to experience during their stay. They may become uneasy with this newness and feel uncertainty as their habitual ways of seeing and thinking are questioned or thrown into disequilibrium. As Ting-Toomey (1999: 8) describes it, 'we must learn to embrace uncertainty and face our vulnerability.' Students often experience considerable stress due to the dissonance between what they have known and what they are experiencing. This type of stress can vary in intensity with each successive experience which, as they accumulate, are constantly present and gradually intensifying. Moreover, the impact of stress on the student and how he or she handles it is significant to intercultural adjustment and general happiness.

Stress does not have to be a negative factor in becoming intercultural, it can serve as an impetus for change, as many researchers in cross-cultural psychology have theorized. Note theories of cross-cultural adaptation, security vulnerability and stress-adaptation growth in which stress is the motivator to encourage a person to adapt to the host environment in order to restore homeostasis (Gudykunst, 2004; Gudykunst & Mody, 2001;

Kim, 1995, 1996; Kim & Gudykunst, 1988; Ting-Toomey, 2005; Wiseman & Koester, 1993, 2001). Kim (2001: 190) explains the changing quality of intercultural identity as the ability to grow beyond one's original culture and encompass a new one while one gains insight into both cultures in the process. Also, note the theory of identity negotiation (INT) (Ting-Toomey, 1999) that follows how stress impacts personal, social and intercultural identities and calls for a state of 'mindfulness'. 'Mindfulness' means the readiness to shift one's frame of reference, the motivation to use new categories to understand cultural, ethnic difference and preparedness to experiment with creative avenues of decision-making and problem solving. Such mental flexibility requires one to rethink assumptions about oneself and the world. During the process it may cause identity dissonance, but it can also lead to personal growth and resourcefulness (Wiseman & Koester, 1993, 2001). The concept of 'mindfulness' comes from Langer's research as appropriate and effective management of desired shared meaning and goals in an intercultural episode. Her model of INT focuses on 'mindfulness' (Langer, 1989, 1997: 49) and includes the importance of integrating knowledge, motivational and skill factors in everyday interaction. Mindful thinking becomes a learned process of cognitive focusing that enables one to experience an 'eye-opening intercultural learning journey in life'.

This chapter explores the evolving nature of intercultural identity in the context of the experience of five women studying in an academic student exchange program and experienced identity change. Such programs offer the opportunity for intercultural experiences that push the individual to respond to the stress created by cultural differences, to confront the differences and, through reflection, gain self insight.

I had the opportunity as an ethnographic researcher to monitor an online internet intercultural communication course that these students were required to take as part of their academic program in applied linguistics. My goal was to follow as an observer the course postings, academic discussions and readings, and to study the interactions of the five women graduate students in an exchange program with each other and the professor, and focus on their final assignment, a mini-ethnographic research project that studied other students in one of their courses (from here on the graduate students will be referred to as 'sojourners' to distinguish them from the students in their mini-ethnography studies). I followed their research about Communities of Practice (COP) (Wenger, 1998) being a primary source of data which it was anticipated would reveal much about the individual and interculturality. This data source including their final written projects and internet postings was not designed for the purpose of talking about one's identity and changes, that is, no one in the course was specifically told to discuss this subject. Instead, what appeared to have surfaced was that the sojourners were moved, in varying degrees and at various moments to comment about the changes in their identities they were experiencing. These comments call attention to the evolving nature of identity change and point to the need to focus future research on this aspect.

Intercultural Communications Course

I would like to pause for a moment to describe briefly the academic context of the intercultural course relevant to understanding its potential for developing interculturality before discussing each of the five women. My attention is directed toward INT and change through interactions in the COPs.

The five women students from a large university in Mexico that offers a masters degree in applied linguistics were active participants in the Mobility Program in Higher Education during a fall semester. They were given a course syllabus online with reading assignments and projects to complete. At the same time they were carrying out their activities, they were interacting with the professor and were in constant daily interaction with all the students in the program in Canada, Mexico and the United States. Much bonding occurred within the group as they posted their observations about daily experiences on the website. The opportunity for camaraderie to develop as they dealt with conflicts and issues inherent in adjusting to new academic cultural environments was very noticeable.

The course design was based on situated learning (i.e. students living in and studying cultures different than their own) and internet technology and included many diverse activities that cross fertilized each other: readings, audiotaped lectures, tasks related to using ethnographic observations and interviews, group discussions, lectures, development of a personal web page, a cultural orientation manual for future exchanges and techniques for studying cultural differences. The final paper for the intercultural course was based on a theme selected by the students related to a mini-ethnography of a COP, and made use of the students in one of their courses at the university where they were studying.

One of the goals was to reach students and teachers of limited actual experience with cultures other than their own and a limited knowledge of basic intercultural communication concepts and strategies for learning about other cultures. The terminal objectives were that participants would have learned and written about aspects of the host culture including a COP in one classroom, practiced and learned critical and ethnographic/ interview research methodology for their study of other cultures, developed greater sensitivity to, awareness of and acceptance of other cultures, become proficient users of web-based technology and become more aware of the shifting nature of their identities.

The components of the course included reading assignments, audio-taped lectures by the instructor, tasks related to ethnographic observations and interviews, group discussion of assigned readings, lectures, development of a personal web page, cultural orientation manual and materials for presenting a COP paper. The goals of the final paper were to acquire learning skills for 'studying cultural differences'. This was to be achieved through learning about a particular COP, while at the same time learning more about themselves. The assignment of the paper was to collect data from one of their classes using interviews and observation, and to plan and write the paper guided by a theme developed by the sojourner.

Central to the readings and discussion was Wenger's (1998) theory of learning based on engagement in social practice as part of the process to become oneself. He proposed a model for his social theory of learning in which learning transforms one's identity through changes that occur with who we are; it involves how members of a community engage with each other, negotiating identities through modes of belonging. In Wenger's words, 'The participants' negotiated response to their situation belongs to them in spite of all the forces and influences beyond their control' (1998: 77).

Wenger makes a connection between identity and a COP in his theoretical model. He states:

> Developing a practice requires the formation of a community whose members can engage with one another and thus acknowledge each other as participants. As a consequence, practice entails the negotiation of ways of being a person in that context. (Wenger, 1998: 149)

He does not imply that negotiation has to be in the form of verbal interaction between its members, rather he stresses that the members deal with it by how they engage in action with one another and how they relate to one another. Essentially, the formation of a COP might be thought of as the negotiation of identities. The parallel between practice and identity is that identity in effect is lived, negotiated, social, a learning process, a nexus and a local–global interplay with an interplay between local and global (Wenger, 1998: 163). Wenger finds that learning transforms one's identity through the changes that occur in who we are (Wenger, 1998: Chap. 3, 227). It is this latter aspect of transforming or changing identity or identities that directly relates to what was observed by the sojourners with their students.

Returning to the course itself, the role of the researcher as a participant observer or non-participant observer in the data collection of the mini-ethnography was not specified in the course syllabus. It could be said that it is not surprising that some of the sojourners expressed aware-ness of their own identity changes with varying degrees of intensity and in different forms in their papers. Two of the five sojourners wrote that the intensity of the experience of living and studying in another country with different cultural groups affected their identities greatly. The other three did not involve their own self-awareness to such a great extent in their papers, rather they were more interested in learning about the students in their multicultural classrooms, and they appeared more detached in dis-cussing their ethnographic data.

Taking this range of differences with respect to self-awareness in the final papers and postings into account with respect to self-awareness, let us look at each of the five students to explore their evolving interculturality guided by three perspectives: first, the intensity of deep self-analysis and mindfulness of self it revealed; second, the stress necessary to prompt INT and change; and third, the openness and willingness to confront differ-ences of others in order to understand cultural differences. Let us focus attention on the INT and change through the sojourners' discussion of their COPs and their personal self-awareness observations.

Five Sojourners

Victoria

> I am not the same person. So. Here I am a graduate student from Mexico thrown into a new country, and into a new set of rules. At the beginning I felt that adaptability was the only thing that was needed to fully take advantage of this program. Little by little, I would figure out the rules and how everything worked.

> Well, no. It did not happen that smoothly. In little time I realized that the task was going to be much more complex than what I imagined. Not only did I need adaptability, but I also needed to understand all the processes that were going on. I was going to take classes in English. I was going to ask for food in English. I was going to go to the movies in English. I was going to go shopping of food in English. English how-ever was not an obstacle. So, why was living abroad that different.

> People asked questions about my nationality, about the language I spoke, about why I was in Portland, and many other cultural things. On the other hand, I had this great opportunity to teach Spanish as a Second Language to a group of people with conditions that I would

never experience in Mexico. Honestly, there were too many things going on.

Victoria's statement in her final paper, *'I am not the same person'*, touches the surface of the process she found herself involved in as she wrote and talked about herself and her experiences during her stay at a university in the United States. She realizes that her identity is changing gradually as she understands more about who she is and what she identifies with as a Mexican. It becomes apparent in her postings and final research paper, the mini-ethnography especially, where she follows Wenger's social theory of learning involving identity change and negotiation. She decided to focus her research on how identity is shaped by the way one positions oneself within a community (Wenger, 1998). More specifically, she planned to position herself at the periphery of the interaction and learning taking place in a course she selected as her COP.

The specific community she selected was her Syntax course at Portland State University. This course was composed of 35 international graduate and undergraduate students along with a professor who was an applied linguist.

Victoria looked at how identity can change using Wenger's definition of a COP as a group of people who are building, negotiating and reinventing engagement, a joint enterprise and a shared repertoire. The students in her COP class were engaging with each other to negotiate meanings and their identities in the process of learning. Her interest was to study aspects of their evolving identities from the perspective of the members of the group.

Victoria explains in her final paper how she would study the learning taking place in her COP:

> In order to understand how learning occurred I will take a look at three important factors: the group of people who are involved in this COP, the time that affects levels of engagement, and the type of arti-facts that were created in order to encourage learning. Time is what limits most of our activities. I knew I was joining this COP for a limited time, however, this fact did not prevent me from sharing and creating histories among the members of my COP. Within time, I was able to connect myself to the aims of this COP and interact with other mem-bers. I participated in study groups and in discussion groups which encouraged and promoted collective learning. Part of this learning was also motivated by several artifacts that we created as a group, and others that we created individually.

Whereas she had first thought that she would remain at the periphery of the group in order to have full access to the engagement taking place among members of the group, she found instead that in engaging with its members she began to move away from the periphery as the semester progressed. In fact, she remarked that she no longer felt like an outsider.

In her final paper, she draws attention to Wenger's concept of 'staying at the periphery', the effect of interaction and one's relation to the community:

> A community of practice with mutual engagement that becomes progressively looser at the periphery, with layers going from core membership to extreme peripherality. The interaction of all these levels affords multiple and diverse opportunities for learning. Different participants contribute and benefit differently, depending on their relations to the enterprise and the community. (Wenger, 1998: 118)

Victoria, as she wrote about her students and their changes, also found herself mirrored in their negotiations and identity changes. She stands out as one of the five Mexican sojourners who recognized that she was self-searching to understand her own changes.

Maria

> It was a self war. I wanted to say something, but I was not sure if I could accomplish it.

Maria entitled her final paper 'The need to communicate orally: Feelings and experiences'. When she arrived at Carleton University in Canada, she was frustrated as she tried to adapt herself to their academic system and the new cultural experiences she was having. Her frustration centered on not being able to communicate well in English. Interrelating with people was very important to her. It is not surprising then that she decided that the topic of her final paper would be communicating orally and that the class for her mini-ethnography project would be her ESL (English as a second language) Teaching Methodology course that included many nationalities: Croatian, Russian, Chinese, Korean, Taiwanese, Turkish, Palestinian, Japanese, Mexican and Canadian. It was a natural setting for studying their oral communication skills in another language using Wenger's social theory of learning in this COP.

She observed three of Wenger's essential elements in the dynamic of a COP: mutual engagement, a joint enterprise and a shared repertoire. 'Mutual engagement' was the source of coherence of the 43 students in her COP as they participated in a 'joint enterprise' with course goals and activities. They created a 'shared repertoire' as they negotiated meaning. She found among the three elements routines, ways of doing things, gestures, symbols and topics and at the same time frustrations, chaos at times and cultural sensitivities. As her paper progresses, it becomes apparent that her personal experiences with frustration, anxiety, uncertainly and fear strongly relate to the emerging theme of the final paper and its extreme importance for her. Being able to communicate orally with others is a primary theme that paralleled her own concerns. This theme emerged from analysis of her interviews, journal reflections, field notes and online postings about the COP.

One of the first experiences she mentioned in her paper was personal. It illustrated how important communicating in English was for her. How different her first experiences were from what she anticipated they would be before arriving in Canada. People did not understand what she said. They often asked her to repeat. On one occasion her coordinator asked her a question, she tried to answer and he immediately told her that he did not understand what she was saying. She wrote in her journal:

> I felt so disappointed and intimidated because he was the coordinator of the program. I didn't want to talk to him. I was afraid he wouldn't understand what I was saying. I didn't want to see him.

She experienced more disappointment and feelings of intimidation when an Iranian student looked at her in a funny way while she was talking to her. Maria noticed it happened again when an Iranian looked at her in a funny way while she was talking to her. Maria mused:

> I thought .... When is this gonna be over? How come people cannot understand me? People in the States understood me by the end of my exchange year [reference to a previous junior year high school exchange program].

> I just assumed that I wasn't speaking right, so I began to be afraid of speaking. It was a self war. I wanted to say something, but I was not sure if I would accomplish it.

As the semester passed and she continued to observe the members of her COP, she realized the frustrations and sensitivities the students were having were not necessarily related to speaking a second language. When Maria first noticed Liliana, a student in Maria's study, Maria automatically assumed that Liliana would not have problems speaking since she was a native speaker of the language, but Liliana had a hard time interacting with new people. It appeared her problems were related to her lack of confidence in building relationships with others in her COP.

> I purposely don't go to class ten or fifteen minutes earlier so I just don't have to talk to people ... I don't know what to say to them and when I do go, I'll just sit there, read something to look busy. (Liliana's interview reported in the final paper of Maria, November 10, 2005)

Maria, as the author of her final project, allowed herself to appear in the discussion quite frequently in her paper. She appeared to find aspects of herself in the participants of her study. In fact, she questioned whether others had feelings similar to hers:

> I was feeling incompetent in class. I felt that I was not able to cope with it. I blamed it all on the language. I wanted to understand every single word. I was not sure if other people were facing the same problems.

Being able to communicate orally was a strong personality trait of Maria. As she said:

> It is something I needed to be me. Lacking this ability made me feel insecure, and this obviously affected my interaction in the class.

The following excerpt posted in Maria's online journal illustrates the strength of her feelings:

> I was feeling incompetent about the whole conversation setting. I was afraid of introducing myself to others, I was afraid of encountering different accents, I was intimidated by the sarcastic style, I was worried about what to say and what to talk about. I don't know these people. I feel uncomfortable. Who should I talk to? Should I introduce myself? I don't know. People look young. People look different from me. I don't want to talk.

Others, such as Liliana, confirmed when she interviewed them that they had similar problems. Even though Liliana was very talkative in class and a native speaker of English, she was not someone Maria would have imagined having a fear of communicating orally. Maria discovered quickly that Liliana felt incompetent in class, that she had a hard time knowing how to start a conversation. Maria shared with her a lack of confidence and a fear of communicating:

> Liliana and I share a similar need to speak in class. It is the way we are used to learning in class. We learn by participating orally. Liliana

is a native English speaker, so she succeeds in her oral participation in class. I am not a native English speaker. I try hard to succeed in it. We both share a similar fear: we don't know how to engage in conversations. I am afraid of pronouncing words wrong. She is afraid of relating with others on a personal level. We have difficulties finding topics to talk about with others. Oral communication requires common understanding. It is an exchange of thoughts, ideas, emotions, feelings and needs. My handicap was the language skills. Liliana's handicap was the ability to build something in common with new people.

In her journal Maria wrote that participation in the COP is tied to asking questions:

Part of the oral communication scene in class – besides listening – was asking questions. Students will speak up in class when they have a question about an issue, but they will also speak up to add a comment to the topic studied in class. As a Mexican student I was used to participating in class orally. In my high school in Mexico, it was very important to talk. You will earn points when answering correctly. I think my school background had a great influence on me. Learning patterns that repeat year after a year are built in my mind. In this vein, I see talkative students with respect and I categorize them as good students.

Maria interviewed Beta who said that when you ask questions at this university in Canada you raise your hand. However, he also said that there are some students who will ask questions of the teachers as they are presenting a class without raising their hands:

[you] raise your hand, she's finished, she nods in your direction … you go ahead. She acknowledges your question. It drives me crazy a little bit [that] students will ask questions to other students without raising hands.

Maria also noticed another student, Micaela who did not ask questions, thinking it is not polite to interrupt the teacher without raising her hand and waiting for the teacher to acknowledge her question: Should students who like to participate orally have problems facing the politeness rule? They forget that the lecture is a class, and they usually feel it is a one-on-one conversation. Liliana, for example, said, 'Yes, I interrupt the teacher. I ask questions as soon as they pop in my head'. Yet, Liliana and Micaela both agree that interrupting the teacher is not appropriate student behavior.

However, an interesting finding is the way the students who interrupt the teacher see themselves. In this case, the students who interrupt the teacher do not think they are being rude. They just follow the communication pattern of one speaker and one listener. That is, they forget about the others and think the communication is taking place between themselves and the teacher as a single dialogue. Liliana said: '[Teachers] say it's not just me and the teachers. But, the more I get into it. It's me and the teacher' (Interview with Liliana, November 10, 2005). Janet, another student interviewed, expressed similar sentiments during another interview: 'Sometimes I do [interrupt the teacher] I forget I am in the class. I feel it is only the teacher and me. Teachers don't like it, but I don't mean to interrupt the teachers' (Interview with Janet [from the final paper], October 20, 2005).

Elizabeth, Graciela and Isabel, the other students from Mexico, did not tend to reflect upon their own personal experiences or their identities in their final papers as had Victoria and Maria. Instead, they tended to keep their discussion of their data close to the theme of the social theory of learning. Participation and non-participation were central to interaction among members of the COP. All agreed that it was essential to engagement in social practice and contributed greatly to identity awareness. Elizabeth followed participation as an important factor involved with identities. She analyzed considerably the nature of her COP and its multicultural members. Her class was like Maria's in its diversity.

Elizabeth

Elizabeth attended courses at the University of Manitoba in Canada. Her perceptions of others grew during the semester and could be seen in her reactions to differences. There were times in her postings and final paper when she expressed amazement about the students and professor of her COP course. She recognized cultural traditions in her multicultural class that involved students from Russia, South Korea, Palestine, Africa (Sierra Leone), the United States and Mexico. She reflected in her final paper that once she was amazed by the professor's awareness of and respect for the cultural traditions of one of the students. She wrote:

Today my classmate from Kuwait is fasting because she is celebrating Ramadan; the professor was aware of that and just at the hour that her fasting ends the professor made a break so that she could eat something. It was six and thirty something minutes. I get amazed because of my professor's awareness and my friend appreciates it.

Elizabeth included herself as a member of the COP she was studying and noticed that even though they were a small group they had created a dynamic among themselves to be comfortable participating:

> Today we didn't work in groups again and I saw everybody complaining about that, it is really weird because we are just eight people and we like to work in more little groups, I think that we were getting used to it and that we feel comfortable because everybody can participate without feeling that you are judged.

As she was becoming more aware of cultural differences, by the end of the semester she drew connections between her own life and the impact of her multicultural class. These connections were made by seeing the students through the eyes of others and listening through their ears:

> This experience in my COP gave me the opportunity to see through the eyes of others and listen through the ears of multicultural classmates how citizenship, culture, and curriculum are seen and implemented in the educational systems of their countries ... From my experience, becoming a COP member, having a 'unique place', and participating with others result in a better comprehension of the content of the course. It permits members to make practical connections with their own lives and cultures, allowing them to take advantage of previous knowledge in achieving learning goals.

She also became aware of the importance of personality. In several observations Elizabeth noted students being aware that they wanted to participate rather than participate just to receive a grade:

> Yeah! So I feel that when, when I participate I feel really I want to participate not because I want to show that I am talking or I am participating.

> Ah ... I am, I am not one of the people that speak a lot in the class, but that doesn't mean that I am not listening, that I am not understanding. Ahm ... my participation I think, to date, has been primarily listening and if I have something to share that someone hasn't already mentioned I will, I will ... share it.

Elizabeth could relate to how significant participation is to Wenger's COP: 'our relations to communities of practice thus involve both participation and non-participation, and our identities are shaped by combinations of the two' (p. 164). Class organization, for instance, promoted a sense of security and participation by the COPs members either in small groups or in full class discussions.

Elizabeth noticed in her observations a tendency for the class to be teacher-centered and although the teacher tended to direct participation, students also showed their own dynamic through the multicultural nature of the group.

Graciela

Being able to adjust to a new environment and culture was the most important phase of my experience abroad. I used to think that adjusting to a host culture, place and university was like any other transition, like moving to a new house or starting in a new job. However, as soon as I had an intercultural experience for the first time, I encountered meaningful difference. (Graciela's journal)

The 'meaningful differences' Graciela found in adjusting to her new environment were part of the experience of being in COPs. She recognized that she belonged at George State University to several at any given time: one COP as a graduate student taking courses, one as a Spanish teacher with classes, and one as a participant in classes such as Yoga and Tai Chi.

As with Maria and Elizabeth she selected an international/multicultural COP. One day when the topic of discussion was compliments, she followed the shared and negotiated meaning of compliments in their discussion to observe the distinct ways cultural backgrounds and knowledge interact. She wrote in her paper:

Our department has a lot of international students so every class that I've taken has had more than one international student in it and I think this class is particularly interesting because we have a lot of international students from China, Japan, Vietnam, Mexico, Brazil, but I think that this is really a great class because we're talking about cultural related issues, so it nice to be able to say. Okay, you are from Mexico, what do you think?

Also, Graciela, like Maria and Elizabeth, had great interest in becoming familiar with the new culture(s) she was experiencing. The three women recognized that they were experiencing elements of a new culture at the surface level of language, ways of communication and behaviors and that they needed to search in depth in order to connect these elements with values, norms and belief systems. Graciela was very attentive to the behaviors she observed. She singled out the raising of one's hand in class to be recognized by the teacher and be allowed to talk:

What I've noticed is that there are few people who would raise the hand and then if Dr. P doesn't see them, she just starts talking. They'll just put the hand down and they don't ever get to speak and they are like they seemed to be very timid and they never get to say anything.

Graciela was fascinated with the different perspectives, points of view and perceptions that surfaced in this multicultural class. She wrote, and at the same time was surprised, that they were completely different from what she would have imagined:

> It is more interesting because it's not only different points of view but there's a completely different perspective with the multicultural class so when you hear another point of view you say, 'I've never thought of it that way' that's, you know, just completely different than what I ever imagine.

Graciela noticed that the professor who was from England often brought chocolates to class. She said that she had no idea if it was a cultural thing or just an expression of personality.

> I've never seen a professor do that in college. I like it, I like it a lot. I think that's so sweet and I think, my gosh, how much money is she spending every week on these candies? I've no idea why she does it, but it doesn't bother me (laughs).

While Elizabeth and Graciela were fascinated with the cultural differences they were learning about their COPs, Elizabeth found that she could decenter herself from her own cultural background to see through the eyes of her classmates. These women individually were amazed and surprised by meaningful differences and by the negotiation they observed among members of their COPs.

Isabel

Isabel studied at Georgia State University (USA) and chose one of her linguistics courses for her mini-ethnography. An incident occurred which caused her to study the theme of individualism versus collaborative learning. In her COP she began to realize that the students were carrying out activities that implied teamwork, but it did not appear to be occurring. Despite the fact that they were divided into three groups, she observed that most of the members kept working on their own. At first Isabel thought perhaps working as individuals connected with their activities of analyzing data using a computer program. However, as she continued to observe she saw students working alone for the rest of the class. Since she herself was a member of the class, she was confused at first about why her partner did not want to work with her nor did the other classmates. Isabel had expected to work as she would have, had she been in Mexico, that is, in teams in cooperation with others.

Isabel's first reaction to the group raised the question of how they were engaging with each other in the joint enterprise. How were they creating in the COP if they were spending most of the class at the computer working individually? She thought about how her COP was a community made up of people not only from different countries, but also people with different training and background and ways to interacting. She thought about the use of the computer to connect all the participants for more than one hour. Every member of the class, when they arrived in the computer laboratory, without waiting for instructions, immediately logged onto the computers and began to run the program. It was a practice at the beginning of the course that became a routine:

> We just do it because we know we use it every class. Then, we don't have to ask to the professor if we are going to use it that day in class because we already know that it is part of the routine every time we are in the lab. There's also another practice: once we get into the lab, we go directly to the professor desk and take the handouts she prepares for every class. We get specific vocabulary we use in class when running programs. Such as, Frequency, Collocations, TI Score, MI score, etc. Those are words that we were not familiar with at the beginning of the course, but after, when we had a conversation in the lab we use those words so naturally.

Isabel found themes emerging from self-reflective, observational and interview data. She asked them in her interviews if they preferred to work individually or cooperatively in groups:

> (Student A in Isabel's class): Well, most of the times I like to work by myself, overall when I have to analyze data from the word bank, or when we have to follow the steps for running a program. I can concentrate better and perform better the assignments.

> (Student B): I was working on a team with two other girls. During the class we had to analyze a word from word bank program. When professor asked us to work analyzing some data, I didn't start working until I started to interact with my partners and decide how to work on it or at least discuss about our opinions. I realized that my two partners were working on their own and seemed like they didn't need or want help. I began to do the same. After 45 minutes working like that (separately) the professor asked us to discuss our findings. That's when everybody turned to their team partners and began a short

discussion for about ten minutes. After those five minutes, everyone turned back to their computer screens.

Isabel found the aspect of individualism and cooperation present in various ways with the different cultural groups in the class. Some explained that people in the United States were often trained from kindergarten to be more independent in their life styles. That is, they were used to working alone. She associated this characteristic with girls she knew from Georgia State University studying in Mexico at the Universidad de las Americas en Puebla. They tended to do everything in a very independent way, whereas the rest of the people around them were doing just the opposite.

Discussion

The five sojourners gradually created a common thread of experiences which tied them together in various ways. It began when they arrived in their host university, continued as they interacted with university people as well as people in their communities and later appeared in their assignments in the intercultural course.

Their identities were changing. These changes surfaced in their final papers, where it was noticeable that they wanted to reflect about their culture shocks, to adapt to dissimilarities between their host country and themselves, and to express their reaction to stress. As they sought to understand dissimilarities, they grew more intercultural through the intensity of their cultural experiences (see Kim, 1995; also Kim, 2001: 59; Weber, 2005).

Ting-Toomey (1999) defines identity as reflective self images. As we have read, the sojourners' reflections in the quotes of this chapter we see snapshots that include problems, ongoing struggles, mindful thinking and negotiation (Ting-Toomey) and the sequence of stress-adapt growth (Kim, 2001). Stressful situations provided the necessary impetus to adapt to the dissimilarities of their host countries and themselves.

Wenger's social theory of learning guided their mini-ethnographies with COP's and aided each sojourner to understand the intercultural process of identity and change. Wenger speaks of the cohesion among members in a joint enterprise as the foundation of a COP and its negotiation among its members, he states, produces the formation of the enterprise. We might list several assumptions that aid in understanding the identity change of these women. First, each individual's reaction to experience is distinct and personal. Second, stress is an essential element creating change. Third, openness and willingness of the person to study one's own processes enhances how the individual will successfully resolve the problem and in turn forces them to create an atmosphere in which change in cultural identity can take place. Finally, time is another essential ingredient through which changes take place as one gains greater understanding about oneself.

Our look at these sojourners gives a glimpse of distinct ways of becoming more mindful of self and awareness of identity. Mindfulness was quite pronounced in Victoria during her stay as a sojourner. She appeared to have reached some conclusions in her self-analysis. This realization did not surface as strongly with the other women. Maria showed great stress that, as Ting-Toomey theorized, is necessary to prompt INT and change, but during the intercultural communications course she herself had not become aware of the extent and impact of stress on her own identity. Elizabeth, Graciela and Isabel followed their interests in learning about cultural differences mainly through the eyes of the students in the COPs. In their final papers they only occasionally associated their own experiences with those they were observing and the subjects they interviewed. In their postings they talked about cultural dissimilarities they were experiencing in contact with new cultures. Elizabeth used analytical skills to focus on her COP and their multiculturality and participation. Graciela analyzed in depth outsiders and insiders in the COP from the periphery. Isabel noticed a challenge to group interaction in the COP where telecommunications guided the activities.

It might be said that out of this look at five women surfaced the importance of reflection as a way of understanding one's self and reaching some awareness. I would like to emphasize self-reflection as an important element for study in future research. It is advisable that pre-training or training courses consider how self-reflection could be included in their programs. A look at the five women and their reflections suggests ideas for future research focusing solely on this aspect.

These final observations end with some insights into the role reflections play as cultural dissimilarities are experienced. As we have pointed out, experience and one's reaction to that experience is individual. Interaction with others in the COP guided each student along the route of discovery. Victoria was involved in deep self-analysis. Maria felt frustrated about herself, but found that other students had similar oral communication problems. In the final papers, the strong desire to reflect about one's personal awarenesses and educating oneself toward interculturality revealed the intensity each participant brought to the course and to the newness of academic study abroad. It might be questionable whether pre-training or training courses could have reached such goals.

References

Gudykunst, W.B. (1995) Anxiety/uncertainly management (AUM) theory: Current status. In R. Wiseman (ed.) *Intercultural Communication Theory* (pp. 8–58). Thousand Oaks, CA: Sage.

Gudykunst, W.B. (ed.) (2005) *Theorizing about Intercultural Communication.* Thousand Oaks, CA: Sage.

Kim, M.J. and Thomas, M. (1988) Identity in intercultural communication: An interpretive perspective. In Y. Kim and W. Gudykunst (eds) *Theories of Intercultural Communication. International and Intercultural Communication Annual* (Vol. XII, pp. 9–20). Newbury Park, CA: Sage.

Kim, Y. (1996) Identity development: From culture to intercultural. In H.B. Mokros (ed.) *Interaction and Identity* (p. 350). New Brunswick, NJ: Transaction.

Kim, Y. and Gudykunst W. (eds) (1988) *Theories in Intercultural Communication. International and Intercultural Communication Annual* (Vol. XII, pp. 213–238). Newbury Park, CA: Sage.

Kim, Y.Y. (1995) Cross-cultural adaptation, an integrative theory. In R. Wiseman (ed.) *Intercultural Communication Theory* (pp. 170–193). Thousand Oaks, CA: Sage.

Kim, Y.Y. (2001) *Becoming Intercultural, An Integrative Theory of Communication and Cross-Cultural Adaptation.* Thousand Oaks, CA: Sage (USBN: 080384488).

Kim, Y.Y. (2005) Adapting to a new culture, an integrative communication theory. In W.B. Gudykunst (ed.) *Theorizing about Intercultural Communication* (Chapter 16, pp. 375–400). Thousand Oaks, CA: Sage.

Langer, E.J. (1989) *Mindfulness.* Cambridge, MA: Perseus Books.

Langer, E.J. (1997) *The Power of Mindful Learning.* Reading, MA: Addison-Wesley.

Ting-Toomey, S. (1999) *Communicating Across Cultures.* New York: The Guilford Press.

Ting-Toomey, S. (2005) Identity negotiation theory: Crossing cultural boundaries. In W.B. Gudykunst (ed.) *Theorizing about Intercultural Communication.* Thousand Oaks, CA: Sage.

Weber, S. (2005) *Intercultural Learning as Identity Negotiation.* Frankfurt/M.: Lang (ISBN: 3631543166).

Wenger, E. (1998) *Communities of Practice: Learning, Meaning and Identity.* Cambridge: Cambridge University Press.

Wiseman, R.L. and Koester, J. (1993) *Intercultural Communication Competence.* Newbury, CA: Sage.

Wiseman, R.L. and Koester, J. (2001) Intercultural communication competence. In W. Gudykunst and B. Mody (eds) *Handbook of Intercultural and International Communication.* Newbury Park, CA: Sage.

Chapter 4
Becoming Interculturally Competent in a Third Space

ANWEI FENG

Introduction

Most chapters in this book illustrate how formal courses or training programmes help nurture willingness and open-mindedness towards otherness and develop intercultural awareness and skills for intercultural interaction. With ever-increasing mobility of people in the new century and widely perceived trend of economic globalisation and internationalisation of education, courses and training programmes provided by educational institutions and organisations are evidently in high demand in all societies. It is hoped that through systematic examinations of the processes to become interculturally competent, as we do in this volume, educators and trainers gain better insights into the developmental stages of this process and will be able to design better curricula and conduct more meaningful programmes.

While the book centres on presenting and evaluating what intercultural trainers and educators do, mostly in formal settings, it is important to keep in mind three observations or facts noted in the literature or in the real world. First, people in need, such as internationally mobile students and workforce, may not have easy access to institutionalised and accredited courses and training programmes designed to develop intercultural knowledge and skills. Second, researchers and scholars including those in this book have demonstrated that programmes developed on the basis of thoroughly researched contexts and well-founded theories do help build up competence for intercultural interaction and extend people's perceptions of the world. Accessibility to educational and training opportunities, however, does not automatically lead to development of the competence desired for the real world. Formal programmes that adopt an orthodox approach, as Jack (2002; this volume) argues, too easily enhance stereotypes and ethnocentricity of the participants. Third, organisations or individuals who perceive the needs for intercultural knowledge and skills and take initiatives to develop them on their own may become interculturally competent to meet challenges in the changing circumstances. Mughan (in this volume), for example, shows with empirical data how under-resourced small and medium-sized enterprises (SMEs) engage in experience-based learning while developing overseas markets. Mughan argues that their intercultural paradigm is driven by the business and market imperatives, rather than following a structured, formal trajectory familiar to a large company or organisation.

The third phenomenon discussed above is also the focus of this chapter, but attention is given to how students living and studying abroad develop intercultural competence and negotiate identity in an academic environment different from their own (see also Ryan, this volume). After an overview of widely adopted approaches to evaluating the experience of internationally mobile students, with an emphasis on theories of thirdness, the chapter presents empirical data collected from a group of students from CHC[1] countries currently studying at a British university. This study takes such notions as Socratic and Confucian cultures of learning as a starting point for analysis. On such basis, the chapter argues for a redefinition of the notion of third space, to refer not only to highly individual, heterogeneous and 'discursive conditions of enunciation' (Bhabha, 1994: 37), which may give rise to something that 'displaces histories' when individuals, particularly those of different sociocultural background, interact, but also to intermediate zones where individuals are found to negotiate identity and mediate between a system of values, beliefs and norms internalised through earlier socialisation and a new system.

Theories of Thirdness

There is a substantial body of literature on globally mobile personnel, including international students, and two major approaches stand out in this literature on evaluating the experience of those living, working or studying abroad. One way researchers traditionally follow is to use models such as those developed by Bennett (1993), Berry (1990) and Kim (1988) to describe or depict developmental stages of acculturation and intercultural sensitivity, or adaptation and accommodation. Numerous inventories or checklists developed on the basis of principles or axioms specified for these models enable researchers to study mobility and diasporas through either or both quantitative or qualitative data. An alternative approach adopted by an increasing number of researchers in recent years is the interpretive paradigm, notably the grounded theory perspective, to evaluate the process and outcome of international mobility (Byram & Feng, 2006; Murphy-Lejeune, 2002). Several authors such as Tarp (2006) and Lam (2006), for example, used grounded theory to analyse patterning or grounded themes of intercultural growth or intercultural tension, or increased understanding or enhanced stereotypes of otherness, that are emergent from empirical data collected mostly through qualitative methods from international students living and studying abroad.

While many of the studies following the first approach have thrown new lights on the lived experience of internationally mobile personnel, immigrants or refugees, critics often question the generalisability or applicability of such models or inventories to studying and analysing human relationships and human behaviour that not only depend on knowledge, skills and psychological inclination for communication with otherness but also a complex web of social factors such as power and dynamics of social and individual identities. Research claimed to follow an interpretive paradigm, particularly the grounded theory perspective, is not without criticisms too. Thomas and James (2006: 767), for example, argue that the perspective constrains and distorts qualitative inquiry for 'what ultimately materializes following grounded theory procedures is less like discovery and more akin to invention'. Strong critiques of this kind do not seem to prevent researchers from adopting this perspective to analyse research data for its theoretical base is generally acknowledged as sound. Dey (1999) in a comprehensive critique of grounded theory sees it as capable of development and as offering a 'middle way' between idiographic and nomothetic theorising. However, criticisms remind researchers adopting the grounded theory perspective of the dynamic and intriguing nature of social science study and the ethical responsibility of researchers, who are also agents having the capacity of action in the research process, to truthfully present emergent theories by uncovering multifaceted and ambivalent phenomena in interplay.

Recent scholarship in foreign language education and intercultural communication has shown a growing interest in concepts such as the third place or a culture of a third kind in language education (Kramsch, 1993, 1999; Lo Bianco *et al.*, 1999), third culture kids in international education (Pollock & Van Reken, 2001), third culture building in intercultural communication (Starosta & Olorunnisola, 1995), and the notion of third space developed by cultural studies theorists and human geographers (Bhabha, 1990b, 1994; Crang, 1998; Soja, 1996). What these concepts, collectively called theories of thirdness in this chapter, and the grounded theory perspective have in common is the emphasis not on using existing schemata or theories to understand social phenomena but on examining spatial, temporal and social dimensions of human communication in the performative present (Bhabha, 1994). Definitions of theories of thirdness differ from one theorist (or academic area) to another, but all these notions suggest in metaphorical language a conception that reflects new insights into each of these academic areas by challenging binary opposites such as the here and the there, self and other, the present and the past, the local and the global, and of course the traditional view that sees 'education' and 'training', 'deep learning' and 'surface learning' as polarities (see Introduction to this volume). Theories of thirdness, in a practical sense, provide us with useful vocabulary to critique binary conceptions of social phenomena and to analyse and problematise culture by turning all physical places, symbols, customs, ideas, etc. into lived zones of trans-cultures and trans-ideologies.

While arguing strongly for the transformational and performative nature of communication between cultures, some researchers and scholars in intercultural communication appear keen to get to the heart of intercultural studies by challenging conventional views of culture itself. Fay (1996), Holliday (1999, 2005), Holliday *et al.* (2004) and Keesing (1998) argue that research in intercultural studies is often dominated by a 'standard' view of culture that is limited to locating essential features of a particular social group, that is, the *shared* values, *established* norms and *patterned* behaviours. This is an essentialist or reductionist approach to theorising culture. Bhabha (1990a, 1990b, 1994) is one of the most prominent critics of the conventional approach. His writings question many frequently used but elusive concepts such as culture, cultural difference and intercultural as opposed to intracultural communication. To begin with, Bhabha (1994: 136) holds the view that culture is first of all '*heimlich*' with 'its disciplinary generalizations, its mimetic narratives, its homologous empty time, its seriality, its progress, its customs and coherence'. It is through cultural translation, appropriation and rehistoricisation by individuals in specific contexts, that is, in the in-between space, that culture becomes interdisciplinary, dynamic, ambivalent and even self-contradictory. Bhabha (1990b: 211) states that 'all forms of culture are continually in a process of hybridity'.

In his critique of cultural unity and homogeneity, Bhabha (1990a: 4) questions the commonly perceived difference between intercultural and intracultural communication arguing that 'The "other" is never outside or beyond us: it emerges forcefully within the cultural discourse when we think we speak intimately and indigenously "between ourselves"'. In theorising cultural differences, Bhabha (1994: 162) challenges traditional views stating that cultural differences 'should not be understood as the free play of polarities and pluralities in the homogeneous empty time of the national community'. Instead, they should be regarded as a process that is built into the very condition of communication in the performative present. In this process, he continues (Bhabha, 1994: 37), the two places ('You' and 'I') are mobilised to produce meaning in the passage through a **Third Space** which 'constitutes the discursive conditions of enunciation that ensure that the meaning and symbols of culture have no primordial unity or fixity; that even the same signs can be appropriated, translated, rehistoricised and read anew'.

The notion that culture has no 'primordial unity or fixity' and 'can be appropriated, translated, rehistoricised and read anew' highlights the openness and heterogeneity of culture, permeable by otherness, susceptible to interpretations in different contexts and times by individuals of a social group and therefore often ambivalent and self-contradictory. In this sense, the notion of 'third place' discussed in length in Lo Bianco *et al.* (1999) and Kramsch (1993) is most attuned to third space. According to these authors, the third place suggests individual opportunities for change by virtue of being confronted with the unfamiliar when learning a foreign language or when living abroad. Kramsch (1993: 257) maintains that the opportunities for transformation are embedded in cultures in contact, but not enslaved in them. Therefore, this third place is located in somewhere different for each learner and 'will make different sense at different times' . Discursive conditions of enunciation as a result of individuality and heterogeneity and ambivalence of culture seem to characterise the third place or third space which, in Bhabha's (1990b: 211) words, may displace histories and give rise to 'something different, something new and unrecognisable, a new area of negotiation of meaning and representation'.

In short, the third space perspective not only challenges traditional views of the elusive notion of culture but more importantly problematises our 'normal', polarised or binary perceptions of the relationships between, for examples, the West and the East, intercultural and intracultural communication, education and training, and deep learning and surface learning as discussed in the Introduction. In what ways will these insights out of the discussion help analyse the perceptions and experience of internationally mobile students? What implications will this analysis have for studies into development of intercultural competence? The pages that follow address these questions by examining the academic experience of a particular group of international students, the CHC students at a UK university. Empirical research data showing their experience will be analysed with the third space concept, but prior to this, let us look at the notion of Confucian culture of learning that forms the starting point for the analysis.

Confucian Culture of Learning

In the scholarship of living and studying abroad, the so-called Socratic–Confucian cultures of learning and teaching (Greenholtz, 2003; Tweed & Lehman, 2002) or other similar binary oppositions such as Western versus Chinese cultures of learning (Cortazzi & Jin, 1996a, 1996b; Jin & Cortazzi, 1998), learning and teaching in individualistic versus collective cultures (Trumbull *et al.*, 2001) and dialogic versus dialectic education (Hammond & Gao, 2002) are notions widely used in studying and discussing the experience of CHC students in their year(s) abroad, often in Western countries such as the US, the UK, Canada, Australia and New Zealand. Many provide empirical evidence to show that between the two broadly defined cultures there are huge differences in terms of values and beliefs in learning and teaching. Hence, they argue that, while students need to be made aware of the differences, educators in Western countries that host the students should take into account the differences in the cultures of learning and accommodate accordingly.

A culture of learning is usually defined as values and beliefs of good teaching and learning shared by a particular social or cultural group and their learning behaviours that are built on these values and beliefs. Many educators and researchers believe that the discovery of these values, beliefs and expectations is the key to developing curricula for intercultural education. Among them are Jin and Cortazzi (Cortazzi & Jin, 1996a, 1996b; 2001; Jin, 1992; Jin & Cortazzi, 1993, 1995, 1998) who have conducted empirical studies comparing perceptions and observable behaviours of Chinese students and their counterparts in the UK and have recently extended their research to include learners from other places such as Japan, Malaysia and Turkey (Cortazzi & Jin, 2001). On the basis of the findings, they propose a cultural synergy model that they define as cultural extension of accommodation theory necessary to 'encourage conscious awareness of the differences in learning and teaching through explicit discussions' (Cortazzi & Jin, 1996a: 74) so that both parties (e.g. CHC students and British lecturers) are clear about each other's expectations and accommodate each other accordingly. Not surprisingly, their writings reporting findings and analyses often show clearly contrastive sets of beliefs and values (Table 4.1) which, they claim, are meant to promote a synergy model to bridge the gaps.

Table 4.1　Contrast of learning cultures in China and UK

China	*UK*
Knowledge from authority	Skills in communication and learning
Collective consciousness	Individual orientation
Teaching and learning as performance	Teaching and learning as organisation
Learning through practice and memorisation	Learning through interaction and construction
Listener/reader responsibility for communication	Speaker/writer responsibility for communication
Hierarchy, face, respect	Equality, informality
Teacher as model and centre	Teacher as organiser

Source: Cortazzi and Jin (1996a: 74)

Different values, beliefs and approaches to learning and teaching typically associated with learners and teachers in these two countries are contrasted in unambiguous terms in this table. The binary oppositions are often claimed to be supported by empirical evidence and raising awareness of the differences, they argue, can help bridge the gaps in communication between the two sets of established norms and between these two cultural groups. Similar contrastive tables can also be found in Trumbull *et al.* (2001) and Hammond and Gao (2002).

Some other researchers, on the other hand, give evidence to counter-argue that the widely believed differences in terms of established norms are never empirically coherent and many are simply 'myths'. Contradictory empirical findings and the debates have led to the questioning of the existence of different norms in educational traditions and the necessity to mediate (the lack of) them in intercultural education. From a survey among a group of teacher trainees from China, Stephens (1997) reported findings that negate many statements made by Jin and Cortazzi. He critiques 'the air of typicality' shown in their selective data and warns of the danger of over-generalisation of differences between 'east' and 'west' orientations. Debates related to the Confucian culture of learning are noticeable in many other discussions and empirical studies reported by language teachers and researchers in direct contact with students from China and other Confucian Heritage Cultures (e.g. Garrott, 1995; Harris, 1997; Hess & Azuma, 1991; Kember, 2000; Littlewood, 2001, 2003; Maley,

1995; Watkins & Biggs, 1996, 2001). Among them, Littlewood's (2001) findings from a large-scale survey are perhaps most striking. A survey of perceptions of and attitudes towards classroom English learning was conducted among 2656 students in 11 countries, eight in Asia (CHC countries) and three in Europe. Littlewood gives graphical representation of his findings to suggest that difference in cultures of learning is perhaps an illusion as the students from different cultures seem to have the same perceptions and preferences as far as learning is concerned.

Apparently, contrastive studies do not seem to provide much valid insight into the dynamics of two cultures of learning in contact. On the contrary, discrepancies in empirical findings as shown above challenge the notion of culture of learning itself. Critics in intercultural studies would ask whether the discussion on the notion makes any sense at all if little valid evidence of contrast or divergence is found between Confucian and Socratic cultures of learning, which have been traditionally believed to be vastly different. This would in turn lead to fundamental questions on culture, cultural difference and intercultural communication, as theorists of third space do. However, if we take their view that culture is on the one hand dynamic, ambivalent and even self-contradictory, but on the other hand it has 'its seriality, its progress, its customs and coherence' (Bhabha, 1994: 136), an interesting question could be whether the application of theories of third space, rather than a contrastive perspective, to empirical studies helps shed new light on the academic experience of CHC students living and studying abroad.

Durham Research

Diverse and even contradictory data from the empirical studies as exemplified above suggest that Confucian culture of learning, like any form of culture, is context dependent. 'Essential features' may be found evident in certain situations but not in others. Quantitative surveys used by researchers reviewed above are unlikely to explain human attitudes, perceptions and behaviour simply because of the context-dependent, multifaceted and dynamic nature of culture. For such studies, adopting an ethnographic approach as defined by Agar (1980) and Spradley (1980) to examine the perceptions and behaviours of individuals or social groups and to study their engagement in a third space is more likely to reveal the dynamics and multifacetedness of the cultures in contact, leading perhaps to a new culture in the forming.

In the following pages, I shall briefly describe the methodological principles followed by this ethnographic study carried out at a UK university starting in the summer of 2004 and ending before the summer of 2005. This study involved 21 students[2], including 17 postgraduates and 4 undergraduates, mainly from three departments of the university: business school, school of education and computer science. Data were also collected from five local lecturers involved in an e-forum group. Three 'foreshadowed questions', in Hammersley and Atkinson's (1983) words, were initially formulated. These are anticipated problems, not for testing or (dis)proving but for sustaining a researcher's curiosity and involvement during the long period of study, and may be reformulated during data collection in the field:

(1) Do CHC students truly experience the differences between Confucian and Socratic cultures of learning and mediate between the two?
(2) Or do they (co)create, with others, a third space that is new and displaces histories?
(3) Or both, or neither?

Methodological principles

The research involved ethnographic interviews or informal conversations with CHC students, complemented by observations of classroom behaviour of a specific group of students in naturalistic classroom settings. The study followed the general principles set by methodologists such as Agar (1980), Hammersley and Atkinson (1983) and Spradley (1979, 1980), which are briefly summarised by Hammersley (1998: 8–9). The first principle is the pursuit of naturalism that primarily aims to capture the characteristics of emergent human behaviour by ensuring that research data are collected from the everyday, naturalistic setting of the participants. The second aims for in-depth understanding of complex human behaviour rather than drawing quick conclusions on causality. This in-field work meant examining the social phenomenon that emerged by carefully studying the context and other factors that may be associated with it, and thick descriptions of the social phenomenon (Geertz, 1973) are expected for data analysis. The third is to give emphasis to inductive rather than deductive inquiry, that is, to discover the meanings of new and unfamiliar social phenomena not to test hypotheses.

Emergent themes

Because of the nature of ethnographic study and the methodological principles followed in the study, many of the data, including the 'quotes' presented below, are field notes jotted down during an observation or after an informal conversation retrospectively. Except for the e-forum postings, none of the data are recorded verbatim. For the purpose of this chapter, three themes are selected for presentation on how the CHC students self-direct their own learning to become competent. These themes focus on studying abroad, although inevitably competence in living abroad is touched upon in some places.

'Norms' versus change

Data from ethnographic interviews (26 interviews, many of which were casual conversations, were conducted) and from about a dozen e-forum postings by lecturers (most are local British) suggest that differences in terms of established norms of learning were commonly perceived and in some cases observed. Perceptions were usually illustrated by such expressions as 'of course, there are differences ...' and 'I knew it is important to speak up here ...'. On two occasions, one Chinese and one Taiwan student said, 'I noticed that here ... but back at home ...', which showed their observations of differences. However, it is important to note that most students and teachers did not find their perceptions proven by their empirical experience. Expressions recorded to show this pattern include 'I was surprised to see some local students were also shy ...', 'In fact, more than half of us are from Asia and even the lecturer is originally from China. I don't see much difference ...', 'The [Asian] student, surprisingly, was quite active ...' (e-Forum P-3, posting by a British lecturer in English literature), these being just a selection from a larger number of similar statements.

More importantly, data suggested that once different norms were observed some developed strategies to address the differences, resulting in a change or transformation in behaviours and beliefs. One MA student in law from China, for example, originally took a local student's behaviour of asking 'simple' questions in lectures as 'shocking' and *'Hou Lian Pi'* (thick-skinned), which means 'not ashamed of looking unintelligent'. In time, she said she saw the advantage of doing this and began to adopt this behaviour. When asked if she actually asked questions in lectures; however, she hesitated a while and answered,

> Well, yes, I never seem to have asked any question in front of so many people during lectures. I would start *asking a friend first*, or ask in a small group. (FN-11, 17/11/04, my translation from Chinese and emphasis)

An undergraduate student of economics with early primary and secondary school experience in Singapore and Hong Kong described her change of classroom behaviour from a relatively reactive listener to a proactive participant. When explaining why, she said:

> In Hong Kong and Singapore, you are expected to be attentive in class. Here, I found all students talk. I began to try to contribute more in the classroom and found it interesting. This can also *impress the teacher*. (FN-26, 12/05/05, original English, my emphasis)

The two examples show self-directed learning in practice. Both students identified issues in their circumstances and made their own decisions to address them. The 'quotes' (translated or lifted from the field notes) indicated that both felt happily transformed, at least partially, by adapting their way of thinking and behaviour in the new environment while maintaining to some degree traditional values of 'face' (by asking a friend first) and respect for authority (by impressing the teacher) as listed in Cortazzi and Jin (1996b). In other words, they brought the two cultures of learning into relationship and mediated between them.

Data from this study show that CHC students and local tutors perceive differences prior to interaction, although the perceived differences in terms of cultures of learning may or may not prove true empirically. The students depend on these perceptions at the initial stage to make sense of specific situations, to bring their expectations into relationship with the experienced realities and to mediate between them. The findings are apparently explicable by the schema theory developed by cognitive psychologists such as Moscovici (1984) and Rumelhart (1980). A schema, according to Rumelhart (1980: 34), is 'a data structure for representing the generic concepts in memory'. The list of values and norms as given by Cortazzi and Jin (1996) could be seen as the 'data structure' internalised through early socialisation. When this schema is challenged in the real world, particularly when the real world is foreign, two processes are activated (Moscovici, 1984: 29): 'anchoring' in which an individual draws things foreign and intriguing and compares them to the paradigm of a system which the individual thinks is suitable; and 'objectifying' which 'saturates the idea of unfamiliarity with reality' (p. 38). In other words, new experience is assimilated to and in turn modifies the existing data structure (Byram, 1989). The data presented above show that few CHC students rigidly followed the set of 'norms' internalised in early socialisation or were found to be transformed entirely. As time went on, many existing schemata were modified. An intermediate zone was created, usually through a repeated process of mediation between the perceptions of the two cultures of learning with the experienced reality.

Classroom dynamics

Classroom observations, participant or non-participant, did seem to present a contrast between cultures of learning; local students tended to look more ready and more articulate in airing views than CHC students in the classroom. The linguistic barrier is undeniably a significant factor[3] in the tendency towards relative quietness of CHC students. A closer observation revealed that in a classroom mixed with local and CHC students of about 15-in size, two patterns might emerge. If a classroom was dominated by local students, CHC students tended to be reluctant to participate, particularly in whole class discussions (FN-23, 21/02/05; FN-4, 22/07/04). When the majority in a classroom were from CHC countries or regions, which is often the case in departments that offer courses popular with Asian students such as business administration, international law and computer science, this difference was less evident. Some CHC students could be as active as their local counterparts.

Classroom behaviour was found to be affected by some other factors such as class activities and tutor's mediation. Small group activities tended not to be dominated by native speakers as 'quiet, foreign' students looked more willing to participate. For whole class discussions (which were common for small classes of, say, less than 20), the first student to speak up would determine the outcome of the discussion, that is, a triggering effect in which contributions that followed tended to trail the line of thinking and be made by those from the same cultural group. Tutors have a clear role to play in influencing classroom behaviour. In an education classroom, for example, the tutor took measures to fill in the cultural gaps to prevent CHC students from getting 'lost'. The tutor also deliberately encouraged quieter voices (usually international students), often by silencing a few 'over-expressive' native speakers (FN-2, 20/07/04; FN-23, 21/02/05; FN-4, 22/07/04).

> Some lecturers make special efforts after seminars or lectures to ensure that learning is taking place. A British lecturer in the Business School wrote in an e-forum posting, ...[classroom debate and discussion] is normally left to the British students. ... , at the end of the lecture I always try to make myself available for about half an hour. So far I have not had a single British student approach me after the lecture. However, I do find that the Chinese students will approach me,

normally in a small group of around five or six and ask for some additional clarification of some topic in the lecture. (e-Forum P-6)

However, not all measures taken by tutors can achieve the intended or desired outcome. Some tutors choose to slow down the pace of presentation for classes dominated by CHC students, or show special concern about quiet students, for example, by asking them individually if they could follow (this happened twice to a computer science student from China during breaks between lectures). Such efforts, according to this student during a casual conversation after a tennis game,

> were OK at the initial stage. In time, many of us got fed up with it ... because slow pace in lectures are *not authentic teaching* and special concerns looked irritating as they made us look stupid. (FN-17, 06/12/04, my translation and emphasis)

The 'quiet' behaviour was found common in the classroom among CHC students. However, of the students approached during breaks or after lectures, not a single student was found to readily remain content with a listener's role in the classroom while others are talking, accept whatever knowledge the teacher presents and remain obedient and submissive in learning.

> ... the majority of my classmates are British. Honestly, I often couldn't follow what they were talking about. They often talk about the local system. But I don't wish to look *Ben* (slow-witted), so I spoke up when sometimes I only *sort of understood* what was going on. ... (FN-8, 26/10/04, my translation and emphasis)

This was given by an MA student in education from China. She was obviously eager to join in the discussion even though she only partially understood what the issue was because of her limited understanding of references to the local system. She tried to negotiate her identity and representation (Bhabha, 1994) according to her evaluation of the situation.

Some CHC students with better fluency in English were in a better situation. An MA student of mass media from Taiwan found herself 'more and more brave' in the UK classroom as she realised that difficult points could be more easily dealt with by being brave in the classroom. 'If a question can get answered quickly, why do I have to waste time figuring it out myself?' (FN-25, 30/04/05, my translation). A most interesting narrative was given by a female student from Singapore, who spoke fluent English,

> ... When I started my study here, I noticed some local students tended to think few Asian students can express views in English in the

classroom. When you do speak up, they would look stunned. ... Though I was relatively quiet in class when I was in Singapore, in the UK, I become more and more active than before. The advantage is that you need to be more alert in class. (FN-23, 21/02/05, original English)

This student apparently created herself a new identity by transforming from a reactive learner to a proactive one, a new self in the new environment. This may be seen by Bhabha (1990b: 211) as a clear example of an individual exploring a third space, which resulted in 'something new and unrecognisable, a new area of negotiation of meaning and representation'.

Surface or deep approaches to learning

A student's behaviour in a classroom is an important indicator of how the student would approach a learning task. A learner who actively participates in classroom discussions is usually believed to be one who takes a deep approach because it is widely argued that active classroom participation requires higher levels of cognitive engagement (Biggs, 1999). On the other hand, a quiet student is often viewed as a surface learner who tends to use lower-order thinking skills such as memorising and note taking. Fleming (in Introduction) points out that, a polarised view of the notions of deep and surface learning, just as the polarised concepts of education and training, 'does not do justice to the complexity of what is involved in becoming intercultural'. Indeed, data from my study suggest that, when facing a challenging concept in learning, an active and 'deep' CHC student with adequate linguistic competence participates in classroom discussions to check, confirm or show understanding. A 'deep' learner without such competence, on the other hand, 'listens attentively', makes use of all available means to figure out the meaning, or finds an answer outside the classroom. The higher-level cognitive engagement of such a learner can be demonstrated by the outcomes such as assignments the learner produces. A 'quiet' student from Taiwan who was observed closely, for example, came up with two highly engaging assignments that showed many features of a deep learner who analyses, relates and theorises competently. It is, therefore, problematic to use classroom behaviour as an only indicator of deep/surface learning.

The strategy of achieving understanding through memorisation (see Watkins & Biggs, 1996, 2001) could also be seen as an indicator that signifies a deep learning approach adopted by CHC students. Evidence of the use of this strategy often emerged in informal interviews with CHC students. Most individuals studied saw it as both a deeply entrenched belief and a sign of commitment to learning that prove effective everywhere. Some claimed that they value and actually use this learning strategy in their studies in the UK. However, the following given by an MA student of finance from China seems to represent the views of most postgraduates in social science departments:

> ... in the UK extensive reading required by all module lecturers in fact helps me retain knowledge even more effectively than memorising hard facts and isolated bits of information. In China, I used to, *better say*, had to memorise a lot of these in order to pass exams. (FN-12, 18/11/04, my translation and emphasis)

This claim is interesting because, on the one hand, the student seemed to negate the approach to memorising hard facts and bit of information, but on the other hand, the notion of 'retaining knowledge' indicates the value of keeping learned knowledge in memory. Retaining what has been learned through extensive reading, rather than through rote learning of hard facts, may well be seen as evidence of appropriating and translating an aspect of a new learning culture to the advantage of the international students.

As stated before, using a foreign language for study and research is the most challenging task faced by CHC undergraduates and postgraduates. Individual learners adopt different attitudes and approaches to meeting the challenge according to their circumstances or priorities. A highly motivated student may feel disempowered for lack of linguistic competence and does not exhibit the features of a deep learner of any kind, irrespective of any particular culture of learning. Therefore, some students, like this MA student in economics, prioritise opportunities to learn the language over all other matters:

> ...Yes, I have to be quiet and passive in the classroom I struggled with some tasks and assignments and only focus on things assessed. My English was quite weak ... I tried hard to improve my English outside the classroom. Though I don't drink much, I often go to the pubs with my British friends and I joined a student tennis club, instead of a Saturday football team self-formed by Chinese students I very much wanted to join.... . (FN-9, 29/10/04)

The social activities this student was involved in may not look directly related to his academic work but for him they were necessary undertakings to acquire the language skills needed for academic work and future career. To categorise this student as a surface learner would clearly reduce the theoretical relevance of the notion of surface/deep learning.

However, the data do yield some 'typical' cases of surface learning. The economic student mentioned that some Chinese students he knew never seemed to care about their English nor to make friends with English speakers or international students of other cultures.

> They often play together, eat together, and even take turns to attend lectures. They compare lectures notes and past exam papers ... What they try to do is to *Hun* (do the minimum to get) a degree before returning home. (FN-9, 29/10/04)

This phenomenon was noted by a few other students as particularly prominent among those who take a one-year master degree course and who live together with other students from the same country (FN 26, 12/05/05; FN-17, 06/12/04).

Discussion

The theoretical analyses and the research findings presented above focus on three aspects in relation to the cultures of learning in contact: norms versus changes, classroom dynamics and learning approaches. Data obtained provide some evidence to the foreshadowed questions for the study. The findings suggest that differences between Confucian and Socratic cultures of learning are commonly perceived not only by CHC students but local lecturers, even though the perceived norms may not be empirically evident. The perceived norms of learning and teaching associated with the Confucian culture of learning, their preliminary schemata, are useful as both students and lecturers seem to depend on them to make sense of the realities they face and use them as the basis for negotiating their identities and mediating learning and pedagogical strategies. During mediation, their preliminary schemata underwent a process of modification and transformation. Furthermore, the data indicate that 'something new and something unrecognisable' did occur when the two cultures were in contact. Quite a number of students were found to be doing something they would never do if they had stayed in their home academic environment. Examples include the 'stunning' Singaporean student who co-created a new identity of proactive learner (perhaps temporarily) with others in the classroom, the MA student in education who decided to take the risk of participating in class discussions to avoid looking *Ben* (slow witted), the student with limited linguistic competence who gave priority to improving language skills over all other matters, and perhaps even the students who tried to *Hun* (do the minimum to get) a degree before returning home. These cases give evidence that some CHC students were exploring 'a new area of negotiation of meaning and representation' (Bhabha, 1990b: 211) in a third space constituting the 'discursive conditions of enunciation'.

As shown by the overview and the data presented in this chapter, the concept of third space is particularly insightful when we study the experience of internationally mobile students. The most relevant of the concept of third space to this volume is its strong proposition to contest binary or polar opposites such as Confucian and Socratic cultures of learning, 'education' and 'training' and 'deep learning' and 'surface learning'. The notion of 'discursive conditions of enunciation' represented in third space allows researchers and theorists to investigate heterogeneity and ambivalence of culture and cultures in contact from different perspectives and from multi-dimensions. The third space concept opens up new and productive ways of understanding the dynamics of identity negotiation in relation to power, language and individuality in intercultural interactions. However, current conceptualisation of third space places disproportional emphasis on fluidity and ambivalence due to hybridity and individuality in defining culture, on the performative present of interpretation in analysing interactions and on 'newness' that is neither part of the continuum of the past nor that of the present in predicting outcomes of cultures in contact. Less stressed by third space theorists are the processes of internalisation of social realities through earlier socialisation, preliminary schemata and modification of them through later socialisation long argued for by schema theorists as reviewed before (Moscovici, 1984; Rumelhart, 1980) and by theorists in tertiary socialisation (Byram, 1990, 1997; Doyè, 1992, 1999, 2008) who maintain that exposure to otherness through learning a foreign language or studying abroad may enable individuals to extend their perspectives to see the world and reconcile their identities in three dimensions: cognitive, moral and behavioural. Excessive emphasis on newness by third space theorists cited in this chapter suggests negation of mediation and reconciliation, although not explicitly stated in the literature.

On the basis of the evidence shown in this study, I would argue that the concept of third space should be reinterpreted to strike a balance between the '*heimlich*' and '*unheimlich*' nature of culture and between newness and mediation of the past and the present as a consequence of intercultural interaction. To be meaningful, third space needs to be seen as interactive space in which intercultural interaction is a process of enunciation, or 'negotiation of contradictory and antagonistic instances that open up hybrid sites and objectives of struggle' (Bhabha, 1994: 25). Through the process enunciation, something entirely new and unrecognisable can arise out of a specific context at a specific moment that is 'blasted out of the continuum of history' (Bhabha, 1994: 38). This space, at the same time, is an intermediate zone where mediated ways of behaving and modes of thinking are identified and individual identities are negotiated and transformed, usually partially.

It is important to note that while the process of enunciation would give rise to something new, which can be desirable or undesirable from the standpoint of international mobility (the latter is illustrated by the observation that some were trying to *Hun* (to do the minimum to get a degree), the process of mediation as the data show would usually lead to competence that is desired for intercultural communication. This study as well as other studies (e.g. Coleman, 1998) show that mere exposure to otherness, by living and studying abroad for example, does not automatically result in intercultural competence. To become interculturally competent, it (exposure) has to go with willingness to relate to otherness, skills to mediate between cultures and actions to explore third space.

Notes

1. Confucian Heritages Cultures are often used to refer to those national groups in Asia that are generally said to share values articulated by Confucius (551–479 BC), a thinker and educator who founded the *Ru* School of Chinese thought. These national groups are often said to include China, Japan, Singapore, South Korea, Taiwan and Hong Kong (Biggs, 1999; Greenholtz, 2003). Some such as Phuong-Mai *et al.* (2005) extend the notion to include Viet Nam and Malaysia.
2. None of the students we studied had attended a regular course or training programme, although three students mentioned that they had once or twice attended occasional talks or lectures on British culture before their sojourn abroad.
3. When asked about the main challenge, many informants immediately pointed to language as the main hurdle for studying and living abroad. Some also listed culture as a chief barrier.

References

Agar, M. (1980) *The Professional Stranger: An Informal Introduction to Ethnography.* New York: Academic Press.
Bennett, M.J. (1993) Towards ethnorelativism: A developmental model of intercultural sensitivity. In R.M. Paige (ed.) *Education for the Intercultural Experience* (pp. 21–71). Yarmouth, ME: Intercultural Press.
Berry, J. (1990) Psychology of acculturation. In R. Brislin (ed.) *Applied Cross-Cultural Psychology* (pp. 232–253). California: Sage Publications.
Bhabha, H. (1990a) *Nation and Narration.* London: Routledge.
Bhabha, H. (1990b) The third space. In J. Rutherford (ed.) *Identity, Community, Culture, Difference* (pp. 207–221). London: Lawrence & Wishart.

Bhabha, H. (1994) *The Location of Culture*. London and New York: Routledge.
Biggs, J. (1999) *Teaching for Quality Learning at University*. Buckingham: SRHE and Open University Press.
Byram, M. (1989) *Cultural Studies in Foreign Language Education*. Clevedon: Multilingual Matters.
Byram, M. (1990) Intercultural education and foreign language teaching. *World Studies Journal* 1 (7), 4–7.
Byram, M. (1997) *Teaching and Assessing Intercultural Communicative Competence*. Clevedon: Multilingual Matters.
Byram, M. and Feng, A. (eds) (2006) *Living and Studying Abroad: Research and Practice*. Clevedon: Multilingual Matters.
Coleman, J.A. (1998) Evolving intercultural perceptions among university language learners in Europe. In M. Byram and M. Fleming (eds) *Language Learning in Intercultural Perspective* (pp. 45–75). Cambridge: Cambridge University Press.
Cortazzi, M. and Jin, L. (1996a) English teaching and learning in China. *Language Teaching*, 29, 61–80.
Cortazzi, M. and Jin, L. (1996b) Culture of learning: Language classrooms in China. In M. Coleman (ed.) *Society and the Language Classroom* (pp. 169–206). Cambridge: Cambridge University Press.
Cortazzi, M. and Jin, L. (2001) Large classes in China: 'Good' teachers and interaction. In D.A. Watkins and J.B. Biggs (eds) *Teaching the Chinese Learner: Cultural, Psychological and Contextual Influences* (pp. 115–134). Hong Kong: CERC and Victoria; Australia: ACER.
Crang, M. (1998) *Cultural Geography*. London and New York: Routledge.
Dey, I. (1999) *Grounding Grounded Theory – Guidelines for Qualitative Inquiry*. London: Academic Press.
Doyé, P. (1992) Fremdsprachenunterricht als Beitrag zu tertiärer Sozialisation. In D. Buttjes, W. Butzkamm and F. Klippel (eds) *Neue Brennpunkte des Englischunterrichts*. Frankfurt a.M.: Peter Lang.
Doyé, P. (1999) *The Intercultural Dimension: Foreign Language Education in the Primary School*. Berlin: Cornelsen.
Doyé. P. (2008) Foreign language education as a contribution to tertiary socialisation. In P. Doyé (ed.) *Interkulturelles und mehrsprachiges Lehren und Lernen*. Tübingen: Gunter Narr.
Fay, B. (1996) *Contemporary Philosophy of Social Science: A Multicultural Approach*. Oxford: Blackwell.
Garrott, J.R. (1995) Chinese cultural values: New angles, added insights. *International Journal of Intercultural Relations* 19 (2), 211–225.
Geertz, C. (ed.) (1973) *The Interpretation of Culture*. New York: Basic Books.
Greenholtz, J. (2003) Socratic teachers and Confucian learners: Examining the benefits and pitfalls of a year abroad. *Language and Intercultural Communication* 3 (2), 122–130.
Hammersley, M. (1998) *Reading Ethnographic Research* (2nd edn). London and New York: Longman.
Hammersley, M. and Atkinson, P. (1983) *Ethnography: Principles in Practice*. London: Tavistock.
Hammond, S. and Gao, H. (2002) Pan Gu's paradigm: Chinese education's return to holistic communication in learning. In X. Lu, W. Jia and D. Ray Heisey (eds) *Chinese Communication Studies: Contexts and Comparisons* (pp. 227–244). Westport, CT: Ablex.

Harris, R. (1997) Overseas students in the United Kingdom university system. *Higher Education* 29, 77–92.

Hess, R.D. and Ryan Azuma, M. (1991) Cultural support fro schooling: Contrast between Japan and the United States. *Educational Researcher* 20 (9), 2–8.

Holliday, A. (1999) Small cultures. *Applied Linguistics* 20 (3), 237–264.

Holliday, A. (2005) *Small Cultures – Small Identities: The Richness of Self in a Changing World*. Key-note speech given at the Interrogating Third Space (ITS) Conference held on 27–28 June 2005 in Leicester University.

Holliday, A., Hyde, M. and Kullman, J. (2004) *Intercultural Communication: An Advanced Resource Book*. London and New York: Routledge.

Jack, G. (2002) Barbie, interculture and global ideology. Plenary presentation given at the Symposium *Thinking Interculture: Practice, Programmes, Policies*. 6 March 2002, American International University, Richmond, London.

Jin, L. (1992) Academic cultural expectations and second language use: Chinese postgraduate students in UK – A cultural synergy model. PhD thesis, University of Leicester.

Jin, L. and Cortazzi, M. (1993) Cultural orientation and academic language use. In D. Graddol, L. Thompson and M. Byram (eds) *Language and Culture* (pp. 84–97). Clevedon: BAAL and Multilingual Matters.

Jin, L. and Cortazzi, M. (1995) A cultural synergy model for academic language use. In P. Bruthiaux; T. Boswood and B. Du-Babcock (eds) *Explorations in English for Professional Communication* (pp. 41–56). Hong Kong: City University of Hong Kong.

Jin, L. and Cortazzi, M. (1998) The culture the learner brings: A bridge or a barrier? In M. Byram and M. Fleming (eds) *Language Learning in Intercultural Perspectives, Approaches through Drama and Ethnography* (pp. 98–118). Cambridge: Cambridge University Press.

Keesing, R.M. (1998) *Cultural Anthropology: A Contemporary Perspective* (3rd edn). London: Harcourt Brace College.

Kim, Y.Y. (1988) *Communication and Cross-Culture Adaptation: An Integrated Theory*. Clevedon: Multilingual Matters.

Kramsch, C. (1993) *Context and Culture in Language Teaching*. Oxford: Oxford University Press.

Kramsch, C. (1999) Thirdness: The intercultural stance. In T. Vestergaard (ed.) *Language, Culture and Identity* (pp. 41–58). Aalbord, Denmark: Aalbord University Press.

Kember, D. (2000) Misconceptions about the learning approaches, motivation and study practices of Asian students. *Higher Education* 40, 99–121.

Lam, C.M.H. (2006) Reciprocal adjustment by host and sojourning groups: Mainland Chinese students in Hong Kong. In M. Byram and A. Feng (eds) *Living and Studying Abroad* (pp. 91–107). Clevedon: Multilingual Matters.

Littlewood, W. (2001) Students' attitudes to classroom English learning: A cross-cultural study. *Language Teaching Research* 5 (1), 3–28.

Littlewood, W. (2003) Students' perceptions of classroom learning in east Asia and Europe. *HKBU Papers in Applied Language Studies* 7, 44–63.

Lo Bianco, J., Liddicoat, A. and Crozet, C. (eds) (1999) *Striving for the Third Place: Intercultural Competence through Language Education*. Melbourne: Language Australia.

Maley, A. (1995) *A Landmark Review of English in China*. Manchester: British Council.

Moscovici, S. (1984) The phenomenon of social representations. In R.M. Farr and S. Moscovici (eds) *Social Representations*. Cambridge: Cambridge University Press.

Murphy-Lejeune, E. (2002) *Student Mobility and Narrative in Europe: The New Strangers*. London: Routledge.

Phuong-Mai, N., Terlouw, C. and Pilot, A. (2005) Cooperative learning vs Confucian heritage culture's collectivism: Confrontation to reveal some cultural conflicts and mismatch. *Asia Europe Journal* 3 (3), 403–419.

Pollock, D.C. and Van Reken, R. (2001) *Third Culture Kids*. Yarmouth, ME: Nicholas Brealey Publishing/Intercultural Press.

Rumelhart, D.E. (1980) Schemata: The building blocks of cognition. In R.J. Spiro, B.C. Bruce and W.F. Brewer (eds) *Theoretical Issues in Reading Comprehension*. Hillsdale, NJ: Lawrence Erlbaum Associates.

Soja, E.W. (1996) *Thirdspace: Journeys to Los Angeles and Other Real-and-Imagined Places*. Cambridge, MA; Oxford: Blackwell.

Spradley, J. (1979) *The Ethnographic Interview*. New York: Holt, Rinehart and Winston.

Spradley, J. (1980) *Participant Observation*. New York: Holt, Rinehart and Winston.

Starosta, W.J. and Olorunnisola, A.A. (1995) *A Meta-model for Third Culture Development*. Paper presented at the annual meeting of Eastern Communication Association, Pittsburgh, Pennsylvania.

Stephens, K. (1997) Cultural stereotyping and intercultural communication: Working with students from the People's Republic of China in the UK. *Language and Education* 11 (2), 113–124.

Tarp, G. (2006) Student perspectives in short-term study programmes abroad: A grounded theory study. In M. Byram and A. Feng (eds) *Living and Studying Abroad* (pp. 157–185). Clevedon: Multilingual Matters.

Thomas, G. and James D. (2006) Reinventing grounded theory: Some questions about theory, ground and discovery. *British Educational Research Journal* 32 (6), 767–795.

Trumbull, E., Rothstein-Fisch, C., Greenfield, P.M. and Quiroz, B. (2001) *Bridging Cultures between Home and School: A Guide for Teachers*. Mahwah, NJ: Lawrence Erlbawm Associates.

Tweed, R.G. and Lehman, D.R. (2002) Learning considered within a cultural context: Confucian and Socratic approaches. *American Psychologists* 57 (2), 89–99.

Watkins, D.A. and Biggs, J.B. (eds) (1996) *The Chinese Learner: Psychological and Pedagogical Perspectives*. Hong Kong: CERC and Victoria, Australia: ACER.

Watkins, D.A. and Biggs, J.B. (eds) (2001) *Teaching the Chinese Learner: Cultural, Psychological and Contextual Influences*. Hong Kong: CERC and Victoria, Australia: ACER.

Part 2

Reflections on Teaching and Learning Programmes

Chapter 5

A Critical Perspective on Teaching Intercultural Competence in a Management Department

GAVIN JACK

Introduction

This chapter presents a discussion of my experiences of teaching a critical understanding of intercultural competence within the context of a management department in a UK university. It is based on a reflective look back at a module I taught on cross-cultural management and marketing (CCMM) to 22 second-year undergraduate students of mixed gender, ethnicity and nationality. The first half of the chapter articulates some of the general principles that underpinned the design, delivery and assessment of the course which I label 'teaching for critical intercultural learning'. These principles derive from my reading of academic work in the discipline of education on teaching for critical learning, as well as certain texts and well-established tenets of poststructuralist and postcolonial theory. The second half of the chapter presents and examines student responses to the course, which I collected through formal and informal evaluation. The positive and negative responses from students paint a complex and contradictory picture of my 'success' in delivering a critical understanding of intercultural competence. I will try to illuminate as honestly as possible how the pursuit of a critical intercultural agenda in the context of a management classroom created a number of difficult and ambiguous cognitive and affective reactions from students towards me, and vice versa.

Teaching for Critical Intercultural Learning

From a pedagogical point of view, the goal of my module was to conduct teaching for critical intercultural learning. The fact that I am an academic from a management school, and that my students study management and marketing, presents a number of important ramifications for this goal. I suppose that one would expect a course that attempts to develop inter-cultural competence within the context of a management school to be based largely, or even exclusively, on the works of Hofstede, Hampden-Turner, Trompenaars and so on and to be geared towards the production of interculturally competent students for future contexts of work and employment. In small part this was the case. However, the goal of engen-dering critical intercultural competence went far beyond this, asking stu-dents to confront and consider social, political and ethical issues associated with a broader conception of the intercultural. This was 'tricky business'. I approached the task with a particular understanding in mind of how the teacher–student relationship might produce a more politicized under-standing of intercultural competence. In this section I attempt to explain this understanding, and thus the term 'teaching for critical intercultural learning', by drawing upon academic work from education and other humanities disciplines.

Critically reflective teaching

Moves towards the professionalization of university teaching within the UK context have forced universities to find mechanisms for encourag-ing academic staff that teach to develop what might broadly be labelled a 'critically reflective approach' to their pedagogical practice. But just what counts as a 'reflective' approach? And even more problematically, what does it mean to introduce 'criticality' into the classroom? It might be argued that there is a little more agreement among writers on the answer to the former rather than the latter question. My own approach to teaching intercultural competence is, at least to some degree, sensitised by this literature.

A 'reflective' approach to teaching would seem to be based on the notion that teaching and learning are inextricably linked rather than dis-parate social and institutional activities. To divorce the two is to create an artificial distinction indicative of Freire's (1972) famous portrayal of the 'narration sickness' of education at the beginning of chapter two of *Pedagogy of the Oppressed*. For Ramsden (1992: 5), one learns by teaching and teaches by learning, and recognising this interconnection means that: 'the aim of teaching is simple: it is to make student learning possible'. For Ramsden, effective teaching and effective learning necessarily involve a change in the ways in which we come to view our respective worlds as teacher and learner. To achieve effective teaching, we need to study carefully how our students learn and reflect this understanding in our conceptions and practices of teaching. Learning about learning, then, lies at the heart of a reflective approach to teaching since it fosters a process in which our emergent understandings of the learning strategies of progressive cohorts of students are purposefully built into our emergent strategies for teaching.

The literature is full of recommendations on the aspects of teaching and learning processes that should be continually inspected in order to facilitate so-called 'good teaching'. Prosser and Trigwell (1999) argue that good teaching in higher education necessitates a continuous awareness of students' present learning situations, the contextually dependent nature of teaching, student diversity (including cultural diversity) in the classroom and the need to continually evaluate and improve teaching *inter alia*. In a similar vein, Ramsden (1992) lists six principles for effective teaching, including concern and respect for students and their learning, appropriate assessment and feedback, clear goals and intellectual challenge, fostering a sense of independence and active engagement among students, and learning from students.

Brookfield (1995) suggests that the extent to which we are following any of the above principles involves gathering feedback from a number of sources or 'different lenses': our own narratives and autobiographical reflections on teaching, from the students themselves, from peer observation, from theoretical writing on pedagogy, and so on. Reflective practice should therefore be dialogical and could be considered critical in so far as it impels us to consider the effects of our teaching strategies on our students in their diversity. From a sociological viewpoint, however, this represents a very narrow conception of 'criticality'. Surely it is more than just monitoring your activities through various lenses and adapting one's practice accordingly?

Learning approaches

A point of departure in responding to this rhetorical question is to consider what is meant by 'critical learning' and, to this end, to take a look at different conceptualisations of student learning. A common way of understanding how students learn is to articulate a student's 'approach' to learning which Ramsden (1992: 40) defines as

> (...) how people experience and organize the subject matter of a learning task; it is about 'what' and 'how' they learn, rather than 'how much' they remember. When a student learns, he or she relates to different tasks in different ways.

An approach to learning describes a relation between a person and the material to be learned, and is not an attribute of that person. A frequently occurring distinction is made between 'surface' and 'deep' approaches to learning. The former indexes a student's intention to only complete the task requirements and no more. Teaching activities are seen as an external imposition and deploying this approach, students are often unreflective about the purpose of learning and how they might develop it further at a theoretical or conceptual level. By contrast, a deep approach to learning describes a student's disposition to perceive teaching tasks as an opportunity to gain new insight rather than to satisfy external demand. This approach to learning is more holistic in so far as it portrays students relating previous knowledge to new knowledge, theoretical ideas to everyday experience and evidence to argument (Ramsden, 1992). A final approach, labelled the 'strategic' or 'achieving' approach (Biggs, 1999), is also commonly encountered and denotes the prime motivation for learning as the competition for the highest marks. In this case, the student adopts a strategic approach by optimizing the organisation of time and effort, using surface and deep approaches as relevant.

At one level, I suspect that most university teachers would assert that they encourage so-called deep approaches to learning through their practice. Inculcating deep approaches to learning signals a departure from a view of students as passive receptacles into which knowledge is poured and a move towards a more active view of students' role in teaching contexts. To some extent, it is reminiscent of Freire's comment that 'the teacher is no longer merely the-one-who-teaches, but who is himself (sic) taught in dialogue with the students' (1972: 53). However, to suggest that encouraging deep approaches to learning is akin to a kind of Freirian critical pedagogy is rather disingenuous. On the one hand, rendering students as active agents in learning processes would indeed seem to be evidence of a democratisation of the classroom and a problematisation of its authority relations. But on the other hand, declaring that one tries to foster deep learning approaches among students, and that this is a sign of introducing criticality into the classroom (i.e. getting students to 'think for themselves'), falls short of addressing seriously a long tradition of critical thought in the wider humanities and social sciences.

Barnett's critical beings

Part of the problem above, in my estimation, is that notions of deep, surface and strategic learning would seem to be underpinned by psychological theories of learning which overprivilege the 'student as individual' as the unit of analysis. For me, this tends to promote an asocial view of the nature of teaching and learning. It embraces the idealistic notion that learners meet as equals and ignores the social relations, and therefore the relations of power, that exist in teaching contexts (Willmott, 1997) and that are also encoded in the kinds of formal knowledges that students are exposed to. In this regard, Barnett's (1997) *Higher Education: A Critical Business* has been instructive for me since he views the aim of education as the creation of 'critical beings'. For Barnett, criticality works on two axes: the first axis is that of the *level* of criticality, whether understood narrowly as critical skills or more broadly as transformatory critique; the second axis is that of *domain*, in other words whether criticality is engaged in relation to formal knowledge, the self or the world. As Table 5.1 shows, bringing together these axes provides us with three forms of criticality: critical reason, critical self-reflection and critical action.

Table 5.1 Levels, domains and forms of critical being

	Domains		
Levels of criticality	*Knowledge*	*Self*	*World*
4. Transformatory critique	Knowledge critique	Reconstruction of self	Critique-in-action (collective reconstruction of the world)
3. Refashioning of traditions	Critical thought (malleable traditions of thought)	Development of self within traditions	Mutual understanding and development of traditions
2. Reflexivity	Critical thinking (reflection on one's own understanding)	Self-reflection (reflection on one's own project)	Reflective practice ('metacompetence', 'adaptability', 'flexibility')
1. Critical skills	Discipline-specific critical thinking skills	Self-monitoring to given standards and norms	Problem-solving (means-end instrumentalism)
Forms of criticality	*Critical reason*	*Critical self-reflections*	*Critical action*

Source: Barnett (1997: 103)

For Barnett, enabling students to fashion themselves as critical beings involves a teacher deploying all three forms of criticality in their courses:

> A curriculum intended to develop critical persons necessarily, therefore, has to find some way of developing critical thinking in the three domains so as to develop critical thought, critical self-reflection and critical action. (Barnett, 1997: 114)

I would say that the production of critical beings is the goal of my teaching, and Barnett's table has proved invaluable to me in specifying the different kinds of critique this necessitates.

If I were to relate Barnett's table to the variety of courses I have come across in the past that attempt to engender, in some way, intercultural competence among students (be that modules in cross-cultural management, intercultural communication, cross-cultural capability, cross-cultural psychology, etc.), I would suggest that most work with levels one and two of criticality. The courses (in both university and the corporate sector) that I am familiar with would typically teach: dimensions or frameworks for articulating cultural differences; use vignettes or case studies to conduct problem-solving activities that involve cross-national interactions; ask students to 'start with the self' and to articulate the oft-unexamined, tacit values and norms that frame their own behaviours; and encourage students to practice self-monitoring in cross-cultural interaction. Often the ultimate goal of cross-cultural training is to foster in students an ability to practice 'mindfulness' in intercultural contexts, using generic (rather than culture-specific) frameworks of analysis, and with an appreciation of both the cognitive as well as the affective aspects of intercultural competence. What these courses do not do, however, in my experience, is to pursue a critical agenda beyond these two levels. My own module set out, with the (retrospectively dubious) ambition to create an understanding of intercultural competence that transgressed convention in cross-cultural teaching (certainly in management).

Critical intercultural learning: A problem of representation?

There are two key reasons why I pursue teaching for critical intercultural learning, both of which reside in the epistemological and political/ethical problems I associate with conventional approaches to cross-cultural teaching. I have written about these problems on several occasions before, so a brief rehearsal of these positions will suffice. Epistemologically, I believe that a 'dimensional' approach to culture, which allows us to plot or map representatives of national cultures onto some kind of continuum, presents students with unhelpfully fixed categories of analysis that essentialize culture and divest it of its key processual and political contingencies. In privileging the individual as the core unit of analysis, the reality-constitutive properties of dialogue and social interaction are steadfastly ignored. With particular regard to Hofstede, moreover, I am convinced that McSweeney's (2002) devastating critique of the methodological basis of *Culture's Consequences* means that it is impossible to take his cultural dimensions as self-evident or statistically sound evidence for national culture.

Politically and ethically, I have difficulties in viewing intercultural competence *purely* as the serial acquisition of skills that can be exchanged in the labour market. To be more specific, my problem lies with the commodification of intercultural understanding and the manner in which an obsession with the marketplace obscures and often distorts a broader discussion of values and relations to the Other. Hegemonic interculture (structural functionalist, positivist, aligned with capital) serves to normalise a particular and problematic view of cultural diversity – one that casts other understandings of the intercultural to the margins. Within the management context, intercultural competence is regrettably a process of managerial internationalisation where institutions shape and edit the managerial self to fit the institutional interest of the organisation.

My aim is to restore a multiplicity of accounts, agendas and values to students' understandings of intercultural competence. Certain principles and concepts from postcolonial and poststructuralist thinking have assisted me in this regard. First, I am interested in encouraging students to 'provincialize' (Chakrabarty, 2000) management thought, including cross-cultural management, and to contextualize it within the contemporary hierarchy of global culture. This work of provincialization would illustrate the lack of epistemic diversity in management thought and practice, the eurocentrism of conventional management theory, and the narrow demography of the management academy, that is, the small number of people (and here I mean white men based principally in the US and Western Europe) who are institutionally authorised to decide what ideas count and what ideas do not.

Second, and relatedly, I am interested in students understanding that intercultural competence is, importantly, an issue of representation and to think about what it means to represent Others. I make students read Said's (1978) *Orientalism* in order that they come to understand: the dialectical and relational nature of identity construction; the role of discourse in enabling and constraining understandings of certain people or objects in the world; the asymmetrical and political nature of knowledge; concepts of appropriation, hegemony and cultural imperialism; the cultural architecture of colonialism. Said's Foucauldian-inspired view of discourse means that Hofstede's work is not simply dismissed out of hand in my teaching; instead his work is viewed as an outcome of a wider regime of truth that enables and constrains a certain view of culture. Finally, I am interested in students understanding the concept of neo-colonialism, and debating the view that cross-cultural training is the latest form of preparation for neo-colonial administration based on the image of a Western coloniser's way of life. To teach interculture competence critically is to ask students to 'unlearn their privilege' (Spivak, 1993) and to contextualise difference within a context being continually re-written by global capital. Barnett's call for transformatory critique takes on a particular hue here.

Critique: Emancipation or practices of liberation?

While I am sympathetic to (often Freirian-inspired) ideas about education as emancipation, it does seem to rest on an overly optimistic, romantic and essentialised view of the human subject breaking free of the shackles of certain ideological structures and practices and re-discovering their creativity. I am not a romantic Marxist, nor a romantic Freirian. From a Foucauldian perspective, there is no external position (some might say utopia) that is free from power or ideology; but, rather we can only ever move from one discursive regime to another, a regime that will itself hail the subject to change him or herself in particular ways. For Foucault (1984/1986), some sense of emancipation or, to use his term, 'practices of liberation', are involved in realising that there are other ways to relate to oneself than those that currently govern us. The sense of liberation comes in moving from one discursive regime to another, not residing there. This 'other place' comes with its own strictures. I find this idea of practices of liberation useful in talking about the kinds of transformatory critique mentioned by Barnett. In this regard, deploying Foucault enables me to view a central tenet of my notion of teaching for critical learning as introducing students to discourses that might help them relate to themselves differently and to engage in the kinds of liberational practices that enable them to view this as a possibility.

Course design

How did these principles and concerns feed into course design, delivery and assessment? Here is the introductory blurb to the module outline (taken verbatim):

> The aim of this module is to provide you with a critical introduction to the theoretical frames and practical issues involved in the processes of

managing and marketing across national and cultural borders. Drawing upon a range of ideas and studies from disciplines like anthropology, literary criticism, cultural studies, comparative/international and radical management studies, you are invited to explore critically academic and practitioner constructions of the effects of national culture on managerial and consumer values and behaviours. At the heart of our explorations of cross-cultural research lies a concern with similarity and difference. What does it mean to say that cultural differences exist between people? Or that some things transcend cultural boundaries and a shared part of humanity? What is the basis of these perceptions of sharedness and difference? How have different answers to this question been deployed in the construction of international management and marketing strategies, or cross-cultural training programmes? What are the effects of these managerialist interventions on the people who constitute target markets or international workforces? What does it mean to have knowledge of another? What are the contingencies of that knowledge? Just whose interests do they serve? These questions of knowing (of epistemology) are central to this course.

Importantly then, this course does not teach the subject of cross-cultural management and marleting as some kind of 'neutral' activity or set of managerial tools/techniques with which to control and manipulate national and cultural differences in work and market-places. Rather it attempts to understand the nature of these activities within the social, political and cultural contexts of globalising markets and workplaces and uses this background to ask questions of a critical nature that explore the social, political and moral implications of this management discourse.

The course was delivered through 12 two-hour workshops. It began with an introductory workshop that explained the overall course narrative, warned students that this may not be what they expected, outlined the reasons why and then set up a dualistic structure that framed the course organisation. The first half of the course was entitled: *Constructing the Other: Classifying, Knowing and Managing Difference.* This section included workshops on Hofstede and national cultures; ideas of the nation-state; language, communication and codes; personal intercultural effectiveness training; the concept of the global manager; application of cultural theory to various elements of management (e.g. motivation, leadership) and marketing (e.g. consumer decision-making, country-of-origin effect). The second half was entitled: *Deconstructing the Other: Postcolonial Discourse and the Politicization of Difference.* This section included workshops on Said's *Orientalism* and

the idea of postcolonial critique; the concept of Othering and appropriation; consuming the Other and commodifying the exotic; place-making
and the re-invention of tradition; the politics of in-between. The students
were given a reading week between the two halves to study Said.

My teaching methods aimed to facilitate as much participation, interaction and discussion from the students as possible in order to foster high
levels of critical debate, analysis and reflection. The majority of the sessions
were conducted around small group work using a variety of materials
including videos, case studies, brainstorming and mind-mapping, text/
vignette-based discussion and some conventional lecture delivery. Often,
the formal classroom is (over-)privileged as the main site where student
learning is supposed to occur. This is very limiting since it ignores the
multiplicity of spaces and times where learning might occur. As such, and
in order to formalize and legitimate a wider topography for learning,
spaces were structured outside formal class time to facilitate collective
learning. In this respect, students were organised into and worked within
cross-cultural learning sets, asked to meet outside class time each week to
prepare tasks, and a web board was set up as a discussion forum. Probably
over-assessed in retrospect, the students were required to do coursework
comprising a group presentation and an individual essay, and then a formal two-hour examination. In the essay, students were required to conduct a Saidian-inspired colonial discourse analysis of a set of contemporary
cross-cultural management texts. In the next section I go on to outline and
discuss student responses to the course.

Student Responses

The 22 students that took this course exhibited a considerable diversity
in terms of gender, ethnicity, nationality and language. Half were exchange
students, mainly from Europe (Germany predominantly, but also France)
and the United States; the other half were full-time undergraduate students
mainly from the United Kingdom (and of multiple ethnicities) and a few
other nations (Germany, Oman, Nigeria). Information about where the students come from is important for contextualising my presentation and
analysis of their responses to the course. I collected these responses through
a number of formal and informal mechanisms including student evaluation forms (see Appendix 1 where I present written comments from these
evaluation forms), informal conversations with students and a recorded
and transcribed presentation I gave about my course at another university.

Overall, and at first glance, students' responses to my course seemed predominantly positive. They reported that they were clear with the structure

of the course, and understood its aims. In terms of organisation and sequence of materials, the construction/deconstruction trope worked well and provided clarity for the students. 'Building up to the difficult stuff', with enough forewarning, allowed students to prepare themselves for some challenging and uncomfortable workshops. Most students seemed to enjoy the challenge and degree of difficulty of the module, especially the full-time students whose other management courses tended to be much more conventional. I listened closely to my students and learned from them through multiple channels, as recommended in the literature on teaching for critical learning outlined earlier. However, on closer inspection and consideration of students' expressions of challenge and the sense of discomfort, the module also clearly created, a number of difficult and ambiguous responses.

Gender, race and class

The module provoked a marked gendered and racialised response from the students. Reflecting on student evaluations of the course, axes of gender/race might provide a key basis for the differentiation of student responses to the module. In short, it was those students who self-identified as being at the 'cultural margins' who expressed the strongest and most positive cognitive and affective connections to the module. For these students, it seemed that the module was an important cultural experience that enabled them to engage in a considerable amount of self-reflection, and to re-interpret their own cultural histories and present subject positions with a greater sense of pride and dignity.

Famida (female, Muslim student from Birmingham with Indian parents), for instance, expressed the view that the course had helped her understand and, to some extent, come to terms with the ways in which she had in the past been discriminated against on account of her cultural and ethnic background. Not only was she a Muslim in a UK context, but she was also an Indian Muslim, itself a marginal ethnic group in the context of Indian culture. She told me that both in the United Kingdom and in India, she had experienced racism on account of her Islamic faith, and in the United Kingdom, she had also experienced racism on the basis of her skin colour. The alternative ways of knowing about cultural difference, where difference is viewed as an outcome of problematic Othering practices, facilitated an understanding of these racist experiences at a cognitive level. Perhaps more importantly though, at an affective level, the course provoked reflection on difficult cultural memories, enabling Famida to come to terms with them to some degree by ascribing a positive value to her subject position. Similarly, Shamsa (female, Muslim student from Oman) also found the ideas of Othering covered on the course useful in helping her understand not only the demonisation of her religion, but also responses to her home culture. In terms of the latter, Said's *Orientalism* taught Shamsa that the kinds of Othering that had been applied to Oriental cultures in the past, continued in the present with regard to her own religion. While Shamsa expressed similar cognitive responses to the course, her affective engagement with it was less emotionally charged than Famida's.

It should be noted though that there were male students from the course whose response to its materials also shared a positive cognitive and affective dimension with Famida and Shamsa. Phil (from South Korea) commented that he felt 'the course has helped me to understand how my culture is threatened'. He explained that this meant two things: first that his culture was threatened by the perceived dominance of Japan as an economic and cultural power in East Asia and second that globalisation had intensified the flow of Western, and especially American cultural symbols into South Korea. Kahaso (from Nigeria) found it a useful basis from which to speak as an African national in the context of a white, UK classroom – it gave him a legitimised space from which to 'enunciate' (a term he picked up in the class, and actively deployed in his discourse). Given his Nigerian nationality, and therefore his superior understanding of the colonial and postcolonial context for many of the ideas on the course, he engaged very productively with ideas of agency, voice and revisionist history. On leaving university, he went on to do a Masters in development studies on the basis of his enjoyment of the course.

It is tempting to sum up these sentiments in the following way: that the postcolonial tenets of the course engendered successful cognitive and affective responses among this sub-set of students who could be thought of as part of the cultural margins of British society (in their positions as either British nationals, or as full-time overseas students in a British context). It could be said that they managed to successfully reach levels two and three of Barnett's table, re-defining and developing a more positive self-image and sense of cultural belonging as they engaged with new traditions of thought. To do this, however, would be to overlook the important issue of contexts for social stratification (or social class). With the exception of Famida, the students mentioned above had privileged backgrounds – they came from the elite strata of their own societies. This privilege gave them access to travel and to a British education. But in coming to the UK, they came to speak, or may well have felt forced to speak, from an alternative subject position in a 'foreign' culture. In other words, while they might legitimately take the position of Other in the context of the British university classroom, they could hardly be viewed as part of the economic or social and cultural margins back home. Interestingly, this view back upon their home culture, and its complicating mediation in their expressions of self-identity in the British context, was only briefly remarked upon in discussion.

Negative emotions, superior cognitions

While the students above expressed a particularly strong personal resonance with the course, this is not to say that other students who did not find the course as enjoyable did not also have heightened emotional responses. It is just that their responses indexed different emotional attachments to learning on this course. To be more specific, some of the other affective responses were considerably less positive than those articulated above. The second dominant theme in the following discussion relates to a distinctly interesting cleavage in certain students' cognitive and affective responses.

In comparison to the students above, it was members of dominant identity groups who were responsible for these 'resistant' responses: Jorn, Philip, Oliver (white, male, German exchange students). Again it would be wrong to push a uniformly gendered picture here, for the two female German students (Marieke and Stephanie) were also particularly reticent about the course. It was Marieke and Stephanie whose responses to the course seemed most emotionally intense in a negative way. Crying, frequent visits to the office, high degrees of uncertainty, checking behaviour and the need for constant reassurance characterised their engagement with the course. As for the male students, their resistance took form in both a kind of 'pleasant' or 'non-confrontational' cynicism and denigration of the course objectives, as well as some pretty outspoken verbal turns in class discussion. Together these responses seemed founded on a considerable degree of anxiety, and to a lesser extent, anger with the course.

I began to understand that such anxiety was not just the product of being unfamiliar with new forms of material and of challenging readings, but was also with the fact that it was seen as a threat to successful *assessment*. For these German students, the spectre of assessment and getting good grades was the source of considerable worry, considerably more it seemed than for students of any other nationality.

It is perhaps ironic then that it was these very students, those of a distinctly negative disposition to the course, who scored the top grades in the coursework and examination process. Although these students felt little personal resonance with the course material and its delivery, they still managed to score very high grades indeed. Those students with more positive responses to the course did not do as well by comparison. For me, this cleavage between the negative affective responses and the positive cognitive ones (as measured by good assessment outcomes) was worrying and caused me to think profoundly about whether the course was meeting its objectives. For one, the question arises of how this situation could come to be. Using the learning approaches model noted earlier, it could be suggested that this was a result of the *strategic* manner in which the German exchange students approached the course. Throughout, the students decided not to explore the implications of the course material for their own being in the world (since this material was not managerially relevant and therefore not 'really' management education, as we shall see below). Instead they objectified the course as a set of knowledges with which they needed to be familiar for assessment purposes only. They engaged in surface and deep learning as necessary and in accordance with my explicit assessment criteria. This suggests, to me, that I had put in place inappropriate structures for assessing the kinds of outcomes I desired on the course. I did not want to encourage this kind of strategic approach to learning about the subject matter, but wanted to reward students for some sense of transformatory critique. I failed at this I think.

Capitalist ideology and student subject-formation

As Foucault reminds us, power is not totalising. It merely provides the conditions of possibility for its formation by social agents, and sits in contiguous relations with resistance. Student responses to the CCMM module suggest that the purported sovereign power of the teacher over the learner is a myth – 'my' exercise of power over 'them' took the form of a tense, uneven and ever-shifting relationship which expressed itself in a number of different forms of resistance. Through the collection of formal and informal feedback, I began to identify a number of strategies deployed by some of the students to 'deal with the political stuff' (retort from one of the students).

As indicated above, while for many the course was interesting, difficult and challenging, for others it was not such a happy experience; indeed, it was sometimes threatening. Some of these sentiments are encoded in the following comments from the students on the course:

- A quirky sideline to real business.
- It is important to have a bit of ethics somewhere.
- Not managerially relevant.

- Its link to management was weak.
- Capitalism has won, so why think about other systems?
- I thought colonialism was over?

A starting point for interpreting these quotes is to note that they work through particular labours of division: that is, divisions between what is relevant and not relevant; what is political and not political; what is part of managerial life and part of private life; what counts as business and what counts as ethics. Students were drawing lines here and demarcating that which they considered acceptable in a management course ('business' and not 'ethics' or 'politics') and that which was not – in the process allowing them a space from which they did not have to politicise their own knowledges or their relations to self. That is to say, they did not wish to create a space in which to continually work with a struggle about competing values and models for understanding economic, social or cultural organisation. Instead they wished to close down such a provisional space with triumphalist capitalist discourse.

What is interesting about the comments above is that they exhibit how some students use the dominant ideology of management education in the UK (and much of Europe) to resist a course that politicises the very assumptions on which it is based. They are clinging to, in some cases, puffed up by a dominant managerialism for resistance, a strategy that disciplines (in the Foucauldian sense) both them as a student and the subject of the market, and me as the teacher. Dominant market ideology provides a very important source of identification for them, one which reassures them of the rightness of conventional management education by excreting the infiltration of political questions. So while I had attempted to eschew conventional management discourse, it found its way back into the heart of my classroom in the form of resistance. It was deployed as a mode of surveillance on the explicitly politicised curriculum I had set.

Returning to the poststructuralist and postcolonial concerns of this course, I would venture an interpretation of these students' behaviour as an unwillingness to 'unlearn their privilege'. Despite *hearing* first-hand autobiographical accounts in their class from students about the effects of Othering, and the dehumanisation involved in the appropriation of minority cultural and ethnic identities by dominant groups, they did not *listen*. They did not seem able, or willing, either to reflect on the fact that they might themselves be considered part of a dominant/privileged identity group (in British and German societies), or to understand that Said's *Orientalism* is more than just a text to be learned about. It is a continuing everyday reality for many across the world. Although Famida, Shamsa,

Phil and Kahaso experienced some sense of emancipation (in so far as these new discourses allowed them to engaged in practices of liberation) on the module, the others stuck steadfastly within their current discursive structures. At best they remained on level one of Barnett's table.

Relating these outcomes back to my initial pedagogical strategy, I would say that my course design proved problematic in so far as it fostered the conditions of possibility for these kinds of student response. Looking back, I think I trapped the aims and objectives of the course too much into the domain of formal knowledge and was rather unsuccessful at importing it into the domains of 'self' and 'world' as prescribed by Barnett. While there were several instances of class activity where personal reflection was encouraged, there was no meaningful space for critical *action* to occur. On reflection, creating spaces in which the members of dominant groups could begin to see their own privilege through a critical engagement with the world may have helped illustrate and create a personal connection with them in ways not possible when such a theme is encoded in heavy theoretical reading of abstract analytical concepts. In sum, the outcomes of the course at best reached level three of Barnett's table (the refashioning of traditions), and at worst remained on level one. None of the students, so far as the evidence allows me to say, achieved a desired level of transformatory critique.

Conclusion

In this concluding section, I draw together my personal experiences and reflections on the course, with the themes already presented above. To begin, here is an excerpt from the transcript of a seminar I did about this very course at an educational network aimed at engendering teaching for critical learning in the context of UK higher education. I talked of:

> …an enormously uncomfortable and emotional rollercoaster over twelve weeks. Some of them have been prepared for it, some of them haven't. It's been antagonistic at times, they've been upset; it has caused debate and tension in the class. For some it has been enormously creative and politically empowering.

For me, this course was always about more than academic achievement. It was an attempt to get management students to think beyond the confines of management discourse, and in particular the dimensionalising impulse that characterises work in CCMM. It was an attempt to make culture intertwine with politics and ethics, as much as, probably even more than, capital accumulation. It was an attempt to bring different stories and different voices into the milieu of a management classroom in a British university. That the outcomes of the course in terms of students' cognitive and affective learning were highly differentiated is testament to the fact that teaching is never an unequivocal success. Perhaps teaching for any kind of learning (critical intercultural or otherwise) is always, perhaps necessarily, ambiguous and imperfect.

But what remains something of a puzzle to me is how it is possible for students who have completed a course explicitly set up to legitimize and carry out a politicization of management theory and practice on the issue of culture, to come to the end and still take the view that management and culture is 'not political'. Perhaps this can be explained as an ideological outcome, or a discursive effect, of living with global capital. Capitalism (despite its many internal contradictions and inconsistencies) is a belief system that, when articulated in everyday life, seems to have the effect of presenting itself as the most desirable form of social and economic organisation (despite evidence to the contrary) and to create the illusion that it is not a political system, merely an economic one (and in the process lead students to believe that questions of politics somehow stand outside questions of economy). Capitalist ideology perpetuates a myth of an eternal present, and refuses to be historicised in ways that might allow for any radical economic or cultural alterity to be properly considered. Perhaps the paramount aim of teaching for critical intercultural learning should be creating a *culture or cultures of disjuncture* in the classroom where students can shake off the ideological shackles of 'present times', and begin to realise that both they and the world around them could be radically different.

To my mind, the students most highly resistant to this course seemed to adopt a cosmopolitan attitude to cross-cultural learning. By cosmopolitan I do *not* mean that these students were open to different ways of being with the Other; instead, I think they resisted these possibilities through the deployment of triumphalist capitalist discourse. By cosmopolitan what I have in mind is a negative sense of cosmopolitanism expressed, for instance, in the work Žižek (1997) for whom cosmopolitanism is capital's latest cynical way of incorporating and thus appropriating (ethnic) differences into the structural organisation of production and consumption. It trades in objectified, commodified, decontextualised and often highly aestheticized forms of cultural difference that continue to organise global culture into ever-changing hierarchical forms. The students' refusal to listen to the highly contextualized, subjective experiences of their peers was a refusal to listen to the global hierarchy of culture at work – an attempt to preserve a status quo in which they all had a stake as they trained to become elite professionals, part of Sklair's (2001) transnational capitalist class.

The cultural difference they came to class to learn about is the cultural difference of an imagined cosmopolitanism, of world cities, airport lounges, exotic foods and comfortable communicative possibility. It seemed to me that courses in CCMM like mine that did not provide this 'shopping-cart' for knowledge, its embodiment and future performance was at best suspect, at worst wasted. Perhaps this is an unfair personal response to some of my students, but it was a firmly held view of mine at the time, perhaps one that enabled me to come to terms with the ambiguity of my own success as a teacher for critical intercultural learning.

References

Barnett, R. (1997) *Higher Education: A Critical Business*. Buckingham: SRHE and Open University Press.

Biggs, J. (1999) *Teaching for Quality Learning at University*. Buckingham: SRHE and Open University Press.

Brookfield, S.D. (1995) *Becoming a Critically Reflexive Teacher*. San Francisco: Jossey-Bass Publishers.

Chakrabarty, D. (2000) *Provincializing Europe*. Princeton: Princeton University Press.

Foucault, M. (1984/1986) *The History of Sexuality: Vol. 3: The Care of the Self*. New York: Pantheon.

Freire, P. (1972) *Pedagogy of the Oppressed*. London: Penguin.

McSweeney, B. (2002) Hofstede's model of national cultural differences and their consequences: A triumph of faith – a failure of analysis. *Human Relations* 55 (1), 89–118.

Prosser, M. and Trigwell, K. (1999) *Understanding Learning and Teaching*. Buckingham: SRHE and Open University Press.

Ramsden, P. (1992) *Learning to Teach in Higher Education*. London: Routledge.

Said, E. (1978) *Orientalism: Western Conceptions of the Orient*. London: Penguin.

Sklair, L. (2001) *The Transnational Capitalist Class*. Oxford: Blackwell.

Spivak, G.C. (1993) *Outside in the Teaching Machine*. New York: Routledge.

Willmott, H. (1997) Making learning critical: Identity, emotion and power in processes of management development. *Systems Practice* 10 (6), 749–771.

Žižek, S. (1997) Multiculturalism, or, the cultural logic of multinational capitalism. *New Left Review* 225, 28–52.

Appendix 1:   Formal Student Feedback

The following comments are taken directly, and verbatim, from the formal student feedback conducted via questionnaire at the end of the module.

Overall comments: (What did you like best/least about the module?)

Best: The invited interaction of the class; that the readings were printed out for us. Least: All the reading!

Very nice course; great class interaction; lectures were helpful and approachable; widened my horizon. But a lot to do!

I liked the fact that everything was made problematic and that we learnt more about the topic and gave me a deeper understanding. It was very enjoyable and interesting.

A very interesting subject to study, however not easy, a challenge. The way in which the classes were conducted was excellent, a comfortable environment and easy to express yourself. Excellent teaching methods.

The course was extremely interesting. It challenged a lot of stereotypical ideas about how I spoke about other cultures.

The course is very well structured with a very different approach to gaining knowledge. What I like most about it is the fact that it lets you think for yourself and come up with your own conclusions about the subject. Overall one of the best courses I have taken.

That is was different from everything I have done so far in the department. Not everybody felt the need to participate; lots to read and the texts were very challenging.

Other courses were more or less boring and appeared to be easy. This course was different. I hated doing the reading but really liked the class. I wouldn't mind a bad mark. Reading material – very challenging but probably necessary.

I have really enjoyed this course. He is a very relaxed and approachable tutor which makes for easier understanding of difficult material involved in the course.

Too much reading and assessment. Challenging and interesting. Suits overseas students.

Very interesting. A lot to cover though. Nice to have an article each week. I have found the ideas easier to present verbally rather than in writing – so a little worried about the essay component.

I really enjoyed the module. It was interesting and really different from other modules. You really know how to motivate students!!! But it was a little bit too much to read.

It was one of the most interesting courses and also very challenging. The tutor is great in motivating students. The topics discussed very difficult but he always found a way to explain it easily.

Best: Learning about a new way of looking at the world and people. Least: It is very hard to understand because it is a very different way of learning in terms of level and language.

Best: Staff approachability. Least: Said is very demanding; it did not focus on the relationship to marketing and that's what I thought the course was about. However the other stuff is also interesting.

I thought we were going to speak about management and marketing! But it was quite interesting.

Hard to get the real point of this course.

It opened up a whole different area of knowledge which was good. But the relevance of this to management is fairly weak and not much marketing in the module.

Chapter 6

Applying the Principles: Instruments for Intercultural Business Training

BARRY TOMALIN

Importance of Models

Business managers work on models. This is what they learn on MBA programmes. International business culture as a part of organisational development also works on a number of proto-models or principles, elucidated by theoreticians such as Hofstede (2003), Trompenaars and Hampden-Turner (2003), Lewis (2003) and Bennett (2003).

The problem is that it is not always clear how to implement their principles in the training room. You can teach them as they are presented in the books but the key issue is how to turn this knowledge into active business skills. Business people need practical immediately applicable business tools that will help them solve business communication problems. This is where training instruments come in.

Training instruments are the means we use to turn principles into active business practice and are the way we effect the mindset change and behavioural adaptation that is basic to intercultural awareness. This chapter presents a number of training activities that can be used to raise awareness of intercultural issues and to put cultural skills into action.

These activities are based on learning theory and on the understanding of the learning cycle as the framework for training, which is what we need to address first.

The Learning Cycle

A basic operating principle of management training is to follow the learning cycle. This has four phases.

- Activity.
- Debrief.
- Conclusion.
- Implementation.

The activity phase is very important. Intercultural training is first and foremost a knowledge-based topic. However, it is also a topic that invites reflection and consideration of one's own mindset and one's own practice. Effective cultural training does not come from merely telling someone how things are done elsewhere. It comes from considering your own mindset, comparing with your counterpart's mindset (or your perception of their mindset) and then deciding how to proceed on the basis of what you have learned.

So the activity phase involves getting trainees to do something that gives them an experience of cultural difference and makes them think about their own practice or mindset by comparing it with others. It is by definition interactive.

The debrief phase offers the opportunity for trainees to discuss their experience with others in the group or with the facilitator. This involves their thoughts about what they did, what they learned and above all how they felt about the experience. This once again involves interaction and discussion.

The conclusions phase is a more reflective phase when trainees think about the implications of what they have experienced, what changes in thinking it suggests and what changes in behaviour it might imply.

However, the key phase is implementation. There is no training without implementation. The way you do it is to ask trainees how they will apply what they have learned to the business environment they work in. This may lead to the establishment of SMART (specific, measurable, agreed, realistic and time based) business objectives and the establishment of an action plan for achieving them.

In summary, the learning cycle as applied here to business cultural training provides a framework for all the activities described in this chapter, which can be summarised in the following steps.

(1) Do something that raises awareness of cultural differences in expectation or behaviour.
(2) Debrief on what happened and how you felt.
(3) Reflect on what you have learned as a result of the experience and draw conclusions as to how your behaviour and expectations might change as a result.
(4) Plan how you will implement these changes in your business process.

Reflection and Action

Business training has both a left brain and a right brain aspect. The right-brained approach aims to promote reflection on differences with the result of kick starting a change of mindset. It speaks about the existence of different customer values and expectations. The left-brained approach focuses on improving performance by adapting behaviour. In fact, the very definition of interculturality assumes both a right- and left-brained approach. Your interaction with me changes my mindset just as mine with you changes yours. That is how mutual understanding is created. Some of the activities discussed in this chapter have a predominantly reflective function: thinking about cultural differences and the attitude change needed to adapt to them. Others have a predominantly behavioural function: making differences in behaviour in order to adapt to business practice elsewhere. Both reflective and behavioural activities have one outcome: improved performance, however you measure it, on the part of the trainee.

Training and Coaching

If training is about getting people to think about and do things differently and is achieved through a single or series of single defined insertions (one day, two days, one week), coaching is a longer term more adaptive and more personal process that has a deeper psychological impact on the coachee.

Good intercultural training will have both a training and a coaching aspect, because very few people get involved with cultural training as a matter of principle. They do it because they have a problem. In this respect, intercultural training is more specialised than mechanistic soft skills, such as time management or appraisals training.

The trainer's job in an intercultural training programme is to drill down to the personal issues faced by the trainee in dealing with other business communities and help him or her find personal solutions to dealing with them. As we will see later, this personal coaching function can be of the greatest importance in a successful intercultural training seminar.

In looking at intercultural training instruments we will divide the activities into

Experiential activities: BARNGA, Towers of Deurdia and Exclusion Zone

Comparative activities: The Communication Matrix, the Cultural Style Profile, the 80/20 principle applied to culture and the RADAR system

Reflective activities: Coaching activities and their role inside and
                           outside the training room in identifying personal
                           needs, personal interviewing, formal and
                           informal role-play and the consultant's circle

Experiential Activities

Barnga

Barnga is a card game devised by Thiagaran and Steinwachs in 1990,
aimed at raising awareness of intercultural issues. The game is played in
small groups and each player moves from group to group and becomes
aware as they do so that other players are playing by different rules.
Success in the game is achieved by understanding those differences and
adapting behaviour to the new regulatory environment. The game needs
a number of groups of between four and six players but can be used with
groups as small as 10 and also very large groups. No one talks or writes
during the game. The only communication is by gestures or grunts. The
game takes about 60 minutes, including debrief.

The advantage of the game is that it needs only a pack of cards for each
group and instruction. One or two 'knowers' circulate between the groups
to facilitate the process. The outcome is that participants discuss how
they felt, when dealing with a situation with different rules, how they
adapted and most importantly, how they changed their behaviour as a
result.

The Towers of Deurdia

This is a simulation game of two teams in which one team prepares and
presents a project to another team. The outcome of the simulation is to see
whether the presenting team gain or lose the contract or get to the second
meeting to re-present or further discuss their proposal. The aim of the
simulation is to get participants to take account of cultural issues as well
as task-related issues. The way this happens is that the team receiving the
presentation are encouraged to develop a particular set of cultural habits
and behaviours that usually the consultants do not know about.

The simulation usually lasts for one and a half hours and is divided up
as follows:

* Preparation 30–40 min.
* Simulation (up to 30 minutes).
* Debrief (up to 30 minutes).

Depending on the groups, each phase can be adapted to maintain the overall timing.

The group is divided into two teams. One team is the consultants, who have to prepare and present a construction project to the Deurdians (the other team). This involves producing a mock-up of a tower, with coloured card sticking tape and staple. The consultant team will elect a team leader, a technical team, who will build the tower and a marketing team, who will sell the product. They prepare under time constraints of 30–40 minutes in a breakout room.

The Deurdians will receive a project presentation for a new tower to be constructed in Deurdia from the consultants. The Deurdians love towers and are enthusiastic about receiving the consultants' visit.

While the consultants are preparing their presentation, the Deurdians are preparing the room to receive the consultants and rehearsing their own cultural traits. First they elect a leader (who will decide when the meeting should end) and their own marketing, finance and technical committees. Most importantly, however, their job is to make their culture as unfamiliar to the consultants as they can and to develop some fairly anti-social ways of greeting, showing approval and showing disapproval (such as hissing like geese when a social norm is broken).

The job of the consultants is to pick up on the Deurdians' cultural characteristics and to adapt their behaviour accordingly.

The final phase of the simulation, the debrief, involves the participants on both sides saying what they observed, what they felt and how successfully they adapted.

One of the great qualities of this powerful and memorable simulation is that it encourages reflection, not only about cultural adaptation but also about leadership and teamworking. With larger groups it may be a good idea to appoint one or two observers on each side to give feedback on how each team has performed.

Trainers using the simulation will introduce all sorts of interesting refinements but the core culture can be based on characteristics of the culture they are training the participants to deal with.

Exclusion zone

This is a simpler and astonishingly powerful activity in which all the participants in the group take part in conversations. First, select a group of fairly outgoing individuals and ask them to go outside. Once outside ask them to choose a topic of conversation and begin discussing it. Then, when they are ready, they should rejoin the others and tell them about their discussion. In the meantime, divide the rest of the group into small discussion groups and instruct them to completely ignore any outsiders until and unless absolutely compelled to.

When the outside group is ready, they join the inside groups and attempt to enter the discussion.

After about 10 minutes of this, stop the discussion, call the groups together and discuss the experience. The results can be quite profound but it illustrates the experience and emotions of the outsider trying to enter another group and the strategies they can use to do so. One of the outcomes is to encourage outsiders more to help them integrate and the activity can help develop a much greater sensitivity towards newcomers.

Analytical/Comparative Tools

Analytical/comparative tools are training instruments that help participants compare their own preferences and behaviours with others.

The Communication Matrix

One of these is the Communication Matrix, the principles of which are derived from E.T. Hall, Fons Trompenaars and Richard Lewis.

The trainer gives out the following chart, which identifies the communication paradigms that differentiate cultures, according to their research. Each paradigm is numbered, as follows:

Worksheet 1

1	High context	2	Low context
3	Formal	4	Informal
5	Concise	6	Expressive
7	Direct	8	Indirect
9	Neutral	10	Emotional
11	Fast paced	12	Slow paced

Participants write down the numbers that describe their own personal style and then write down the numbers of the general business style of the culture they are studying.

For example, if a group of British managers were studying Japanese business culture, the results might look like this:

Worksheet 2

UK	Japan
2,4,5,7,9,11	1,3,6,8,9,12

The only point of contact is number 9. Both the Japanese and the British adopt a fairly neutral style of expression, although there will be differences in detail. However, where the British generally prefer to explain things in detail, the Japanese like to work by suggestion and allusion. Where the British are rather informal, the Japanese prefer formality. Where the British prefer to say what they want and then give reasons, the Japanese prefer to explain the background first. Where the Japanese prefer to avoid saying 'No', they find the British style almost brutally direct (although many Americans find the British indirect). Finally, whereas the Japanese style of communication is slow and reflective, with lots of use of silence, the British style tends to be faster and silence is something to be filled.

Some readers will criticise such an analysis as simplistic, bordering on stereotyping. I will respond by saying that business people need platforms from which they can investigate cultures in more detail. In this case, the trainer is making general statements that can be subjected to further analysis when needed, rather than creating stereotypes that resist adaptation to the individual or situation.

Critical incident methodology

This is basic to the approach of exploring cultural differences. The EU European Intercultural Workplace project launched in 2007 to provide an analysis of the cultural problems faced by migrant workers in integrating host country workplaces in the EU. It contains a series of typical situations dramatised on DVD. These scenarios, as they are called, do not tell the migrant worker or the host country manager how to behave but simply identify the issue and raise it for discussion. It is for the workmates viewing the scenario to say what they would do in that situation and work out what would constitute best practice.

The aim of critical incident methodology is to create scenarios in print, verbally, audio or visually and to invite participants to explore how they would respond in that situation. The outcome is a statement of best practice that will inform the behaviour of people dealing with that situation or that culture in future.

Trainers interested in the European Intercultural Workplace as an example of critical incident methodology can refer to www.eiworkplace.net.

Insights and guidelines

This technique, taught by US trainer George Renwick, is an excellent group activity for mixed nationality groups and it is extremely simple to use. Its aim is to increase awareness of differences and also to establish the principle that the best informants about a business community's culture are the members of that community themselves. The process is straightforward. Seminar participants simply ask each other for a core value or expectation of their community and a couple of behavioural guidelines. And then compare notes with the rest of the group. It involves preparing a worksheet, which looks something like this:

Worksheet 3: Insights and Guidelines
Name
Country
. . . .
Guideline
. . . .

You then ask the participants to find someone from another culture (or who is familiar with another culture and ask them three questions).

(1) Tell me something that is really important to people in your culture.
     You might get answers like hospitality, family, transparency or respecting privacy.
(2) Tell me something I can do in your culture that will make a good impression.
     You might get answers like 'Turn up on time', 'Phone before you come', 'Bring a gift' and so on.
(3) Tell me something I can do in your culture that will make a bad impression.
     You might get answers like, 'Set your opening price too high', 'Fail to bargain', 'Arrive without notice', 'Outstay your welcome'.

Depending on the time available, participants can ask the questions of several of their colleagues.

At the debrief stage, all the participants come together and discuss what they learned about the cultures of the people they talked to. In some cases there may be apparent contradictions but these can also be discussed. The outcome might be a list of core values, recommended behaviours and behaviours to avoid by culture.

Finally, at the implementation stage, participants discuss how they would adapt their behaviour to cater to the core values, adopt recommended behaviours and avoid the behaviours advised against.

This then allows participants to pass on to the next activity, the values and attitudes chart.

Values and attitudes chart

The Values and Attitudes Chart allows seminar participants to check their view of a country's core values and attitudes against key indicators. It comes from Tomalin B and Nicks M 'The World's Business Cultures and How to Unlock Them' (2007). We present these indicators in the worksheet below:

Worksheet 4
Core value
Cultural fear
Time sensitivity
Space sensitivity
Motivation (money, status, power, security, job satisfaction)

This activity works well with both mono-cultural and multi-cultural groups. It focuses on the key elements that make up values. Core values are the key beliefs of the community under consideration. You should appeal to these. Cultural fears are the key beliefs about what is wrong. You should avoid appealing to these. Time sensitivity describes attitudes to time, punctuality and planning, and space sensitivity describes attitudes to comfortable personal space. Motivation describes what are considered the key motivations of people. Is it money (particularly common in communities such as the US or India where there is little or no social security)? Is it status (common in countries where social esteem is considered as important or more important than money)? Is it power (where your position in society is denoted by what and how much you control)? Or is it job satisfaction (where you have agreeable working conditions and a feeling of professional development in your work)? All societies have combination of these motivations but usually one or two are dominant.

Here is how it works. Invite participants to complete the grid and then discuss their conclusions. In the debrief they draw the key conclusions for the communities they are dealing with and in the application phase decide how they will act when they are dealing with workers from those countries.

Often my core value may be your cultural fear. For example, my national pride may be seen by you as arrogance or aggressiveness. My reserve may be seen by you as coldness or disinterest. That is why some trainers add an extra column to the values chart to show how these characteristics are perceived by others. In this case the values chart might be presented like this:

Worksheet 5

		Perceived by me as ...
Core value	National pride	Arrogance
Cultural fear	Invasion	Aggression
Time sensitivity	Loose	Rude/inefficient
Space sensitivity	60 cms	Over familiar
Motivation	Money	Greed

This allows for a further dimension of the discussion and emphasises the importance of explanation of why one thinks and acts as one does in order to ensure proper understanding. 'Say where you are coming from', is a key piece of advice for anyone dealing cross-culturally.

The cultural style profile

This is one of the most powerful tools developed for the comparison of cultural traits. It consists of 12 paradigms adapted from the work of Lewis, Trompenaars and Hofstede and grouped into three core categories, communication, leadership and organisation. Participants chart their own cultural style and then map against it the perceived cultural style of the community they are dealing with. The worksheet looks like this:

Worksheet 7

Cultural style profile

Communication

1 Communication style

Direct . . . . Indirect

2 Working style

Formal . . . . Informal

3 Discussion style

Fast moving . . . . Slow and measured

4 Emotional style

Neutral . . . . Emotional

Leadership

5 Leadership style

Flat . . . . Vertical

6 Decision-making style

Individualistic . . . . Collective

7 Basis for decision-making

Facts . . . . Instincts

8 The business relationship

The relationship . . . . Task

Organisation

9 Attitude to risk

Accepts risk. . . . . Dislikes risk

10 Attitude to work

Progressive . . . . Traditional

11 Attitude to time

Scheduled . . . . Flexible

12 Work/life balance

Live to work . . . . Work to live

Here is how it works. First participants chart their own personal cultural style by making a cross somewhere on each line. When they complete the task they join up their dots, making a zigzag line down the page. Next, they think of their perception of the cultural style of the community or people they are dealing with and map that on the same chart against their personal map and join up the crosses.

It is important to remember that this may or may not be an academically accurate representation of a culture. What it does is to visualise the perception of the person doing the chart, which is what matters here.

In the debrief phase the participants note the gaps between the two lines. Where the gaps are narrow we can assume that no difference in perception exists. Where, however, a large gap exists then there may be cause for further investigation. In this case, you can ask three questions:

(1) Is the gap important? If it is not, ignore it. If it is, go to question 2.
(2) Do I need to change? Or, do they need to change? Remember the supplier normally has to adapt to the client although there are exceptions to this maxim.
(3) If I do need to change, how much? (See the 80/20 principle applied to culture, below.)

Through this process participants will probably identify three or four areas of change that may improve cultural co-operation between groups. In the application to the business phase they then write 'I' statements to establish what change is needed.

For example, if someone has a very informal style and is working in a formal environment, they may write 'I need to be more formal'.

Or, for example, if your company has a strong culture of consultation and consensus decision-making and the company you are dealing with is very individualist in their decision making and your organisation is the client, you may write, 'I need them to consult more before taking decisions'.

The procedure is very simple, as it needs to be in business organisations but the psychological effect is very powerful as it simultaneously helps the participant identify where behavioural and attitudinal change is needed and suggests what action he or she needs to take.

However, the question is always 'Do I have to make a 180 degree change?' and the answer is no. This is where the 80/20 principle applied to culture is so useful and re-assuring.

The 80/20 principle applied to culture

Vilfredo Pareto (1848–1923) was a 19th century Italian economist who made the assertion that 20% of a nation's population contribute 80% of its wealth. The 80/20 principle, as it came to be known, has since been applied to a range of other environments and I have found it can usefully be applied to management culture and communication. In this environment the statement is 'a 20% change in behaviour will lead to an 80% change in attitude'. It is, of course, a rule of thumb but it does work and is easy to apply.

When a workshop participant has completed the cultural style profile and identified the areas where change is necessary, he or she simply has to estimate what 20% change in behaviour is needed to change attitudes.

For example, if you are too individualistic and you are working in a consultative management culture, then consulting with colleagues 20% more will quickly change attitudes.

If in a Japanese company you go home to your family and never go out with your team you may be considered an individualist. If, however, you change your behaviour 20% and go out with your team once or twice a month, you will earn the accolade, 'good team player'.

The question, therefore, is 'What 20% change do I need to make?' to make a cultural difference.

The RADAR system

This is an exercise that helps managers remember the importance of cultural; change in improving communication at work. It is a mnemonic, like KISS (keep it short and simple) and SMART objectives to help you remember key principles and it describes the procedure of dealing with communication issues at work. The nmemonic is RADAR and it works like this.

R Recognise	You have a cultural issue
A Analyse it	Use the cultural style profile above to analyse it. You will probably find two or three gaps between your style and the person you are dealing with

D Decide	Decide if the gap in behaviour or attitude is important, who needs to change and what 20% change in behaviour is needed by you or by them
A Act	Make the change
R Review	Assess the impact of the change in behaviour. Did it achieve the desired change in the other person's attitude? If so, continue. If not, try something else

Coaching

The third type of cultural training activities involves a coaching element. A key element in good training is the ability of the trainer to identify and focus on personal issues that are important to individual trainees in doing their job and this is particularly important in training executives to deal with other cultures. In this final section we shall examine four types of activity:

• Need to know.
• Personal interviewing.
• Role-play.
• Consultant circles.

Need to know

Need to know is a simple on site diagnostic activity that supplements and makes more precise any needs analysis completed before the training course. It allows participants on the programme to identify key issues of CURRENT CONCERN and to seek answers.

Participants work in pairs and identify issues that have arisen for them or which they think may arise for them in projects they have been or may be involved in. They write these down on library cards and present their issues to the group. The aim is to make the issues as specific as possible and to present them as questions or as situations.

The need-to-know cards are then posted on the wall in the training room and are referred to at various points during the training programme. The important thing is that participants are encouraged to take responsibility for their own learning and to seek the answers they need during the training session.

At the end of the session, working in groups or individually, they take the need-to-know cards and present their conclusions, which constitute a summary of the personal learning that has gone on.

The public presentation of the results attests to the success they have had and may also trigger ideas in other participants that help them resolve issues they have raised.

Need to know is one of the simplest and most successful diagnostic activities we have found.

Personal interviewing

Sometimes issues are too confidential to be raised in a public fashion, as they may involve communication problems with another member of the group or with someone who others in the group know. In this case, it is worth giving time in a two- or three-day programme for an hour's personal interview for each group member. This can take place at the end of each day's training so as not to disrupt the day's work.

Another approach might be to plan one or two telephone or face-to-face coaching sessions of an hour per participant. These need to be pre-planned, as participants in open plan offices may need to get to a private phone.

Coaching conversations tend to have three aims:

• Update on progress (particularly re-action planning).
• Reinforce training messages.
• Troubleshoot issues.

In each case the trainer's aim is to be less directive and more consultative, less giving direct advice and more asking questions to help the participant come to their own realisations and conclusions.

Many participants find that the personal follow-up is one of the most useful outcomes of the training as it helps them apply the training directly to their personal situation.

Role-play

Two kinds of role-play are used in inter-cultural training:

• Formal.
• Informal.

In the more formal role-play, role cards are handed out and people play different roles to act out a typical situation. To do this successfully, it is important to have people from the culture or sufficiently familiar with the culture to take the necessary cultural role. For example, in interviewing a Japanese manager from a Western viewpoint it is important to have a Japanese manager or someone very familiar with Japanese management culture as the interviewee.

In this situation, the subject matter and the parameters of the role-play are clearly laid out and the interaction can be filmed and played back. It is an excellent opportunity to study the body language and behaviour of the person whose culture the group is studying.

In an informal role-play the trainer identifies a problem and 'slips into' the character of a typical member of the culture under study, sometimes without the other participants realising it. Fairly quickly, they realise what is happening and they respond appropriately.

A good example was a German explaining the sales strategy he wanted his US colleagues to adopt. The trainer immediately slipped into the role of the American and disagreed in a vigorous but a culturally appropriate fashion to the explanations being offered by the German manager. Immediately, the German could experience the effect of his cultural style on his US counterpart and was able to begin to adapt his style to his colleague's in order to get an effective result. What was happening was that the German approached the issue from a company policy angle without taking into account the US manager's personal aspirations and without personalising the message in a way that the American could take on board. The effect of the encounter was electrifying and brought home to the German manager in a dramatic and effective fashion how his style could have negative results and how to change it to get a positive outcome.

The informal role-play strategy may be highly effective but it is also high risk. The trainer may not be an 'actor' and may find it difficult to slip into this kind of training role. Done insensitively, it could have negative effects on the group and the seminar as a whole or cause embarrassing personal issues to be raised. It is a highly effective technique with the right personalities but needs to be introduced and handled carefully and with respect for the parties and cultures involved.

The consultant's circle

At the very beginning of this chapter we introduced the need-to-know activity as a valuable way of identifying issues that needed to be addressed by the group. The consultant's circle is a way of ensuring that those issues are addressed. In this exercise the expertise of the participants is called into play to advise each other on solutions to communication issues.

Let us take the example of a group of health care practitioners, several of whom are of a different nationality to their patients and who feel they suffer discrimination from patients as a result.

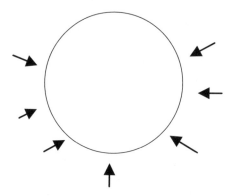

Ask the participants to arrange their chairs in two circles facing each other. So you have an inner circle facing outwards and an outer circle facing inwards:

Worksheet 8

Some of the participants, it does not matter who, sit in the inner circle and some in the outer circle.

The outer circle takes their 'need to know' cards and ask the person opposite them for their advice. Then they go sideways (the inner circle stay where they are) and ask the next person's advice and so on round the circle. In this way they receive a range of advice from different 'consultants' in the inner circle. Finally, they summarise the advice they have received.

Then the inner circle and the outer circles change positions and the process is repeated, with the original outer circle now playing the role of consultants. The value of this activity is that it mobilises the expertise of the group in working on solving specific problems and enables people to get a range of different experiences and expertise to bear in a short time.

Conclusion

Good cultural training involves three skills. One is cultural knowledge. One is learning skills and one is interpersonal skills. The cultural knowledge is the basic information you need to get across to your trainees. The problem with cultural knowledge is that it tends to encourage a lecturing and hectoring approach. You sit there, I tell you what's what and you listen. You do not, however, necessarily learn.

Another is learning skills. That's why you need to know about learning engineering skills (presentation, group working, reinforcement and coaching strategies) to help your trainees get the best out of their own learning by entering different situations and learning from colleagues as well as the trainer.

Above all, however, a good cultural trainer needs to cultivate their interpersonal skills. They are helping their participants and their families through potentially life-changing experiences that will help their careers and enhance their lifestyles and their sense of themselves.

In business terms, cultural training, like all business training, is about improving performance. In life terms it is about becoming a more rounded, more internationally minded individual. In a short training session, you may feel that is a tall order but it is still what every intercultural trainer should be aiming to achieve.

References

Bennett, M.J. (2003) *Basic Contexts*. New York: NTC.
Hofstede, G. (2003) *Cultures and Organisations*. London: Harper Collins.
Lewis, R.D. (2003) *When Cultures Collide*. London: NB Books.
Sivasailam, T. and Steinwachs, B. (1990) *BARNGA*. Yarmouth, Maine: Intercultural Press; and London: NB Books.
The European Intercultural Workplace (2007) *EU Leonardo Programme*. On WWW at http://www.eiworkplace.net.
Tomalin, B. and Nicks, M. (2007) *The World's Business Cultures and How to Unlock Them*. London: Thorogood Publishing.
Tomalin, B. and Stempleski, S. (1995) *Cultural Awareness*. Oxford: OUP.
Trompenaars, F. and Hampden Turner, C. (2003) *Riding the Waves of Culture*. London: NB Books.

Chapter 7

Intercultural Teacher: A Case Study of a Course

ULLA LUNDGREN

Introduction

Is it possible to become intercultural by attending a course? If so, how does this process happen and how do we get to know what happens? This chapter will deal with these questions with the help of students' reflections on a pilot course that they attended at the Teacher Education Programme at Jönköping University, Sweden, in autumn 2005.[1]

As internationalisation of Swedish higher education expects universities to integrate native and foreign students there is an expressed demand for more English-medium courses. The statuary documents of our Teacher Education Programme state that teacher students should acquire intercultural competence (IC). This buzz-word like so many others has too long been taken for granted and the concept had not been questioned.

Against this background the planning of *The Intercultural Teacher*, a full-time one semester course of 30 ECTS,[2] started in spring 2004. Four lecturers from different disciplines formed a planning group, all with a personal commitment to international and intercultural issues. *The Intercultural Teacher* was offered to students for the first time in autumn 2005 and ran as a pilot project.[3] After having been responsible for the planning team I was appointed as the course leader.

General Description and Aims of the Course

The general description of the course plan[4] was written to meet with current Swedish societal demands and academic policy of internationalisation:

Becoming a teacher in an internationalised world and in a multicultural society requires intercultural competence. Personal as well as professional development is called for to enhance the teacher's intercultural understanding. The aim of this course is to create possibilities for the student to develop knowledge, skills and attitudes to meet these new demands through theoretical and practical tools as well as through experiential learning.

A combination of Swedish and international students in the course will create an intercultural learning environment. The course contents as well as the team reflect a multidisciplinary approach allowing for flexibility.

A course is evaluated against its aims. As IC is a core concept of the course it had to be defined as aims. The aims are drawn on the theoretical framework of Byram (1997). In addition to Byram's components of IC, consisting of knowledge, skills and attitudes, the aims were extended to specifically include religion and living conditions. The course description states that:

through this course the students should acquire:

- Culture specific and culture general knowledge.
- Knowledge of self and other.
- Knowledge of interaction: individual and societal.
- Insight regarding the ways in which culture affects communication and education.
- Insight regarding the ways religion affects values.
- Knowledge of living conditions in different societies.
- Skills to interpret and relate.
- Skills to discover and/or interact.
- Attitude to relativise self and value other.
- Positive disposition towards learning Intercultural Competence (IC).
- General disposition characterised by a critical engagement with the foreign culture under consideration and one's own.

We have drawn on Byram's theory of IC as we have considered it practice oriented, developed and flexible and well matching the purpose of promoting an intercultural dialogue. Byram advocates the intercultural speaker (IS) as a norm for intercultural communication. An IS 'has a capacity to discover and relate to new people from other contexts for which they have not been prepared directly' (Byram & Fleming, 1998: 9).

Participants

Students

The course attracted in all 14 students. During 2005 we had three Linneaus-Palme[5] agreements with Vietnam, Malawi and India. One

Erasmus student from Spain and six Swedish students enrolled, preparing to educate age groups between pre-school and upper secondary (Table 7.1).

For a group with the objective to develop intercultural understanding there was a good mixture of students regarding future teaching profession, age, gender, nationality, religion and interests. A heterogeneous group is a tremendous resource for a course like this, but it is not entirely easy to satisfy all individual needs.

Teaching staff

The four teacher educators, (two male and two female) in the earlier planning team formed the course team representing Science of Religion, Biology and Environmental studies, Swedish Language/Literature and Education (Language and Culture). Seven other Swedish lecturers gave sessions on, for example, citizenship education, conflict resolution, media and the Global School. They also helped the team to supervise

Table 7.1   List of students attending the course

Name (gender)	Age	From	Specialism	Field studies in
Bin (M)	21	Vietnam	English, 16+	Sweden
Jav (M)	33	Spain	English, 7–12	Sweden
Joh (F)	28	Sweden	Early childhood	India
Kal (F)	25	Sweden	Elementary school	El Salvador
Kap (F)	23	Sweden	English, 16+	Jerusalem
Mar (F)	37	Sweden	English, 16+	India
Pem (M)	37	Sweden	Social Science, 16+	Jerusalem
Pik (F)	32	Sweden	Early childhood	El Salvador
Poo (F)[6]	29	India	Education, tertiary level	Sweden
Rah (M)	26	India	Education, tertiary level	Sweden
Tha (F)	25	Vietnam	Special education, all ages	Sweden
Tik (F)	22	Malawi	Religion, 16+	Sweden
Tow (F)	21	Malawi	Religion, 16+	Sweden

the students' field studies as well as their final papers and to examine the latter.

We were also fortunate to involve some foreign guest lecturers, who gave between two and 10 sessions each. Two were from Vietnam (the Vietnamese school system and Global Health education), one from India (Women in India and Citizenship Education in Indian schools) and one from the USA (African–American women, Critical thinking, Social hegemony, ICT skills).

Course Contents

The course was divided into four modules (7,5ECTS each).

Module 1: Introduction of theoretical and practical tools

The time resource was concentrated on this first module. We felt that it was important for students and teachers to get to know each other and to get a thorough introduction to set the structure of the course. The module was described in the course document as including:

The concepts of culture, multiculture and interculturality;
A socio-cultural perspective on communication in education;
Living conditions and environment;
Values and religion, ethnicity and identity;
Citizenship education in an international perspective;
Conflict solving;
ICT skills;
Ethnography in practice.

Module 2: The teacher as Ethnographer: Field studies

The second module was the core module of the course. Now the students were offered the opportunity to observe and analyse their observations with the help of the theories and methodological tools they had acquired in module 1. During the field studies the students collected data for their final paper written in module 4 but were not required to teach. Course documents said:

Field studies (5 weeks) in various educational contexts according to the student's special interest, in various countries abroad for Swedish students and in Sweden for international students. The aim of the field studies is to offer the students insight in daily life and educational conditions for citizens in an unfamiliar society in order to develop a deeper intercultural understanding. During the field study the student will be mentored by a local instructor in the field. Prior to the field study a personal plan will be made for each student.

The international students were offered placements in Swedish schools in accordance with the age level they were being educated for. Swedish students went in pairs to Jerusalem, El Salvador and India. A member of the course team visited the Swedish students abroad for about a week and the international students were visited on two occasions in their local schools. With two exceptions, one Swedish and one Indian, the mentors were extremely helpful to the students.

Module 3: Intensified theoretical studies

According to the course document module 3 should:

build onto previous field studies within common areas (below) and other specific areas in agreement with the group

Religious traditions in transition
Media
Gender
Sustainable development
Citizenship education (basic values in education).

This module was restructured for the second course in spring 2007 and focused specifically on power from the different perspectives above.

Module 4: Final written assignment

This last module was designed to tie the previous modules together and it worked out according to the plans.

The final assignment will permit the student to inquire into a selected area of personal interest, which is prepared in module 1, investigated in module 2 and further developed in module 3.

Fully aware of the fact that the autumn semester of 20 study weeks does not end officially until the third week of January, we managed to squeeze in the module before the holidays to allow the international students to go home. This was an emergency solution that we changed the second time.

The 2007 course was moved to spring semester (January–June) to solve the time problem.

How Do We Know What Happened to the Students?

Becoming intercultural implies an ongoing process and, according to Stier (2002: 13), this process is 'dynamic and must be understood in a given social and cultural context'. It is unique for each individual and takes place in the interaction between individuals and in self-reflection of the individual. Dialogism (e.g. Dysthe, 2002, who draws on Vygotskij, Bakhtin and Wertsch) is the theoretical background for group discussions and continuous written student reflections. The main data used for this article are the students' final reflections based on what they had experienced and felt during the semester. The quotations in the article are taken from these reflections. Naturally, a critical stance has to be taken towards what informants say in their written reflections. This is specifically the case if the writing also may be understood as an assignment. In the Discussion some quotations are taken from the course evaluations done by the students. Personal communication with the students and my own observations are well in line with these accounts.

Every Friday the students posted a weekly reflection on a web-based discussion forum, titled Ping Pong. According to the students' wishes they could only be read by the teachers. Finally, they were asked to go through all their weekly reflections and write a final 'reflection on reflections'. Within a month after the course the students posted this last reflection on Ping Pong for everyone to read.

Teaching and Learning in an Intercultural Communicative Perspective

Drawing on dialogism, learning and communication could be regarded as two sides of a coin. You learn in interaction with others and your own self-reflection. Thus we tried to create a multi-voiced learning environment in the course. The teaching methods were a variety of lectures, seminars, group studies and practical assignments. The electronic forum, Ping Pong, was not only used for posting students' reflections and assignments, but also for texts and messages for the group, for interactive discussion groups and for questions and answers. This forum seemed to be very useful and appreciated both by students and teaching staff. It was specifically popular with the international students to whom it was new. Some of them had had very limited access to computers. The level of ICT skills within the student group varied, but was in general improved for everyone, including the teachers.

To the international students the difference in teaching style and academic culture between home and Sweden was a great intercultural challenge:

> The first time I attended the classes, I found everything very strange because the way classes were being conducted was very different from the way we do. ... This explains why at first I found it very hard to participate in Swedish classes where they emphasize on class discussions and group discussions. The teachers believe that students too have knowledge and even the teachers can learn something from them rather than in Malawi where students are viewed as blank jars waiting to be filled with knowledge from their teachers. ... The interesting thing is that as time went on, I started participating in both class discussions and group discussions. The most important thing that I learnt was to be confident. At first I was not participating in class because I was doubting myself if what I will say is right or wrong but due to the type of teaching methods I was exposed to, I started having confidence in myself. I always told myself that I can also contribute something to the class. (TOW)

In fact the reactions of the international students certainly were a real intercultural experience even to the Swedish teachers and students. During the first week one Swedish student approached me about her worries that the Swedes dominated too much. Should they keep themselves back to give space to some of the international students, who said very little in class? A long time afterwards this specific student who has a native speaker competence in English after living in Britain for years came back to me about the matter. She said that for the first time ever she experienced a great deal of disadvantages by being a near-native speaker. Among African English and Asian English speakers it actually put communication barriers up instead of taking them down and it was very frustrating but at the same time a very important lesson for her to learn. Her opinion was that a near-native language competence littered with idioms and culture-specific expressions often resulted in unintelligibility. She had understood the concept of IS through experiential learning.

To make a more communicative learning environment, we tried to promote group discussions to give everybody the possibility to voice their opinions:

> It was in the smaller study groups that the discussions were good and I think it could depend on the cultural differences. So it was during these discussions I got the most of the knowledge. In the bigger class

it was not until the end of the course that all told their personal view. So that was a system that suited the Swedish students more, while the international students got a cultural experience which we could see that they succeeded in adjusting to. (KAP)

The fact that foreign teachers took part in the course made the Swedes realise what it meant to be exposed to unfamiliar teaching style. They were able to put themselves into the position of 'the other':

Due to the fact that we early in the first module had two professors from Vietnam enhanced the social understanding of their culture. From what I could understand I saw that the some of the exchange students were not accustomed to our teaching culture where we students are free to question the teacher or discuss during the lectures. That made it hard for me in the beginning to interpret if they did not understand, was not interested or simply just were not used to the system. After that we had the lessons with Mr T. and Mrs T., it became easier to understand what a student in Vietnam was used to.... I noticed the difference the week when the African-American professor gave classes, which meant I as a Swede also had to make a greater effort since her way of teaching was different and she expected the class to act differently from how I know the Swedish teachers expect me to act. It made me realize our different starting-points in the class regarding the teacher-student communication. (KAL)

To get the group together we arranged a camp the second weekend where Swedish and international teachers took part. The weekend included lectures and leisure activities and developed a further understanding of the group dynamics.

One of the unforgettable events was the weekend course we had. This was nice because I was able to interact with my classmates and I learnt how to cook different Swedish foods and for the first time in my life I went canoeing. (THA)

I had no idea that you can learn so much about a person just sitting in the same canoe for a couple of hours. Jav and I shared some of our dreams with each other. (PIK)

Every Friday the students posted their reflections of the week on Ping Pong. One purpose was to make them aware of their own reactions. By saving them as a portfolio students and teachers could follow their individual intercultural development. The reflections also turned out to serve as a kind of continuous course evaluation. It was a new learning method for the Asian and African students who came to like it. One of them also said that the reflections made things clearer and improved his English language. He said that he wanted to use this method for his future teaching to 'understand students' problems and their opinions'.

There were some problems connected with language skills. At the beginning some of the students did not feel comfortable with English as the course language. One of the international students had obviously not enough language skills to benefit fully by the course. Though the prerequisites stipulated 'very good knowledge of spoken and written English' – in fact TOEFL test was required – the partner university concerned had not taken its responsibility to control this. Unfortunately, this student seemed to be quite unaware of his lack of communicative skills. Others were on the contrary very conscious about their English:

> The language was my main handicap during the first weeks of the course. I was absolutely terrified when I had to talk in public. It was also difficult for me to understand the rest of the international students, except X and Y, due to their unfamiliar accents. It was very strange for me because I am a participative and communicative person and it seemed like I was shy. For me it was a big pressure when I was asked to say my opinion about something. This affected me not only at the University but it also affected me in the rest of the time outside the class. As the time passed by I was more and more participative, more the 'real' Jav. (JAV)

On the other hand, being confronted with different Englishes was a true intercultural experience to the Swedes, mostly used to British or American native speaker norms. They were challenged to understand accents that were strange to them like African, Vietnamese and Indian English. It really trained their ability to develop as ISs.

> I have also learned that it is very difficult to express one self in English, there are always nuances in languages which often are important if one wants to express one self clear. … I now better understand how difficult it must be for foreigners to make them selves understood in Sweden and I also understand that many of the misunderstandings and conflicts between foreigners and Swedes are in fact linguistic problems. (PEM)

Also the rules for what you are supposed to say and what not to say became obvious.

> Other cultural rules exist in our way of communicating and expressing ourselves. I have met some straightforward answers to questions

this term that both made me smile and realize the differences. I have also been surprised when confronted with non-expected questions, understanding that the surprise stems from that I would not normally be asked the same question by a Swede. But by being asked the question, I can understand something new both about my own culture as about the culture of the person asking me the question. (KAL)

Students' Development of IC

Byram's framework of IC (1997) does not only form the theoretical base of the course but has also been used to analyse the students' development of IC. An accessible and easily applicable theory of IC as a model for analysis is a crucial tool to find out and to describe what happened to the student.

> To some extent teaching the intercultural dimension is a matter of seizing opportunities, being systematic in developing those opportunities – i.e. drawing on theory for help and guidance – and evaluating the results against clear and explicit criteria. (Byram *et al.*, 2001: 4)

For this chapter the reflections of the students have been organised according to Byram's more simplified and somewhat overlapping criteria of IC as knowledge, skills and attitudes (Byram *et al.*, 2001: 4–7).

Knowledge

Apart from formal factual knowledge from course literature and lectures the students developed culture general and culture-specific knowledge (Byram, 1997) by communicating and observing in class and outside. Formal and experiential learning went hand in hand.

Students learnt about cultural rules different from their own, like different views on what time means and learnt to adapt to the local culture.

> Another important thing that I learnt is to be on time. At the beginning I was always late for classes. Since the Malawians are not good at keeping time this affected me during the first few weeks but later on I learnt to use time properly and also always tried to be on time. (TOW)

> The first time I went to church in El Salvador, I sat one hour waiting for the service to start. The second time I went there I arrived one hour late on purpose and at that time they were just about to start. I felt I had adapted quite well to the existing view of time in this particular church. (KAL)

They were able to make comparisons based on first-hand experience between educational systems, social and economic conditions.

> Studying with international students has also opened my eyes for many things. I have read about the poverty in Malawi, but it wasn't until I sat down with Tik and Tow and discussed the situation in their country that I understood how bad the poverty is. I knew about the female situation in India but got it directly shown in class by Rah and Poo. I knew Vietnam was a communist republic and Bin and Tha showed me what respect for your country really is. Jav told us about the water problem in Spain, I had no idea earlier. .... I have got a deeper understanding, even though I knew it before, about democracy and how fortunate we are here in Sweden. (PIK)

Taken-for-granted concepts of their own society were re-valued and looked upon with new eyes. The students said that the course had made them aware of new points of their own personalities and given them new views of other people.

> It demands a lot of energy to reconsider one's cultural values all the time. I think that I became a bit disappointed at myself when I realized that I did not always have the energy to plunge deep into other cultures. (KAP)

> My intercultural journey was more of emotions than theory. To stay in Palestine is an emotional experience most of all, I learned that it is very easy to have the academic and political correct answers then you are in the calm and peaceful Sweden. But in the eye of the storm there is a reality which you always need to deal with. I am now more humble and I can separate small problem from big ones. (PEM)

> When studying abroad, I found that I very proud of my country. I could tell about it day by day. In my first presentation, I showed the flag of my country and our Great Father – Ho Chi Minh. ... Many people I met often asked me about the war in Vietnam, our Party and what I thought about Americans. Therefore, I thought I had responsibility to tell them more about my country, not only the past but also the present. ... In addition, I become more confident Europe now is no more strange for me. When away from home, I recognized my family had an important role in my life. (THA)

> I have learned about other cultures and about my own. You think you know your culture, and deep inside you do, but it is when somebody

starts to ask you about it that you become aware of how it's really working. (PIK)

I am not the same person I was when I left Spain in August. ... the main thing for me, I have met incredible people from all continents. We worked as family and we became friends. The stereotypes have been broken in pieces. (JAV)

When returning from El Salvador I had learnt for example that although we claim to be individualistic in Sweden, we actually depend a lot on the state. I believe it is when people refuse to learn about their own culture in the encounter with another culture that prejudice is created. (KAL)

They had changed and they were able to analyse their own development.

Skills

Students developed their ability to interpret and relate with the help of theoretical input, which they sometimes referred to. They were able to decentre and see a different perspective of events through discussions and experiences.

Coming from different cultural backgrounds in our class this semester, I have noticed that like it is said in *The Silent Language*, rules are made visible when they are broken. In El Salvador for example people left the table when they had finished eating and did not wait for the others around the table to finish. Since I am used to people leaving the table when everybody has finished the meal the broken rule became visible to me, a rule I was not very aware of that I apply in a Swedish lunch or dinner context. (KAL)

People are not first and most different; we are very similar, with the same needs and interest. When you can see other in your self its easier to understand people's behaviour. People act very similar in similar situations but they live under different circumstances. (PEM)

Students developed meta-cognitive strategies to direct their learning. These strategies were made possible through the theories on interculturality and learning, as well as through ethnographic methods presented and practiced during the course.

In conclusion I must say that my intercultural ability has changed during this course. Within the course I have received tools for how I can step out of my own culture to evaluate why I am reacting as I do, as well as I have learned methods of evaluating other cultures. (KAP)

Looking at what I did in Jonkoping; I remind myself of good ethnographic eyes through which I used to look at a new world in four months and also the eyes for having a new look at the familiar things in my home country. (BIN)

I learnt how to observe things objectively and avoid using my meanings, beliefs to evaluate what I see. Now, before giving my opinions about something, I often ask why it happens like that and do continued analyzing. (THA)

Attitudes

Students developed attitudes to relativise themselves and value others. Customs and behaviour, which they earlier thought unacceptable and incomprehensible, were made possible to understand once they got the cultural background from their peers, even if they did not agree with them. Differences were accepted to a greater extent. Preconceived notions were moderated. Gender issues stirred the group.

Throughout the course we have discussed gender questions and during my field studies I met another look upon women. The first time I talked with Poo the woman student from India, we talked about arranged marriages. From my point of view it was totally incomprehensible, but after that she described it for me several times I got to understand her arguments. It is when I put myself into her culture and listen to her values that I can comprehend how arranged marriages can be suitable. (KAP)

I was shocked to hear that (the Indian woman student recognized arranged marriages), it was really difficult for me to accept the fact that an educated woman thought that, but I tried to think that she had been told all her life that an arranged marriage was the best and probably the only option. In Malawi there were not arranged marriages but one point took my attention. It is common that men have lovers and their wives or girlfriends were aware of that, in a European country these situations means most of the times divorce or separation. In Malawi it was not that easy for women. (JAV)

The students gained an awareness of their own values and how these influence their views of other people. They expressed an understanding for other values even though they did not agree with them.

I understand that for many people religion and national identity are important and I accept it as I accept most of opinions. To be intercultural is for me to respect all individuals but not always agree with other. On the contrary; I think it's better to take part, have an own opinion, and of course be prepared to change opinion in interaction with other opinions. In a wider perspective intercultural education is a way of realizing human rights. (PIK)

The students realised that values are contextual. They got new perspectives on conditions that they had never questioned before.

In the class we made a revelation about skin lotions that women use all over the world. Suddenly the question about beauty seems humoristic and not as serious as before. I mean although I am pale in Sweden and considered less beautiful because according to the Swedish beauty ideal I should look tanned, I am still beautiful in a Vietnamese or an Indian context.(!) I think a great advantage from my intercultural development, is exactly about this. From now on I have much more experiences to compare with in my daily life and these relativise my own life and surrounding. I am sure similar revelations can be made in other more serious areas as an effect of an intercultural dialogue which in its turn will give a greater possibility to impact our societies and break down existing lies. (KAL)

There was a development towards an intrapersonal, processual competence (Stier, 2002), when the students could leave their own feelings behind and decentre from their own culture.

In meeting with the Salvadoran culture I have had to develop my *intercultural competence*, especially the *processual competencies*, for example, when meeting with a lot of dictation in the schools or the fact that our host family had an employed housemaid. As a Swede I am not used neither to dictation nor employed housemaids. My first reaction in both cases was feelings of judgement but fairly soon I realized that thinking in this way was not the intercultural way of dealing with these issues. I had to try to see it with the Salvadoran's eyes and detect from my own culture. It is in my encounter with this reality and when the housemaid's service is offered to me, that the problem arises. It was hard accepting the fact that she was going to do things for me that I could do and is used to doing myself. After some time I could focus on the positive aspects and see her point of view. She was lucky to have a job that she liked and where she was treated well. (KAL)

> I have learnt to appreciate other people's culture and religion because at first, I thought my values and religion are perfect but I came to understand that even other people's values and religion are perfect. (TOW)

This group of students naturally had a positive disposition towards learning IC, as they had enrolled for the course from their own interest. Their reflections tell us that this disposition had improved and affected their professional pedagogic views and future action in class. They also realised that developing IC is an ongoing process.

> Even though I have developed my intercultural competence during this semester I would not say I am finished, the process has just started and will probably not be completed but continue to develop. As students of this *Intercultural Teacher* course we might not specifically have changed our opinions, but we have kept our minds open to take in new impressions and opinions that have developed and broadened our intercultural competence. (KAL)

> I realize that I can't change the world, but I can change myself. If I treat everybody the way I want to be treated I can make at least a little difference. ... To be a good intercultural teacher I have to be open towards, curious about and tolerant of other people's behaviours, beliefs and values. But it is also of great importance that I am aware of my own behaviour, beliefs and values. (PIK)

Discussion

How do we know that students have improved their IC?

The ways that we can discover whether people have become interculturally competent – questions of evaluation and assessment – are crucial issues of the entire field of intercultural education. The uncertainty and lack of knowledge about good methods in this respect are key issues why teaching IC in practice is so difficult. I cannot avoid thinking that intelligent students were fully aware of what we were aiming at and fulfilled our expectations to make a favorable impression. This is especially the fact as aims, theories and discussions throughout the course were focused on IC. The whole point was to make them interculturally aware and this was an open agenda of which they were very conscious.

The culture-content competencies, the knowledge aspects of a particular culture or culture in general (Stier, 2002), are not problematic in this respect. However, IC is to a great extent a process where the student develops knowledge, skills and attitudes that cannot be quantified. It is not possible to define the development of processual competencies (Stier, 2002) by showing evident measurable results. In this course we used students' final reflections as the last stage of a kind of self-assessment portfolio. I have access to all students' previous weekly reflections and would say that they coincide with and validate their final reflections. In the second course we made sure that the critical skills of self-reflection were more thoroughly dealt with at the course start. Students became familiar with dialogic learning theories and more aware of the benefits of self-reflection to be better trained to use reflections in practice as a learning method.

To give the students' written reflections higher validity I would like to add some personal observations. As time passed the students became more interested in each other, showed more open-mindedness and understanding of different perspectives in discussions. The strong anti-feminist view of the Indian students and the devoted cult of their communist leader of the Vietnamese caused some tension within the Swedish group at the beginning. There was initially a certain Swedish resentment against the reluctance among the international students to engage in class discussions. After the field studies the Swedes, having themselves been exposed to intensive cultural and linguistic experiences in foreign surroundings, became more understanding of alternative perspectives and showed much more empathy with the international students' personal situation. Many Swedish students talked to me about the fact that their own feelings during their field studies of being isolated and left without the taken-for-granted keys to society, culture and language had been an eye-opener to how their friends might feel in Sweden. This experience had made it possible for them to take the position of the other. After the field studies they actively engaged themselves to make life easier for the international students. The group socialised outside class to a much greater extent. For example, at coffee tables in the student cafeteria, and at informal parties in the Swedish students' homes, eager to include everyone. One student arranged for the whole group to attend a big national ice-hockey match, which was a great cultural experience for the international students. The day after, the Swedes were as just happy as the others. The happiness of the former though was caused by having had the opportunity to experience the international students' reactions of the local event. A familiar ice-hockey match and all that was going on around it had now been watched by the Swedes with ethnographic eyes because their international friends were present at the event.

Is it possible to become intercultural by a course?

The evaluation of the course tells us that at least 10 of the 12 students consider themselves to be more interculturally competent after the course. Their reflections quoted above give evidence of their intercultural development. Two of the students said that the course has not changed them, but still something they say indicates the opposite.

> There is a Swedish mode of expression, 'you can't teach an old dog to sit', and maybe this phrase expresses my intercultural journey. I haven't changed my mind that much and haven't received much new thoughts but I have developed and refined my old thoughts. (PEM)

PEM already had a deep international engagement. However, the fact that he has 'developed and refined' his previous thoughts, tells us that the course has fulfilled its aims. The same student says that it is very easy to have the right answers when you are safe at home but being in 'the eye of the storm' has made him more humble (5.1)

The other student says:

> I had hoped to develop myself somehow interculturally, both on a professional and a personal level. Not in the way of a radical personality change, it's unfortunately too late for that ... But at least to have one or two of my many personal opinions challenged, twisted around and to be forced to observe them closer or in a different light. ... Reading and reflecting over the general description of the course, my final thought is that there are never any built in automatics that a course or a classroom is to become intercultural simply by the students/pupils being from different cultures. This is a classic trap to walk into! (MAR)

The final passage shows that MAR has realised one of the crucial aims of the course: to 'create possibilities ... to develop knowledge, skills and attitudes through theoretical and practical tools as well as through experiential learning'. The quote below also shows that MAR thinks that she has learned a lot.

These two students are the oldest ones, in their late 30s, and have lived abroad and travelled a lot. When they say that they have not changed, does this indicate that they are so interculturally competent already that they have nothing new to learn or does it mean that our course could not meet with their high expectations because they needed 'more' than the others? Are there levels of IC towards an ongoing and never ending development or are there just two stages of being intercultural – incompetent and competent? Fortunately their continuous reflections of these two students show a more positive picture of their development than their evaluation of the course.

Can IC be taught?

If you support 'a sociocultural understanding of learning as negotiated, situated and mediated' (Dysthe, 2002: 341) and refute knowledge as transferred then you have to answer: No it can only be learnt. How this happens has no general answer but in this case study I have tried to present how it may happen.

Certainly the intercultural learning environment and the deliberate use of self-reflections supported the students' process of developing IC. The latter was a means to decentre and look back upon one's own reactions. For this the electronic discussion board, Ping Pong, was a very useful medium. The use of Ping Pong was further developed in the next course. Continuous discussions in small groups were arranged to create more frequent interactional learning opportunities.

I would like to return to MAR whose critical voice is heard above.

> Learning happens during interaction between people. Research has shown that to maximise the conditions for lasting learning you need to be emotionally involved to a certain degree and in a semi relaxed state of mind. This might be difficult to achieve in a traditional educational setting; and probably the reason why most of the really important learning actually takes place outside the classrooms. This is true also when I look back at the past months spent at the course Intercultural Teacher. It is during the social moments like lunch breaks and coffee drinking that I have learned the most, not during the lectures. (MAR)

Many of the students say that they learnt so much outside the lecture room. Then, could they have done just as well without a course? No, with no course there would not have been an 'outside'. I feel convinced that the combination of a formal course, including theories and methods, experiential learning in an unfamiliar society, combined with continuous reflections and organised informal discussions in peer groups have a good potential when it comes to developing IC.

> I must say the whole semester has been an authentic experience, not an academic one only based on literature, but an intercultural course experienced in real life and with authentic actors. It has been an encounter between people, eye to eye and in a natural way. I am glad to be able to draw that conclusion. (KAL)

Having had the privilege to teach this course I have learnt a lot about our students, about myself and about my profession. By now I realise to a deeper extent that intercultural education as all education is highly dependent on intrapersonal and interpersonal communication which has to be trained.

During one of our first classes Vygotskij was quoted:

'You develop your thoughts deeper with the help of others'. I have never been in an environment where this has been more true than in this course. Spending time with people from different cultures, countries, ages, beliefs and values makes you start to think in a broader perspective. (PIK)

Notes

1. I owe a deep and sincere gratitude to the students who have made this study possible.
2. European Credit Transfer System (full time studies for one academic year are 60 ECTS).
3. The course was offered a second time in spring 2007.
4. www.hlk.hj.se
5. An educational exchange programme with developing countries financed by the Swedish government.
6. She left the course after module 2 for family reasons.

References

Byram, M. (1997) *Teaching and Assessing Intercultural Communicative Competence.* Clevedon: Multilingual Matters.
Byram, M. and Fleming, M. (eds) (1998) *Language Learning in Intercultural Perspective. Approaches through Drama and Ethnography.* Cambridge: Cambridge University Press.
Byram, M., Nichols, A. and Stevens, D. (2001) *Developing Intercultural Competence in Practice.* Clevedon: Multilingual Matters.
Dysthe, O. (2002) The learning potential of a web-mediated discussion in a university course. *Studies in Higher Education* 27 (3), 339–352.
Stier, J. (2002) *Going International – Becoming Intercultural.* Växjö: Växjö University, School of Education.

Chapter 8

Using 'Human Global Positioning System' as a Navigation Tool to the Hidden Dimension of Culture

CLAUDIA FINKBEINER

Introduction

Culture has often been referred to as 'hidden dimension'. The metaphor of the iceberg explains that culture at its core is invisible (Weaver, 1993). Formerly, the construct of culture only existed in the singular and the focus was on the center of a specific culture. Today we talk about many different cultures as dynamic systems that are constantly renegotiated (Kramsch, 1998).

In order to successfully navigate in a world in which the major part is hidden and invisible, we need adequate strategies as well as clever and efficient tools. As teachers we want our learners to become aware of the hidden parts in order to prevent them from stumbling across them. We want to help our learners see and discover phenomena that at first glance seem invisible (Finkbeiner, 2006) and make them look beyond their existing horizons (Alred *et al.*, 2006; Byram, 1999). We want them to become interculturally competent. But how does this happen and which facilitators can we use to make it happen?

GPS is a global positioning system that helps one locate and navigate in regions unknown. In this chapter I will transfer the GPS concept to 'Human GPS' and explain what the adaptation requires. In a second step I will show how 'Human GPS' relates to culture as well as to the self and the other. I will follow by elucidating different approaches that implement the 'Human GPS' approach. This includes both an intrapersonal as well as an interpersonal level (Finkbeiner, 2006). The chapter refers to the ABCs (Autobiography, Biography and Cross-Cultural Analysis) of cultural understanding and communication (Schmidt, 1999; Schmidt & Finkbeiner,

2006). A variety of exercises will be given that support the 'Human GPS' approach and promote meta-cognitive language awareness and cultural awareness (Fehling, 2008; Finkbeiner & Fehling, 2006; Hawkins, 1984; James & Garrett, 2000).

The Trickiness of Navigating Through a Diverse World

More and more people navigate through different places, cultures and time zones. Being exposed, surrounded and influenced by many different cultural representations and perspectives has a huge impact on the acculturation process of each single person in the world (Finkbeiner, 2006). This continuously influences our self image and has an impact on who we think we are at a given moment in time. It also influences our image of the other person (Finkbeiner, 2006).

Human beings are multi-facetted and often non-predictable in their actions. There are always components that remain unknown to the self as well as to the other. Misunderstandings happen in private, professional and intercultural interaction without intermission. This is due to the fact that important phenomena are hidden, unknown, blind, not tackled or silent (Furstenberg *et al.*, 2001; Weaver, 1993).

For example, in the Johari window (Luft & Ingham, 1955), which exists in four quadrants, the unknown is represented: (1) by the quadrant 'hidden', which stands for things unknown to others but not to oneself as well as by (2) 'blind spot', which remains unknown to oneself but is noticed by others and (3) by 'unknown', which is neither known to oneself nor to others. Only one quadrant out of four is 'open' to all.

A closer look at the perception of the self and the perception of the other reveals quite some discrepancies in both readings (Finkbeiner, 2006). Discourse and negotiation about the perception of the self and the other make hidden things visible (Finkbeiner, 2006). It can help clarify misunderstandings that are caused by non-adequate or non-proficient choice of words, grammar, tone, medium and body language or by non-logical utterances of thoughts and ideas. Such misunderstandings are likely in unequal linguistic power situations (Fehling, 2005; Hawkins, 1984; James & Garrett, 2000), such as, between native speakers, second language speakers and foreign language learners. They are also probable among speakers of different levels of education, gender and/or different socioeconomic groups. Misapprehension is predictable between experts and novices, and between doctors and patients or teachers and students. For example, it might be caused by the wrong choice of media or when a written code is used instead of an oral one.

A lack of proficiency, sensitivity, empathy and/or even just a poor choice of words said or implied can be completely misunderstood on the situational, the propositional or the literal level (van Dijk & Kintsch, 1983; Finkbeiner, 2005). An utterance can even be misinterpreted as dislike, criticism and disrespect, thus causing conflict in private, public as well as in political life. For example, there are so-called taboo topics, such as religious beliefs. People of a specific belief might feel offended by any kind of satire, comic or persiflage on their religious belief.

In short, the more diverse the world becomes the more difficult it is to act adequately depending on context variables such as time, people and location. Leave all the factors in a scenario stable and simply change one context variable, and the meaning attributed to each single factor will change. What this means is that the sociocultural context highly determines our world view as well as our attitude (Lantolf, 2006; van Lier, 2004). It also has an influence on whether we consider the glass half full or half empty, whether we are optimistic or pessimistic. What we need to learn is how to be more precise and more successful in orienting and locating ourselves in a network of possible places, premises and sites.

'Human' Global Positioning System (GPS)

I remember a walk I took in the high Alps a few years ago. High Alp climbing is never a straight way up. It can be particularly burdensome due to mountain as well as weather conditions. I recall the weather was absolutely fine when I started out. I felt privileged to even see the summit from the distance. Right below the summit was a tiny spot: it was the hut I planned on staying overnight. Once I started climbing I lost complete sight of the summit. I had to descend many times in order to finally ascend and head for the mountain top. During the last leg of the hike temperatures dropped, thick fog rolled in and I could not even see my hand in front of my face. I knew the summit was close but I could see nothing. If it had not been for the red markings blazing the steep and rocky trail I would not have made it to the hut. At that moment I learned that each single step was crucial before I would take the next one. If I took one step of the trail wrongly I could have fallen. I also knew I had to watch and learn about former, present and future markings in order to prevent myself from walking in circles. I finally made it up to the top.

Today we have a tool that can at least prevent us from walking in circles and help us to find our way more easily and thus make outdoor activities safer: GPS. It is a GPS that can help us navigate both on roads as well as on paths in the backcountry. However, there are important pre-conditions for

GPS to operate successfully: GPS only works if: (1) it receives and processes information from at least three satellites positioned at different locations around the globe; (2) the most essential navigation data have been fed into it; (3) it is powered; (4) it is switched on; and (5) the user follows certain application rules. The deployment of a fourth or even fifth satellite is non-mandatory yet it is highly advisable for reasons of monitoring and controlling. If these pre-conditions are fulfilled GPS can help us locate ourselves. Yet it cannot tell us our future goal: we need to know where we are heading.

An analogy to this is that one can conclude that in the process of cultural beings trying to position themselves culturally, 'Human GPS' comes in handy (Figure 8.1). But in order for Human GPS to function, we have to adapt the technical pre-conditions to the human factor. Let us assume that we all carry an inherent Human GPS device in us. In order for the Human GPS to function with the same efficiency as the technical GPS, we must consider the fulfillment of the following pre-conditions: (1) we need to receive and process information from at least two different perspectives,

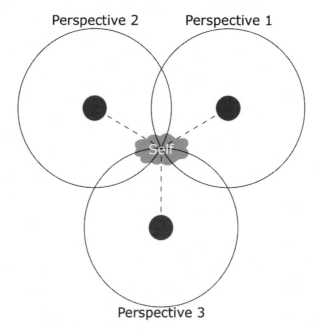

Figure 8.1   Human global positioning system

which are represented by Perspective 1 and Perspective 2 as in Figure 8.1; (2) the 'navigation data' through this processing have to be fed into our 'Human GPS' device to form a third perspective represented by Perspective 3 in Figure 8.1. As we assume the self at the core of the navigation process of cultural positioning (Finkbeiner, 2006), we need to consider two disturbances in order to enable our 'Human GPS' to function well; either the new data conflict with the learners' prior knowledge, belief systems and values or they are not even detected and ignored. Thus, learners need to be continuously 'powered', which means they need a rich and an authentic linguistic and cultural learning environment (van Lier, 1996).

Learners' switches need to be 'on' in order for their human GPS to function. This implies that learners need to develop language and cultural awareness (Cots, 2001; Fehling, 2005; Hawkins, 1984; James & Garrett, 2000; Svalberg, 2007). They need to be able to receive and digest data. They need to become aware of similarities and differences (Schmidt & Finkbeiner, 2006). And they need to control and monitor that the switches are on during the whole process. Furthermore, learners need to follow certain application rules. These are the cultural game rules of a specific cultural system or sub-system. Often these rules, just as cultures themselves, are tacit, non-explicit and hidden. The monitor and control system is crucial for the clarification and constant evaluation of the success of intercultural communication.

Locating the Self and the Other

The Human GPS has its starting point within the self. Before we can start the navigation we have to locate the self. Therefore, the first most important focus is on the perception of the self. This leads us to some basic questions: Where does the self take its start? Where has the self come from? These questions are connected to further question: Who are we? What are our values? What are our wishes and attitudes? How do we perceive ourselves?

The self and its sociocultural context are key to the acculturation process (Finkbeiner, 2006). This process starts in the womb and ends at death. It is highly dynamic, uneven, continuous and social. The mother is the first cultural facilitator. Families, friends, peers and colleagues continue to influence acculturation in the different phases we go through (Finkbeiner, 2006). People are often unaware of how much they have been influenced by their 'inner child of the past' (Missildine, 2007). It seems to be hidden away in most individuals. Values and attitudes that have been acquired in earliest childhood sway us in our future life. The way teachers perceive themselves influences their future actions in the classroom. Yet, the reproduction of learned patterns often remains undetected and large parts of who we actually are might remain undiscovered (Kristeva, 1990).

In order to understand and perceive others one first needs to understand oneself. The journey to oneself can be rocky but it needs to be traveled. This can be done by applying the ABCs of Cultural Understanding and Communication (Schmidt, 1999; Schmidt & Finkbeiner, 2006; see below) which follows the paradigm: 'Know thyself and understand others' (Schmidt, 1999). There are activities that promote a critical approach to the discovery of the perspectives of the self and other. These activities actively involve learners making them navigators who dive deep below the surface of culture to find out about the hidden. It takes a framework of language and cultural awareness activities to make that happen.

Switching the Human GPS On: Using Language Awareness as a Key

There are many people who have always lived in the same, isolated world who might not understand that there are worlds outside different from their own. As a result, they may not see what the difference does to those that are perceived as different (Byram, 1999; Finkbeiner, 2006). This 'blindfolded' cognition is caused by the fact that perception focuses on the known and the familiar, particularly when there is a biological and cognitive need for quick categorization. This can be caused by memory overload, existential threats, simplification and so on.

How do we break that vicious cycle of being trapped in one's own world? We need to ensure that we implement language and cultural awareness activities (Fehling, 2005; Finkbeiner & Fehling, 2006; Svalberg, 2007) for intercultural teaching programs to be successful. And we need to check that the three different satellites are active.

According to James and Garrett (2000) there are five domains of language awareness: the affective domain, the cognitive domain, the social domain, the power domain and the performance domain (Fehling, 2005; Svalberg, 2007). The affective domain deals with the emotional side of languages. It focuses on language learners' preferences for languages as well as their motivation and interest in languages. This is often influenced by the status the language holds in society. The social domain has to do with the fact of being aware of multilingualism as well as the acceptance of language minorities in one's own society. The power domain reveals facts of manipulation with language as well as power distance through discrimination. The cognitive domain represents the cognitive side of language and focuses on language as a construct. Finally, the performance domain covers the implicit and explicit knowledge of language as it is operated.

From Satellites to Perspectives: Implementing a Multi-perspective Approach

The systematic implementation of language and cultural awareness activities automatically relates back to the multi-perspective approach of the Human GPS. As mentioned above just as technical GPS needs three satellites, the Human GPS needs three perspectives to function. A binary, bi-perspective comparative approach to culture can be a start but must be complemented by further diversification in order to understand the whole image.

What is referred to as a multi-perspective approach was already discussed by Comenius (1992: 256; Finkbeiner, 2005: 122–125). Comenius stated that we comprehend phenomena only if we learn about their constituents. We need to grasp how phenomena as well as their parts relate to and differ from each other. This requires a tri-perspective process: synthesis, analysis and syncrisis. Phenomena can only be fully understood if we perceive them holistically. A telescope, on the one hand, allows us to see things clearly even if they are distant. This is why we sometimes solve problems more easily once we step back. The microscope on the other hand supports the same process by helping us to see things that at first glance seem invisible. The final step relies on the mirror to make things perceptible: it is for phenomena that are positioned outside our vision and without the mirror would remain unnoticed.

The understanding of the multi-perspective anchoring of culture, language and people enables us to locate ourselves more intelligently and others culturally and socially. Bhabha's (1994) concept of third space supports this non-binary approach to understanding of oneself as well as the other. In diverse learning groups different perspectives can be conveyed and articulated by the learners themselves on the basis of their ethnic, cultural, linguistic and personal background. Pre-condition and question are whether these learners are willing, capable and motivated to share their opinions, attitudes and perspectives with others. This requires the teachers to consequentially follow a paradigm of a multi-perspective teaching approach (Finkbeiner & Fehling, 2006) to create an open and non-threatening classroom atmosphere where learners are willing to contribute with their expertise (Finkbeiner, 2004).

If the classroom itself is non-diverse or mono-cultural, it can be transformed into a diverse classroom. This can be done in several ways, for example, by opening classroom doors and (1) having people of a background different from the learners come in to present and listen to their stories (Young & Helot, 2003); (2) making students go out and do field studies; (3) using media and the possibility of communicating via chat, forum and blog; (4) following a multi-ethnic literature approach; (5) using a topical, cross-disciplinary multi-perspective approach; and (6) offering content and language integrated learning classes that do not simply teach the subject matter in the target language but are based on target language, mother tongue and heritage language and relate these to the subject matter.

Implementing the Human GPS

The following examples will illustrate how the Human GPS can be applied and implemented in the classroom. The examples are illustrative and need to be adapted depending on the age group and learner type.

Stories about critical incidents involving racial prejudice and stereotyping

The following authentic stories are about critical incidents in people's lives involving racial prejudice and stereotyping. They are given as examples to implement the 'Human GPS' approach. Learners need to be able to relate to the stories. It is important to make participants comment and reflect on what happened in the stories with reference to the sociocultural and sociolinguistic context as well as to the perception of the self and the other.

Megan's story   Megan (5) was playing with her mother in the hotel pool in Phoenix, Arizona. Her mother told me that they were from London, but they had been in the USA for two years. Megan attended a kindergarten in the USA. After talking a while to Megan's mother I tried to include Megan in the talk and addressed her: 'So, you are a British girl?' 'No', she replied. 'I am Caucasian White'.

Megan's interpretation of herself is political-racist. Despite the fact that she is only five years old she has already internalized the political and racial categories of the US census system.

Rick's story   Rick (55) (Norwegian ancestry) had worked for the US Navy for 25 years. He told me he easily tans and often had been taken as a Hispanic when he worked in Southern California. He transferred to the Northwest (USA) to work at a naval shipyard. This shipyard is for nuclear submarines and restricted to US citizens only. The first day he went there to get his work papers the security officer in charge addressed him: 'I would just suspect that you are a US citizen, now that you are a Chief

Petty Officer?' 'Being born in Minnesota, I have always been so,' Rick replied.

In Rick's story the interpretation of the officer about Rick is ethnic-racist. It is based on phenomena that can be observed on the surface, such as skin color. Surface phenomena are often mistakenly related to categories such as ethnic, national or cultural belonging (Kramsch, 1993, 1998).

Anna's story   One of my best friends is black, and although her father is from Senegal she's never been there. Her mother is from Lleida (Catalonia, Spain), and she was born and raised there with her brother. She never had any kind of problems due to her color. People just assumed she was Spanish. However, when immigration began in Spain and there was the boom, people began to act oddly toward her. Once she went to buy some cigarettes and spoke in Catalan. The woman in the store told her she spoke great Catalan. Obviously, she answered that she was born in Lleida. Since then, anecdotes like this have not stopped. Some weeks ago, we went to a shop. The shop assistant was talking to a client in Catalan. When Anna (yes, people also think she calls herself Anna because her real name is something strange, that: her real name is Aisha) was about to pay she asked him in Catalan 'could you please give me that?', the shop assistant automatically switched into Spanish, because he thought that Anna was an immigrant and could not understand Catalan.

As discussed above, Human GPS requires certain information to be fed into the system in order for the system to function properly. Learners need to build up knowledge as an advance organizer (Ausubel, 1976) to understand the texts.

In Anna's story, for example, the following background information might be useful. Lleida is a town that is situated in the western part of Catalonia, which is a Catalan–Spanish bilingual area in the northeast of Spain: 'Catalan is legally considered the language of Catalonia since 1979, when the first Catalan Statute of Autonomy after the death of Franco in 1975 was passed. Besides, the 1978 Spanish Constitution also acknowledges the right of Catalan people to use it. Spanish is the official language of Spain ... and all its citizens have the duty to know it and the right to use it' (Armengol, 2007: 4). According to Armengol (2007: 5) both Catalan and Spanish enjoy high vitality and status and are taught in primary and secondary schools in Catalonia, although Spanish is the dominant language. English is the most important foreign language.

Once enough information has been given to understand the socio-cultural context, teachers need to make sure that their students' Human GPS is 'on'. They learn that Rick's and Anna's stories are similar if not identical in their underlying deeper structures. Even though both stories are situated in completely different sociocultural contexts, certain surface factors are dealt with and interpreted the same way. In both stories visible phenomena, such as skin color are simply related to other phenomena, such as national belonging. As a consequence, the civic status in the society (immigrant versus citizen) is deduced. This remains unchallenged without any further proof.

All three stories, including Megan's, show more than one perspective. They illustrate the perception of the self and the perspective of the other within a given sociocultural context (Finkbeiner, 2006, in print; Kramsch, 1998). The interaction of the two perspectives leads to a third perspective, which is a third place in Kramsch's (1993) term for the self or a third party who is caught in the interface of the two perspectives. Once stories like these have been read, students can be encouraged to collect and write down their own stories.

The stories give evidence that perceptions are based on implicit assumptions about prototypical representations and interpretations of certain categories within a certain sociocultural context. 'Very often these categories are outdated and do not reflect 'current racial/ethnic realities' (Kramsch, 1998: 43) nor linguistic and cultural truths. In our globalizing world students need to learn that they cannot just glance at the surface and assume they understand others (Finkbeiner, in print). They need to switch on their Human GPS and then dive deep to locate and understand others as well as themselves (Finkbeiner, in print; Schmidt & Finkbeiner, 2006; Weaver, 1993). Also they need to address the role of concepts such as the 'nation-state' in an increasingly denationalized political and disciplinary reality.

Learning gallery

The 'Learning Gallery' (Finkbeiner, 2005: 469–470) has been developed for language teachers to gain a better understanding for themselves and for their students to construct a new third perspective with them. It is a tool for the students to start reflecting on their self as a foreign language learner. The 'Learning Gallery' (Finkbeiner, 2005: 469–470) makes use of mind maps because they are an intelligent way to structure and visualize concepts and ideas about one's own self.

The question here is: 'Who am I as a language learner?' The process is triggered by the following instruction: 'Draw a mind map, a picture or write down a list of keywords of how you see yourself as a language learner. You have 15 minutes.' Once each participant has produced a mind map, they are posted around the classroom walls, spaced just as in an art gallery. The mind maps are anonymous. There is a phase of silent visiting followed by a class evaluation. In the evaluation phase learners are asked to pick one 'piece of art' that seems striking, surprising or provoking to them. They then interpret what they think the author wanted to express. The author is allowed to comment on the perception of the other and contribute with his or her own perception. He or she can also choose to remain silent.

After a few mind maps have been chosen, the class discourse starts. The teacher guides the learners to detect similarities and differences of all the mind maps. This takes account of the perspective of the self and the perspective of the other in each single mind map in order to end up with a new third perspective. The latter is not the author's nor the interpreter's perception but a new one constructed in a reciprocal cooperative class effort. An example will follow.

I used the learning gallery in one of my applied linguistics classes right at the beginning of the course in 2007. The class was on the topic 'How languages are learned'. Ceylan, who is one of my Turkish-German students, was born in Germany, has always lived there, and is studying English and Physical Education to become a teacher. Her German is on the native speaker level, which means Ceylan is fluent, and speaks and writes Standard German on an academic level. Her English is academic and highly proficient in both speaking and writing.

The first thing that is striking about Ceylan's mind map is that she labeled the center bubble with 'me, myself and I' (Figure 8.2). Most of the other students simply wrote either 'me', 'I' or just 'myself'. It was important to Ceylan to portray herself in a differentiating way. The whole description of herself as a language learner is proficiency oriented and includes three languages: German as a second language, Turkish as mother tongue and English as a foreign language. Ceylan does not explicitly mention the three languages but uses the generic terms throughout the mind map, creating an inner distance to her mind map.

Her mind map is joined by five major lines with the center bubble. The first line is on the improvement of foreign language learning.

In the second line she compares her mother tongue (Turkish) and her second language (German) proficiency. By adding an emoticon with a sad face next to the statement that she has mastered the second language better than the mother tongue she makes it clear that she is very self-conscious and sad about this.

The third line is neutral by stating that she has been exposed to two languages as she grew up bilingually.

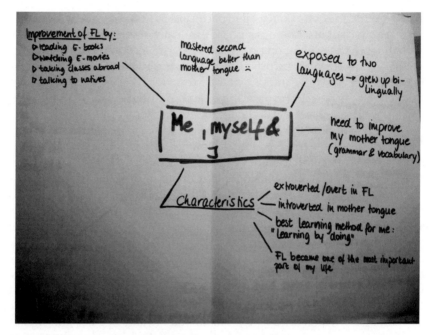

Figure 8.2   Ceylan's mind map

In the fourth line she steps beyond the second and third line by setting a strong goal for the future. She states that she needs to improve her mother tongue both with respect to vocabulary as well as grammar.

The fifth line, which is kind of a summary, is dedicated to her learner characteristics and refers to all three languages. Ceylan reveals that she is introvert in her mother tongue and extrovert in the foreign language. Additionally, she underlines that foreign language learning has become one of the most important parts of her life. The fifth line in her mind map in effect says that learning a foreign language allowed Ceylan to evolve into a different person. It helped her develop from an introvert into an extrovert person that can reach out.

Ceylan's mind map was picked for comment by another student for classroom evaluation. After the perception of the student was finished, Ceylan identified herself and wanted to clarify a few issues. For example, the students were interested in what had caused her to write that her mother tongue proficiency was so poor and caused her to add the emoticon. She explained that she had become friends with Semra, a young female exchange student from our partner university in Turkey. Together they prepared presentations and papers that term. Up to Semra's visit Ceylan had never met a university student from Turkey of her age. Ceylan quickly learned that her own Turkish language proficiency was completely different from Semra's. She became aware of the fact that her Turkish was not academic, low standard and on the level of child language. She had not known this before and had never thought about it. Semra's visit had brought her new friendship but also the hidden pain that she detected the moment she had to reflect on it and draw the mind map. This helped her articulate and start talking about the unease connected to it for the first time. The result of which was that Ceylan determined to do something about her mother tongue. Having been to US American and British universities she applied for an exchange to our partner university to Turkey. She will now gain what ought to be hers: the academic command of her own mother tongue.

During the classroom discussion that followed Ceylan's revelation two more students who had grown up bilingually reported similar language deficiency feelings they had had to face. One male student had just come back from a family visit to Afghanistan and the other one from Italy. The student who considered himself Afghan-German told the class that he had hardly succeeded in communicating in his heritage language. He had the hardest time both linguistically and culturally. His mind map mirrored this experience.

The German-Italian student spoke his mother tongue Italian fluently. However, he was upset with the fact that he had learned that he did not speak standard Italian as he had thought he would but Italian with a very strong Sicilian accent. The talking and sharing of these experiences in class allowed Ceylan as well as her fellow students to step back, be more aware about their proficiency in their mother tongues and develop a new third perspective together.

The phenomenon described here is very frequent among second- or third-generation immigrant children. They might still be fluent in their mother tongue but very often they are not literate in it anymore and mostly do not speak the academic language. It is important for children to gain ownership over their own mother tongue even if late. It is never too late to discover what is an important part of the self.

The ABCs model of cultural understanding and communication
The ABCs is a complex model to promote understanding of the self and other (Schmidt, 1999; Schmidt & Finkbeiner, 2006). It is highly adaptable and can be conducted both face to face, online and hybrid. It can be used

both for students and teachers and other target groups alike (Finkbeiner, 2006; Finkbeiner & Koplin, 2002; Finkbeiner & Knierim, 2006, 2008; Schmidt, 1999; Schmidt & Finkbeiner, 2006; Wilden, 2008). The question is what adaptations have to be made for the ABCs to function within a Human GPS approach.

How to conduct an ABCs

In the ABCs 'A' stands for 'Autobiography', 'B' for Biography and 'C' for Cross-Cultural Analysis (Finkbeiner, 2006; Schmidt & Finkbeiner, 2006). At the beginning, the participants must be willing to write an auto-biography that contains critical life events from their early childhood and which they are willing to share with the teacher or project leader (Banks, 1999). If the participants are non-literate they can use iconic and symbolic narration or oral history.

Step A is followed by an interview with a partner of a cultural and/or linguistic background different from one's own (Bogdan & Biklen, 1994; Spradley, 1979). The interviewer writes a biography of key events in the interviewee's life. Here the focus is on the development of unbiased, non-dogmatic cultural sensitivity. After B has been finished there is time for monitoring and control (Finkbeiner & Koplin, 2002). The partner reads the biography to the interviewee and there is space for clarifying misunder-standings or misinterpretations. In the European ABCs adaptation, we use a reciprocal approach which means all participants are involved in all pro-cesses being both interviewer and interviewee (Finkbeiner, 2006).

In step C each participant studies his or her own autobiography and compares it with the biography he or she has written about the other per-son. On the basis of this, an in-depth cross-cultural analysis of similarities and differences will be conducted. The focus can be either on comparing two life stories or on finding out about the differences of the perception of the self and the perception of the other (Wilden, 2008). In the latter case, one's autobiography (perception of the self) has to be compared to the biography a partner has written about oneself (perception of the other).

Formerly I used the Venn Diagram (Edwards, 2004) for supporting the creation of the list of similarities and differences, which is a pre-condition for the cross-cultural analysis. In the Venn Diagram two or more circles are used that overlap. The overlapping part is for the similarities and the non-overlapping parts are for the individual differences. Over time I learned that the Venn Diagram seems to trigger an analysis that is above the sur-face of the iceberg (Weaver, 1993) rather than below. For some students it has been particularly difficult to dive deep on the basis of the list. This is why we have implemented Weaver's iceberg model into the Venn Diagram

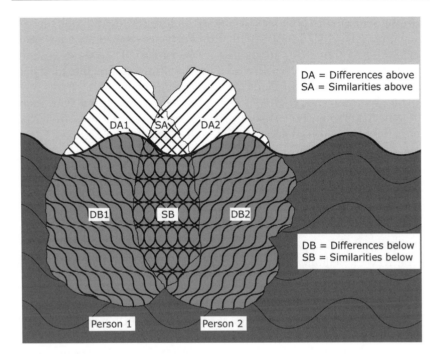

DA = Differences above
SA = Similarities above

DB = Differences below
SB = Similarities below

Figure 8.3   Cultural Venn diagram

(Figure 8.3) to make students become more aware of the differences between cultural surface and deep structures. There are now two or more icebergs, which do not necessarily have to collide in Weaver's (1993: 159) sense but rather overlap and partially transform into each other. The Cultural Venn icebergs remind and guide students to dive deep below the surface of iceberg in their analyses.

To summarize, the ABCs embrace different perspectives. The first perspective is the view on oneself, which is captured with the autobiography. The second perspective is the story told in the interview by partner B and then written down in a biography by partner A. The question is whether the third perspective can be developed in the cross-cultural analysis which is based on the comparison of the two stories (two perspectives) and how the Human GPS can help to trigger this.

Reporting on an ABCs project

The following is a brief report on one of our most recent ABCs projects (Finkbeiner & van Lier, in progress).[1] The project was situated in a hybrid learning setting with both face to face and online phases and took place in the winter 2006/2007 over three months. Forty-two university students in Germany and the USA participated in the project. They were grouped together in pairs and met in an e-learning environment that included both synchronous and asynchronous media to conduct the ABCs.

The experience not only with this most recent project but with many different ABCs projects over several years has shown that the ABCs experience has a deep impact and is often life changing. It is sometimes the first time students have reflected on their own inner self. These reflections are highly elaborate and detailed. The biographies are another important experience as they allow for a complete change of perspective. The *cross-cultural analysis* is the most difficult step to be taken. It ought to entail students going beyond the surface and the binary comparison of the two stories, step back and develop a somehow new third perspective. This most difficult step will be documented with extracts from a few examples and a way to facilitate this process with the help of Human GPS will be developed.

Illustrative results on the topic vegetarianism

The following is about ABCs process data from a Chinese student (D) who has now been to Germany for three years for her studies and an American student (E) who has been to Europe but has never visited Germany. The scenario mirrors a typical sociocultural context in any university in the USA and in Germany. There are a lot of international, bi-cultural and multi-lingual students at the university. I have chosen one of the several topics that were discussed: vegetarianism.

D's and E's Forum entries in their personal forum

E: 'Did you study German in China? I understand you want to go home to have real Chinese food. I like Chinese food too (American Chinese food; emoticon: smile). Since I don't eat meat, I don't think I would like most traditional German food. It sounds like a lot of sausage and heavy food. But maybe I'm wrong and it's good?? I haven't been to Germany but I've traveled a lot in parts of Europe, especially France.'

D: 'You don't like German food either? I am not a vegetarian but I don't eat much meat. That is too heavy and fat. I have to say in my mind, the German food is exactly what you image, lots of sausage. They are proud of their German sausages. Once a German told me there are more than 100 kinds of German sausages. But to me, they taste all the same' (emoticon: shy).

D learns that E is vegetarian by reading her forum entries. She does not respond on this directly to E but leads the topic into a slightly different direction talking about 'typical' German food, a neutral and safe topic for both as neither one of them is German. The entries show that both students relate to prior knowledge to typical traditional German kitchen, which therefore is stereotypical. German food is not picked up anymore at a later point of the process, yet the topic of vegetarian food is dealt with in D's biography on E as well as A's cross-cultural analysis.

Extract from D's Biography on E: 'E. has been vegetarian since 1993. There was an e-coli outbreak at a fast food restaurant in Seattle and she started reading about it and learned a lot of disgusting information about how the meat was processed and about meat in general. She was really shocked with the cruelty to animals and the factory farming. After that she really didn't want to eat meat … During our conversation, E. did never suggest to me to become vegetarian, even though I told her that I don't eat much meat either. She is a kind of person who will never force her own opinion on the others. She doesn't really "preach" about vegetarianism but she is happy that her boy friend is vegetarian because it's important to her.'

Student D evaluates and gives detailed background information on the fact that E is a vegetarian. In this context she starts evaluating E's personality style. In the cross-cultural analysis D reflects on the topic of vegetarian food, again. Here is what she wrote.

Extract from D's cross-cultural analysis on E: 'At the beginning, E. told me that she has been vegetarian since 1993. Since our conversation was based on answering questions which we posted in our forum, I could not ask her the reason immediately. Therefore, before she told me why she did become vegetarian, I was uncertain how I could get along with her during the project, because I have had a very negative image of vegetarian people before. The sister of my friend in high school is vegetarian, who is quite sensitive and hard to get along with. She refuses to eat meat, because she believes once people eat the animal, their spirits would come back to revenge. I thought E. must be also sensitive and I would probably hurt her or she would feel be insulted in certain situations which I could not realize. As a consequence, I was very careful while I talked to her, I did not ask many questions about this topic. However, as a matter of fact, as we went on to working together, I found she is a very nice person and culturally tolerant. She became vegetarian because she is passionate about animals and could not bear the inhumane treatment of animals.'

D compares her autobiography with the biography she wrote on E. In her analysis D describes the process she has gone through. She was judgmental at the beginning when she first heard that E was vegetarian. This was due to her prior experience with her sister's peer at school. This shows how much former stages in our acculturation process have an impact on our thinking at later stages in life (Finkbeiner, 2006). The cross-cultural analysis forces students to re-think. It causes student D to step back form her first perspective that she revealed in her analysis. There was no misunderstanding or conflict caused by D's presupposition. And her caution and hesitation resulted in the problem not being tackled nor detected during the whole process. In her analysis D succeeds in distancing herself from her rather negative preliminary perspective on vegetarians. Her perception about E as a vegetarian finally nearly seems exaggeratedly heroic. It seems as if she felt guilty and wanted to balance out the stereotypes she first had felt inside when she had heard that E was a vegetarian.

A look at E's cross-cultural analysis on the same issue gives us further insight into the discrepancy of the perception of the self and the other (Finkbeiner, 2006).

E's cross-cultural analysis: 'The observations that D made about me being a vegetarian and vegetarians in general were interesting. She said, 'In my opinion, vegetarian people are normally conservative and most of them may have been suffering emotional disorder. In contrast, D is very open-minded and optimistic.' My first reaction to this was to laugh. It struck me as funny and was definitely something I hadn't heard before. … I believe that could be something in the Chinese culture. I'm not sure how many vegetarians there are in China but it is probably not common. I was happy that she didn't think that I was conservative and had an emotional disorder. It's such a strange concept to think that I could be perceived that way in another culture just because I choose not to eat meat. To relate this to the self-image and image of the other, my self perspective was that as a vegetarian, people may think that I was sensitive to animals or healthy and maybe liberal. However, the perspective of the other in this case was that vegetarians often have emotional disorders and that, therefore, as a vegetarian I was likely to have an emotional disorder … I don't mean to come across as harsh toward D. because I believe it could be as simple as a language issue here and either way, it didn't upset me. After all, I don't know exactly how she defines an 'emotional disorder'. It could be something different and much less severe than it sounds to me. This leads me to the idea that this is only my interpretation of what she wrote about it. To get a clear understanding about this, she would have to explain what she meant.'

E based her cross-cultural analysis on the comparison of her autobiography and D's biography on her. She is shocked by how she is perceived as a vegetarian and wonders why that is so. She reflects about the perception of the self and the other and how that is influenced by culture. Vegetarianism symbolizes a liberal, open mind in the USA versus a closed mind with emotional disorders in China. There are some challenges in the data that I will sum up and a solution will be developed.

The role of 'Human GPS' in the ABCs

A lot of emotional turmoil and thinking was created during the ABCs process described here. The discrepancy of the perception of the self and the perception of the other, which is usually mostly hidden, became visible throughout the data and as a consequence hurt the participants. Maybe it is true that only when it starts hurting does it start working. For E it was revealing to learn that the perspective of the other on herself would be so different from the perception of herself. Even though D had been to Germany for three years already, we found her to be in the critical stage of culture shock (Hofstede, 1993).

The ABCs obviously have enormous power in contributing to the insight that there are different viewpoints in the world. But still, it takes some fine tuning to overcome some of the hurdles that seem to prevent the participants from fully developing the third perspective. It now takes further studies to test if the Human GPS can help to do this.

In the European adaptation of the ABCs we introduced an extra step after B that allows for clarification of misunderstandings once the biography is written (Finkbeiner & Koplin, 2002). Another step has to be added for the Human GPS to function. There are several options to do this:

– So far the ABCs are a reciprocal effort. The ABCs design could be transformed into a triangular design with partners G, H and I of different cultural background (Finkbeiner & Koplin, 2002). G would interview H, H would interview I and I would interview G. In this way three different perspectives would be included right from the beginning.

– No matter whether reciprocal or triangular design, we need to make more use of the authentic learners' data. What this means is that it takes another step to reintegrate the outcomes of the cross-cultural analyses into the learning process. This might lengthen the ABCs process, which is already time consuming.

- As the cross-cultural analyses are very personal, they have to be made anonymous and then handed back to the class. Another option is for the teacher to take critical examples and bring them back into the classroom for meta-reflection. In this way we can offer a multitude of perspectives to the class on certain topics, such as the value attributed to religion, to family, to career and so on.
- Just as in the technical GPS, the human GPS needs to include systematic help of an in-process control and monitoring system. The control outcomes have to be directly fed back into the system during the process.
- Two of the whole row of control buttons will have to carry the labels 'cultural' and 'personal'. What human beings say must never be simply reduced to cultural or personal values. We need to find out for each single intercultural and interpersonal event which role culture plays in personal traits. Relating back to the topic of vegetarianism: What is considered a 'healthy' living approach is always culturally as well as personally biased. It is influenced over time by constant change in the socio-cultural context of, in the knowledge about, as well as in the access to, certain foods.

Conclusion

This chapter introduced the reader to the 'Human GPS' idea, which follows the technical GPS and adapts it to human beings. Yet, in contrast to the technical GPS the learners cannot simply go to the shop, buy their little GPS, rely on it to function and be happy. They themselves have to do much more. They have to become active during the whole process. This is so because the Human GPS is an authentic tool. Learners only 'own' their Human GPS if they gain control over it and understand its potential. Language and cultural awareness are the software that helps learners synchronize the different positions. If this is successful Human GPS will help to locate the inner self. The Human GPS journey is never over. It is a journey of a lifetime. The Human GPS approach complies with the concept of lifelong learning, demands for the software to be updated all the time and security patches to be developed to avoid viruses getting into the system that would cause a biased view of the world. Only if we take care of this and keep our system running will we finally know how to locate ourselves and the others in a diversifying world. If we can do this we will more clearly see, embrace and protect our true human values, which lie in the richness of a diverse world.

Note

1. I want to thank Professor Dr. van Lier, Monterey Institute for International Studies, Cal, USA, for his cooperation in three transatlantic online projects (Finkbeiner & van Lier, in progress).

References

Alred, G., Byram, M. and Fleming, M. (2006) *Education for Intercultural Citizenship*. Clevedon: Multilingual Matters.

Armengol Castells, L. (2007) The use of languages in think aloud protocols produced by multilingual writers living in a bilingual environment. Dissertation, Universitat de Lleida Departament d'Anglès i Lingüística, Lleida.

Ausubel, D.P. (1976) Die Verwendung von, 'Advance Organizers' beim Lernen und Behalten von bedeutungsvollem sprachlichem Material. In M. Hofer and F.E. Weinert (Hrsg) *Pädagogische Psychologie. 2. Lernen und Instruktion* (pp. S. 218–226). Frankfurt: Fischer.

Banks, J.A. (1999) *An Introduction to Multicultural Education* (2nd edn). Boston: Allyn & Bacon.

Bhabha, H. (1994) *The Location of Culture*. London: Routledge.

Bogdan, R.C. and Biklen, S.K. (1994) *Qualitative Research for Education: An Introduction to Theory and Method* (2nd edn). Boston: Allyn & Bacon.

Byram, M. (1999) Acquiring intercultural communicative competence. Fieldwork and experiential learning. In L. Bredella and W. Delanoy (eds) *Interkultureller Fremdsprachenunterricht* (pp. 358–380). Tübingen: Narr.

Cots, J.Mª (2001) Language awareness: From the curriculum to the classroom. In D. Lasagabaster and J.M. Sierra (eds) *Language Awareness in the Foreign Language Classroom* (pp. 101–138). Zarautz (Gipuzkoa): Universidad del País Vasco.

Dijk, T.A.v. and Kintsch, W. (1983) *Strategies of Discourse Comprehension*. London: Academic Press.

Edwards, A.W.F. (2004) *Cogwheels of the Mind: The Story of Venn Diagrams*. Baltimore and London: Johns Hopkins University Press.

Fehling, S. (2008) *Language Awareness und bilingualer Unterricht: Eine komparative Studie* (2nd edn). Frankfurt: Peter Lang.

Finkbeiner, C. (2004) Cooperation and collaboration in a Foreign Language Teacher Training Program: The LMR plus model. In E. Cohen, C. Brody and M. Sapon Shevin (eds) *Learning to Teach with Cooperative Learning: Challenges in Teacher Education* (pp. 111–127). Albany, NY: State University of New York Press.

Finkbeiner, C. (2005) *Interessen und Strategien beim fremdsprachlichen Lesen. Wie Schülerinnen und Schüler englische Texte lesen und verstehen*. Tübingen: Narr.

Finkbeiner, C. (2006) Constructing third space. The principles of reciprocity and cooperation. In P.R. Schmidt and C. Finkbeiner (eds) *The ABC's of Cultural Understanding and Communication: National and International Adaptations* (pp. 19–42). Greenwich, CT: Information Age Publishing.

Finkbeiner, C. (in press) Culture and good language learners. In C. Griffiths (ed.) *Lessons from Good Language Learners* (pp. 109–117). Cambridge: Cambridge University Press.

Finkbeiner, C. and Fehling, S. (2006) Investigating the role of awareness and multiple perspectives in intercultural education. In P.R. Schmidt and C. Finkbeiner (eds) *The ABC's of Cultural Understanding and Communication: National and International Adaptations* (pp. 93–110). Greenwich, CT: Information Age Publishing.

Finkbeiner, C. and Knierim, M. (2006) The ABC's as a starting point and goal: The online intercultural exchange project. In P.R. Schmidt and C. Finkbeiner (eds) *The ABC's of Cultural Understanding and Communication: National and International Adaptations* (pp. 213–244). Greenwich, CT: Information Age Publishing.

Finkbeiner, C. and Knierim, M. (2008) Developing L2 strategic competence online. In F. Zhang and B. Barber (eds) *Handbook of Research on Computer-enhanced Language Acquisition and Learning* (pp. 379–405). Hershey, PA: IGI Global.

Finkbeiner, C. and Koplin, C. (2002) *A Cooperative Approach for Facilitating Intercultural Education*. Newark, DE: International Reading Association. On WWW at www.readingonline.org (Reading Online, New Literacies).

Finkbeiner, C. and van Lier, L. (in progress) *Comparative Intercultural Analysis: A Collaborative Online Project*.

Furstenberg, G., Levet, S., English, K. and Maillet, K. (2001) Giving a virtual voice to the silent language of culture: The CULTURA project. *Language Learning and Technology* 5 (1), 55–102. On WWW at http://llt.msu.edu/vol5num1/furstenberg/default.html. Accessed 09.11.04.

Hawkins, E. (1984) *Awareness of Language: An Introduction*. Cambridge: Cambridge University Press.

James, C. and Garrett, P. (2000) Language awareness. In M. Byram (ed.) *Routledge Encyclopedia of Language Teaching and Learning* (pp. 330–333). London: Routledge.

Kramsch, C. (1993) *Context and Culture in Language Teaching*. Oxford: Oxford University Press.

Kramsch, C. (1998) Between self and other. In V. Berry and A. McNeill (eds) *Policy and Practice in Language Education* (pp. 43–62). Hong Kong: University of Hong Kong, Department of Curriculum Studies.

Kristeva, J. (1990) *Fremde sind wir uns selbst*. Frankfurt: Suhrkamp.

Lantolf, J. (2006) *Sociocultural Theory and the Genesis of Second Language*. Oxford: Open University Press.

Luft, J. and Ingham, H. (1955) *The Johari Window: A Graphic Model for Interpersonal Relations*. Los Angeles, CA: University of California at Los Angeles, Extension Office.

Missildine, W.H. (2007) *In dir lebt das Kind, das du einmal warst*. Aus dem Amerikanischen von Josef Wimmer. 17. Auflage. Stuttgart: Klett Cotta.

Schmidt, P.R. (1999) Focus on research: Know thyself and understand others. *Language Arts* 76 (4), 332–340.

Schmidt, P.R. and Finkbeiner, C. (2006) Introduction: What is the ABC's of Cultural Understanding and Communication? In P.R. Schmidt and C. Finkbeiner (eds) *The ABC's of Cultural Understanding and Communication: National and International Adaptations* (pp. 1–18). Greenwich, CT: Information Age Publishing.

Spradley, J. (1979) *The Ethnographic Interview*. New York: Holt, Rinehart & Winston.

Svalberg, A.M-L. (2007) Language awareness and language learning. *Language Teaching* 40, 287–308.

van Lier, L. (1996) *Interaction in the Language Curriculum. Awareness, Autonomy and Authenticity.* Harlow: Longman.

van Lier, L. (2004) The *Ecology and Semiotics of Language Learning: A Sociocultural Perspective.* Amsterdam: Kluwer.

Weaver, G.R. (1993) Understanding and coping with cross-cultural adjustment stress. In M. Paige (Hrsg) *Education for the Intercultural Experience* (2nd edn) (pp. 137–167). Yarmouth, ME: Intercultural Press.

Wilden, E. (2008) *Selbst- und Fremdwahrnehmung in der interkulturellen Onlinekommunikation. Das Modell der ABC's of Cultural Understanding and Communication Online.* Frankfurt am Main: Peter Lang.

Young, A. and Helot, C. (2003) Language awareness and/or language learning in French primary schools today. *Language Awareness* 12 (3–4), 236–246.

Chapter 9

Professional Training: Creating Intercultural Space in Multi-ethnic Workplaces

CATHARINE ARAKELIAN

In 1998, in response to labour shortages, the UK government encouraged large-scale recruitment of international nurses to work in the National Health Service (NHS). To satisfy the Nursing and Midwifery Council, which registers overseas nurses as fit to practise in the United Kingdom, each employing hospital had to supply an adaptation programme which would enable these staff to integrate professionally into their new environments. This chapter describes an intercultural skills programme designed by Arakelian Programmes Limited from the intercultural education theories of Byram (Byram, 1997; Byram *et al.*, 2001). It was delivered in 16 hospitals in the United Kingdom between 1999 and 2003. The programme consisted of two complementary courses: an intercultural communication skills programme for new international staff, together with an intercultural skills programme for their supervisors, team leaders and managers. This chapter briefly describes the curriculum, methods and tools used on these courses including reflective diaries, ethnographic methods, My Personal Lexicon and role-playing practice scenarios. The teaching methodology derived from cognitive behaviour theory and ethnographic research is described.

The Multi-ethnic Workplace as a Learning Space

Hospitals are institutions where people with a range of skills and knowledge work under pressure to care for other people. Hospitals are simultaneously workplaces where people negotiate their roles and performance of their roles within a rule-governed environment. The workplace is a contested place. Learning is not usually prioritised, and for reasons of gender, age, affiliation and ethnicity, there is inequitable distribution of learning opportunities and career development. Some types of learning in a hospital are offered as mandatory such as health and safety training, fire awareness training and manual handling training. Other training needs such as numeracy, literacy and interpersonal communication skills are discretionary and generally expected to happen outside the workplace, in colleges of Further Education for example.

There is now a statutory duty on public bodies to promote race equality after the 1999 MacPherson enquiry into the death of Stephen Lawrence that found 'institutional racism' in the police service. The Race Relations Amendment Act 2000 (and later the Equalities Act of 2006[1]) recommended reform throughout public services, including the NHS. These Acts ushered in a variety of diversity training courses. Diversity training is focused on sharing information about different ethnic and religious groups in the community. In a hospital the visible evidence of such attention to promoting race equality is the provision of multilingual signage, and guides on topics such as the treatment of the body after death for different religions. These short courses, typically a three-hour in-service session, and knowledge guides, do not aim to address underlying intercultural skills.

In some cases, diversity training is framed as a guide to the legal sanctions governing race relations with the careful avoidance of certain language used to discipline discussion. One of the consequences of this type of training in the 1990s was that some British staff reported feeling guilty about their everyday working practices. In fact, some reported that after diversity training they felt increased anxiety that has led to the avoidance of any issue in the workplace that could result in an accusation of insensitivity to someone's background. This type of approach might be seen to have resulted in a diminution of intercultural skills as discussing intercultural conflict became tantamount to admitting that discrimination existed in the workplace.

In the light of this historical context, our programmes are not marketed as 'diversity training'. Our approach aims to improve intercultural skills and intercultural communication skills by following a skills-based syllabus rather than a knowledge/information-based syllabus. Also, the training aims to build on the communication and interactive skills of the participants and to develop their own awareness of their strengths and weaknesses as colleagues working together in the same setting for a common goal. Our syllabus does not seek to emphasise the quasi-legal framework around relationships in the workplace, that is, it is not promoting a rule-based performative model. The teaching methods are designed to develop intercultural skills in observable behaviour in the workplace and to assist the whole staff in the internalisation of habits of 'sustainable learning', so that the institution itself begins to reproduce culturally safe practices.

The Intercultural Communication Skills Programme

Migrant workers, in our case mainly nursing staff, coming to work in the NHS are normally recruited by an external agency with their employing hospital personnel department. Such nurses are qualified and registered to practise in another country. They often bring up to 10 years experience with them and are categorised as 'highly skilled workers' in the British immigration system. This means they are allocated work permits through their NHS employer which normally tie them to that specific employer's contract. If they want to move jobs the new employer would need to apply for a new work permit. This immigration requirement fundamentally shapes the social, psychological and working relationship between the nurse and their employer.

In addition, before being allowed to join the professional register to work in the United Kingdom, there is a period of supervised practice during which time the skilled migrant worker is normally allocated a relatively low status role on low pay under a mentor who is a UK-registered nurse. After successfully completing a portfolio of evidence according to a list of 'core competencies', the nurse is recommended by their employer for registration with the Nursing and Midwifery Council. With so many different legal and professional hoops to jump through sometimes it takes up to a year before the nurse is able to work at any level of professional autonomy, let alone command the status they had in their previous workplace.

Our intercultural communication skills training is intended to be holistic: to help skilled migrant workers in the UK health sector to integrate socially, psychologically and professionally into their new professional settings as efficiently as possible. So much is new to the migrant worker. For example, task allocation and responsibility differentiation between nurses and doctors is different in different countries and between health systems. It is culturally specific.[2] British patients expect information and invoke their 'rights' in a way that may not be the same as in the nurse's own country, and of course the drug names and equipment, jargon and local systems of working in the NHS are unfamiliar. It is also imperative to learn quickly the legal frameworks that govern what nurses can and cannot do in the United Kingdom.[3]

We do not expect nurses to pick up this new workplace culture in a classroom. Since there is such a wealth of information in the environment around them, and they are well motivated to pick it up, we focus on providing cognitive tools to achieve this in the most efficient way possible. We use a specific method based on cognitive behaviour theory (schema and scripts) that can help produce and internalise appropriate 'cultural maps' (O'Grady & Millen, 1994). Our approach helps individuals recognise the differences between their previous professional work and their new role. This entire process results in each nurse re-shaping their *professional identity* for the UK hospital system (Sarangi & Roberts, 1999). Following Wringe, in this process both education and training are happening concurrently in that the nurses are led to discover what changes they need to make through direct learning from managers, informal peer-to-peer mentorship, formal mentorship and the structured experiential learning opportunities afforded by the intercultural communication skills programme (Wringe, 1991).

The nurses are actively and consciously constructing their new professional identities in their new workplaces from the start. To have succeeded in being recruited, they have already demonstrated some level of intercultural awareness and adequate English language skills to function on a day-to-day basis. The programme assumes they are willing to keep professional diaries and other reflective documents, which, as Byram (1997) identifies, is a prerequisite for intercultural work.

The precise curriculum and assessment is agreed with each NHS employer and the schedule of classes fits around any in-house new staff induction and mandatory training, such as fire safety. The nurses are formatively assessed through the tools: My Professional Identity Notebook (PIN), My Personal Lexicon and when taking part in scenarios and other activities in class. Summative assessment consists of the completion of five assignments, including a researched talk on a clinical subject. The course is workplace-based with normally 10–18 study days over three months, depending on the hospital employer. The curriculum is normally covered in 60 hours of class teaching and 40 hours self-study. The process of con structing one's new professional identity is, of course, an ongoing effort.

The tools: Reflective diaries 'PIN'

Students are taught a method of structured reflection in which to record events in their working lives. In the reflective dairies, kept in a bound book called PIN, we are able to note a number of developments, and are able to discuss incidents in the classroom, to praise successful encounters and to analyse through role-plays perplexing or difficult encounters. The range of encounters is wide, but the communicative intercultural challenges recorded include dealing with ancillary staff, line managers, doctors, patients and relatives. Issues with immediate line managers are particularly urgent. Frequently, these encounters appear to illustrate aspects of discrimination and inequality which need careful examination. In the complementary course for managers, we deal with the power issues explicitly through a game called 'Learning the Rules'. This game cannot be 'won' by the overseas nurses without changing the political nature of the relationship between overseas and British staff to one of negotiated supporter rather than critical friend. Because these situations are fresh and relevant to the entire group, they are motivating and the nurses participate willingly in the role-plays that are derived from them.

The tools: Role-plays 'practice scenarios'

Using the records in the reflective diaries, we are able to develop scenarios (role-plays) quickly that have a direct bearing on the lives of the students. The scenario work that emerges directly from real-life encounters stimulates wide ranging discussion of workplace behaviour in its social, political, affective and legal aspects. The context for learning in this way is the assurance of confidentiality in the psychologically safe environment of the classroom, and the mutual trust of the nurses and their intercultural skills teachers. The teachers are not required to act as 'experts' or 'judges' of behaviour but as facilitators and interpreters. This relationship is one of peer to peer, adult to adult. The process of learning is shared and the power hierarchy implied in teacher–student is negated as far as possible. The teacher's role is to facilitate an exploration of the issues by creating a safe and supportive atmosphere, and as a British person and English speaker to help interpret a sociocultural understanding of professional expectations of language and behaviour.

The aim of using scenarios drawn from real life encounters is to explore in depth as a group the impact of certain relationships and conflicts. Teachers need skills of interpreting the group dynamics as well as maintaining a sense of direction and time management. Talking about behaviour is not the same as experiencing or rehearsing new behaviour. The overseas nurses provide the subject matter and work actively on the scenarios through an iterative process. There is noise and laughter as the nurses are on their feet moving around and engaging with the topic to solve its explicit and implicit problems. From the outside such a physical class looks quite anarchic. In fact, a session can be controlled effectively with minimal direct instruction if the aims are clearly understood by all. As the programme progresses, the nurses come to see how scenario work develops professional intercultural skills and they request more of this work, and note more complex scenarios that they want to develop in the classroom. Training intercultural teachers to be successful leaders of scenario work is essential, although many former English, as a Foreign Language, teachers have used fictional dialogue and role-plays in their teaching. A minimum of six hours of the 30-hour teacher preparation course run by Arakelian Programmes is spent considering the strengths and weaknesses of role-play and the teachers engage in scenario work themselves and reflect on their learning through this loop-input (Woodward, 1991).

Cognitive Behaviour Theory: Cultural Maps as the Basis for an Intercultural Teaching Methodology

Psychologists assert that our knowledge and experience of the world as part of a particular culture or group are accumulated into structures in our minds that are called schemas (cf. Beck, 1975). Schemas are referred to as 'cultural models' by health writers Holland and Quinn (1987) among others. Cognitive anthropology ascribes a powerful effect to operation of schemas:

> One can say a schema has motivational force for an individual in the same way one can speak of a request as having directive force. An appropriate request does more than just describe what someone wants: if has the paradigmatic effect of instigating the other person to action. In a similar manner, a schema can serve as more than a recognition device: its activation can be an instigation to action. (D'Andrade, 1995: 231)

Schemas are cognitive maps of behaviours and beliefs which are culturally accurate. In our programmes we use the term *cultural map* because it draws attention to the representational aspect of the internal model created by each person and the use of the model to orientate and direct his or her action in the world (O'Grady & Millen, 1994). *Cultural maps* exist in the form of expectations that help us to make sense of what is going on and to help us know how to interact. In cross-cultural encounters people share fewer schemas and are therefore more likely to misinterpret each other. This means that more strategies for noticing and learning new cultural maps and for checking and negotiating meaning must be put in place.

Scripts refer to what it is appropriate and allowable to say and do (or not do) in a particular context. When people share the script there is much that does not need to be said. The other can fill in the gaps. Scripts anticipate the expected sequence of events associated with an activity including the relative power sharing and direction of the interaction. Schemas and scripts reflect underlying belief systems, values, attitudes and assumptions of the culture in which they have grown (O'Grady & Millen, 1994).

The teaching methodology is modelled on the non-directive counselling approach used in cognitive behaviour therapy. This explicit negotiated approach is part of the cognitive-behavioural method. There are a number of other 'client' attitudes which must be in place for successful outcomes. Clients must have ready access to their thoughts and feelings; they have to have identifiable life (work) problems to focus on; they must be willing and able to do homework assignments; and be willing to engage in a collaborative relationship with the teacher. Finally, clients' cognitions must be flexible enough to be modified through established cognitive behavioural procedures (Beck, 1975).

These ideas are applied to the pedagogical issues raised in teaching intercultural communication skills in the following way:

Clients must have ready access to their thoughts and feelings

The programme teaches formal techniques for reflecting on events and behaviour. We teach critical incident analysis. We develop a supportive classroom atmosphere, with a non-judgmental peer group and an empathetic style of facilitation. Public rehearsal of expressive behaviour, particularly negative emotions such as anger, disrespectful language or gestures or frustration, or where other people in the encounter lose control, is not comfortable for many people and is not required by the method we employ. Scenarios are presented as a dialectical method of inductive teaching standing at one remove from the emotional responses that may have dominated the original encounter. Confidentiality is assured and a relaxed, playful context encouraged.

For example, an interpersonal problem such as an incident of perceived bullying might be modelled in a scenario. It is played through with the nurse who was directly involved standing outside the event. She or he determines how many people were involved, where it took place (public or private space) and identifies the critical moment. With the teacher this person directs the scenario, feeding the words and actions that were used to other participants who walk through the situation as directed. The situation can then be 'played back' several times modifying the language and behaviour to model more or less assertive responses. The sharing of an event like this often elicits an immediate empathetic response from the rest of the class who thus support emotionally the originator of the scenario, and the iterative work contributes to how each of them would deal with this situation, or have dealt with similar situations in the past. In addition, the results seem to be immediately absorbed into the behavioural repertoire of the group. Once this technique is mastered by a class, it is the selection of the most valuable scenarios proposed by the class that becomes part of the teacher's role.

Clients have to have identifiable life (work) problems to focus on

We use the entries made in the reflective dairies, PIN, for noticing and recording intercultural events. Communicative incidents and behaviour of oneself and others become a wealth of data collected in the field. Nurses are highly motivated in the workplace to achieve recognition (and registration) and to engage in the co-construction of their new professional identity through the competency framework required to gain registration referred to in the introduction. The nurses soon begin to construct personal development objectives through a process of self-identification of needs. For example, a nurse who realises that the names of drugs and protocols for drug administration used in the United Kingdom are unfamiliar, and seeing this is a requirement of the competency framework, will actively seek support from the intercultural teacher and nursing mentor.

Clients are willing and able to do homework assignments

'Homework' in this curriculum frequently means ethnographic research in the workplace, as we shall see below. This brings up issues of time-management in the workplace. The workplace-based assignments require supportive senior colleagues to mediate the power imbalance in the workplace (Sarangi & Roberts, 1999: 354–381).

Clients engage in a collaborative relationship with the teacher

The intercultural teacher is not a clinical expert and so to build a collaborative relationship the differentiation between areas of expertise needs to be maintained and respected. Each will become a 'legitimate speaker' for 'speech always owes a major part of the value of the person who utters it' (Bourdieu, 1977: 648). The empathy and integrity of the teacher is critical to the success of this relationship.

Clients' cognitions must be flexible enough to be modified through established cognitive behavioural procedures

Flexibility is governed partly by previous learning experiences: 'face' issues (Goffman, 1967) and self-awareness of linguistic, cultural, gender or other barriers. The curriculum addresses increasing self-awareness and helps the nurses develop socially integrative acculturation strategies.

Ethnography: Sojourner as Cultural Researcher

Ethnographic research is most commonly associated with anthropology (Hammersley & Atkinson, 1995). It is a technique of participant observation whereby patterns of behaviour (social, political, interpersonal) are revealed to the observer through everyday contact with the new culture and society. It is carried out by researchers who live in the community they are researching, who often deliberately define themselves as 'novices' seeking help from 'gatekeepers', from whom they learn the language and concepts of the group they wish to join. The use of ethnographic approaches in language learning has been explored more fully elsewhere (Byram & Fleming, 1998; Sarangi & Roberts, 1999). The description of 'sojourner' (Byram, 1997) or 'professional stranger' (Agar, 1980) is used to distinguish the ethnographic researcher from the tourist or visitor.

In taking the role of professional stranger or ethnographer in their workplace for a period, the nurses are put in a psychologically robust position. There are several benefits. First, the nurse gains confidence by assuming an 'expert' status, as researcher, rather than 'novice' status, as newcomer. Second, by explicitly acknowledging the learning process it is legitimate for a nurse not to know much about the culture and to get things wrong, and to ask clarifying questions. Third, it gives permission to the nurse to admit that they do not know colloquial language or how local people use it, and so they can jot down new idioms and question assumptions in My Personal Lexicon.

Other ethnographic research principles can be utilised, such as the injunction on participant observers not to interfere with or pass judgement on the target group and to remember that their presence will change the behaviour of others. Using their notes and observations, nurses are trained to reflect on what they have gathered, make sense according to the intercultural principles developed in classwork and refer the more curious British rites and rituals to the teacher.

We develop the intercultural communication skills in international nurses through this 'intercultural fieldwork'. Our approach to fieldwork is a modification of the experiential learning cycle (cf. Byram, 1997: 68–69). We identify a series of five socio-psychological stages in 'intercultural field-work' aimed at constructing new cultural maps: *opening up, noticing, hypothesising, risk-taking* and *gathering feedback*. Each of these stages can be enhanced through teaching interventions. First, *opening up* refers to becoming open to new experiences, and a willingness to accept that each culture has its own way of doing things. Second, *noticing* is the skill of being able to separate out specific behaviour from the general flow of activity. In language learning these communicative events are described as functions such as greetings, apologising and so on. Noticing the different ways in which others seek clarification, contradict politely, give and take instructions, means noticing formal and informal politeness markers, body language and timing, length of utterance or gaze. These different ways of actively seeing add up to 'noticing'. Third, *hypothesising* is a stage where an assumption about the intentions or purpose of the observed behaviour is explicitly made. The hypothesis should be discussed or checked before being brought into one's own performance repertoire, as it may be an aberrant observation or may be that certain features of the relationship were not known.

Fourth, *risk-taking* is a point in the cycle of building and internalising a new intercultural map which is extremely difficult, the adoption of the new behaviour for oneself. An example might be an Indian nurse who is expected to adopt a more assertive manner in the NHS context and in particular to look people in the eye when taking or giving instructions. For some Indian nurses this is counter to their previous professional socialisation. They find that they cannot adopt the behaviour in the workplace on command, and this is where the relatively risk-free environment of the classroom scenario work enables someone to test behaviour or a communication strategy new to them without risking their dignity. Even with such rehearsal of a new cultural map it takes a long time for new professional behaviour to be comfortably internalised.

Finally, the fifth stage is *learning from feedback* on the success (or otherwise) of putting the new cultural map into operation. In the workplace nurses need constructive and accurate feedback. They usually receive this feedback in respect of clinical skills from their managers and mentors. In respect of cultural knowledge and intercultural skills they need to actively request feedback.

Practice Scenarios as an Intercultural Teaching Tool

During the formative input in practice scenarios, the teacher works by monitoring and supporting the development of the new cultural maps.

Two key techniques are *feed-in* and *feed-back* which are differentiated by the timing. *Feed-in* is when the teacher contributes cultural ideas, comments on appropriate behaviour or language exponents as the scenario work is in progress. This develops the complexity of the role-plays and stimulates discussion on intercultural differences. The second technique, *feed-back*, is when, after a scenario session, the teacher reflects with the participants on how communicative strategies might be 'read' in host culture. This involves discussing the balance of transactional and interactional communication, the awareness of ethnocentric assumptions, the tolerance of ambiguity of intentions and the negotiation of meaning, ways of seeking clarification through elaboration and repetition.

Cognitive behavioural training is effective through harnessing experiential activity (doing) and cognitive activity (reflecting) to change patterns of behaviour. The content of the scenarios originates initially from ethnographic fieldwork. It is authentic, meaningful, already problematised. The scenarios represent goal-focused learning and so are motivational.

The scenario work promotes deep learning as discussed by Fleming (in this volume). Through the enactment of the scenarios we can look at body language, language choice, strategies for approaching people, rapport management, conflict resolution and countless other culturally determined schema. This could include building simple cultural maps for everyday use, such as changing an appointment, or more complex professional skills, such as listening actively for core messages (empathetic listening), which are also culturally determined. The assessment of such learning has to be in the careful interpretation of the achieved objectives, rather than a tick list of knowledge items. Our intercultural communication skills programmes work on the cognitive level of identifying and changing aspects of the nurses' existing cultural maps, the participants and their work colleagues enter into a conscious redefining of their professional identity which is a re-education rather than a training process that aims to leave the fundamental personal schema intact.

The One-Day Workshop: Working Alongside International Staff

This workshop is the complementary programme offered to managers and mentors of international. The one-day (six-hour) workshop can be delivered flexibly as one full day or two half days or as required. The full menu of activities is too great to be covered in the six hours, so a customised selection of about two thirds is negotiated with the group. (The full programme of activities and learning objectives offered is in Appendix 1.)

In a limited period it is important that the work is kept focused on actual workplace experience. Throughout each session participants are asked to reflect openly to the group on the application of the input to their specific setting. The aim is an atmosphere of shared learning. In post-course evaluations, this peer-to-peer ethos is normally rated as highly valued.

While all participants are notionally equal participants in the programme, there is often a self-selecting sub-group who initially at least 'speak' for the rest. The teacher needs to take this into account when developing methods to engage all staff in dialogue about intercultural relations so as to avoid merely reproducing the existing hegemonic-dominating discourse of the workplace in the classroom. If the hierarchies of the institution are transferred into the classroom, then a degree of censorship over what it is permissible to discuss in front of senior staff is self-imposed. There are normally 16–20 participants in each workshop. The more junior participants, frequently mentors of overseas staff, are normally 'volunteered' by their departments. The senior staff, managers of overseas staff, are normally in the programme by choice, prompted by curiosity or because they feel they are facing certain challenges dealing with their international staff.

One of the aims of the complementary intercultural skills programme is to identify and counter mistaken cognitive assumptions. For example, a commonly reported cause of frustration among managers is why some international staff *say* they understand what is being asked of them but then show quite clearly by their actions that they have not understood. Initially this is (charitably) assumed to be a problem of English language level. When this is not an adequate explanation other assumptions are made by an interculturally untrained manager including concerns about the overseas nurse's honesty, lack of self-awareness of own knowledge levels or even laziness. After learning about schema theory and scripts as the basis for behaviour, a manager may be able to reinterpret the behaviour they are worried about. They can use these cognitive tools to consider the behaviour from another perspective A nurse using a 'respect' schema, which included a notion of professionalism centred on refraining from asking questions, obedience and deference strategies, had been interpreted as servile and dishonest. In the UK schema of 'professionalism' asking clarifying questions and being assertive, making eye contact and negotiating the sharing of tasks is seen as positive professional behaviour. Both parties needed to be able to be explicit about these crossed schemas. Another case involved a highly experienced overseas trained therapeutic radiographer who was used to working in silence in the radiotherapy room. He found the continuous stream of chatter with the patient and discussion of what was happening distracting and fundamentally unprofessional. He was seen by his British colleagues as authoritarian, aloof and lacking in patient empathy, in a word, unprofessional. Once again the intercultural skills programme allowed a dialogue which opened up the different interpretations of what constituted professional behaviour. In the examples above there is a lack of intercultural skills on both sides, specifically a lack of a tolerance of ambiguity which is the realisation that cross-cultural interactions are intrinsically ambiguous, need clarification and that there is no need to feel uncomfortable about this process of interpretation.

But why should it be so difficult for a new international staff member to ask questions and to learn? The rules of the encounter are in the mentor or manager's hands. The learning has to be authorised to be made visible, otherwise all parties continue to act as though learning is not happening. Bourdieu describes workplaces as a type of social field.

> A field is a structured space of positions in which the positions and their interrelations are determined by the distribution of different kinds of resources or 'capital'…The individual who participates in these struggles will have differing aims…but will share common certain fundamental presuppositions. All participants must believe in the game they are playing, and in the value of what is at stake. The very existence of a game or field presupposes a total and unconditional 'investment', a practical and unquestioning belief in the game and its stakes. Hence their conduct presupposes a fundamental accord or complicity on the part of those who participate in the struggle. (Bourdieu, 1982: 14)

Power in the workplace is not exercised as physical force but is transmuted into symbolic form founded on the recognition of shared belief and language. The legitimacy of a certain type of language is recognised or authorised. Bourdieu elaborates on the concept of 'legitimate speaker'. When a person speaks the speaker wishes not only to be understood, but to be 'believed, obeyed, respected, distinguished'. To be a 'legitimate speaker' you must be empowered to speak by those around you: 'those who speak regard those who listen as worthy to listen and that those who listen regard those who speak as worthy to speak'. This idea tries to explain why in some settings and contexts otherwise competent speakers appear institutionally silent (Norton, 2000: 113).

Reproduction of the power structures of the institution is the responsibility of the dominant group. This is illustrated in hospitals where international nurses work alongside British trained nurses at the same grade. International staff rarely share the invisible symbolic power because they are not recognised to possess the social capital of prestige which accrues to the dominant elite. This can be seen in the treatment of workplace problems. Managers reported that whenever there were problems in the workplace, it was always the British managers and British nurses held to account. This suggests that although all the registered nurses were deemed to be equally responsible in principle, in practice the institution recognises that symbolic control is held by the British staff: whatever has happened an overseas nurse cannot be at fault because they were not in true positions of responsibility.

Symbolic power requires, as a condition of its success, that those subjected to it believe in the legitimacy of power and the legitimacy of those who wield it. This seems to be the attitude of the overseas staff on our courses. Asked about their plans for the future many overseas nurses we worked with in 1999–2001 said they did not want to develop a career in the NHS. Effectively they recognised that their status as immigrant workers in the institutional hierarchy would make this difficult. However, after four years when residency rights allow applications for citizenship many of these same nurses transformed their positions by being taking British citizenship and by publicly joining the 'elite' their career aspirations were legitimised. They were now enabled to assume the dominant roles in their workplaces, and become mentors and managers themselves, because the discipline of the institution permitted it.

Conclusion: Creating Space in the Multi-ethnic Workplace

As described in the introduction, the notion of 'core competencies' in UK nurse induction prescribes a finite list of discrete skills which can be assessed objectively by a peer. The nurse who has a portfolio of (largely written) evidence, gathered under supervision, is 'fit to practice'.[4] Managers with funding decision responsibilities categorise teaching and learning activities as training or continuous professional development. NHS hospitals make training needs assessments, often have a training room and teachers are called trainers. Commissioners of training are ordering suppliers of training and expecting to measure numbers of attendees. This commodification of workplace learning into discrete training units which can be criterion referenced and objectively assessed is an accounting exercise to produce statistical data to place against spending targets. The cost-effectiveness of this programme is in its impact on reducing the supervised weeks between induction and registration (when the staff are treated as supernumerary and therefore an additional cost) and the long-term retention of staff. In 2003, an independent report on workforce planning commissioned by the Director of Nursing at the Oxford Radcliffe Hospitals Trust concluded that retention of international nurses at the end of their first contract was improved as a direct result of this adaptation programme.

However, the aims of intercultural skills training and intercultural communication skills training are holistic and seek to bring about a change in the relationship and ethos of the working relationships and the political context in which these are forged. The educational impact of the programme is therefore not confined to individual summative assessment. In Feng's chapter (this volume), he discusses the creating of a third space in which intercultural imagining and understanding can take place. One of the most important outcomes of this programme is the way in which the physical presence of the key tools, the books: My Personal Lexicon and PIN, legitimised discuss of the intercultural learning process with colleagues and managers in two spheres. Socially, the real time use of the two notebooks offers opportunities for informal conversation. Pedagogically, the presence of the ethnographic record encourages asynchronous sharing of critical incidents with mentors. The third space might be realised in the establishment of a learning ethos in the professional workplace over the 12-week programme that empowers all staff to participate in intercultural dialogue.

However, the overall effectiveness of the programme varies with the ethos of each clinical setting. Staff in different units in a hospital experience the programme in different ways. Although all students can complete the formal tasks, the quality of intercultural learning is affected by staff interpersonal relationships and how much time and resource is allocated by the managers to these tasks. Where managers are indifferent to or dismissive of the intercultural skills programme, the international nurses find it difficult to integrate the programme as part of their working lives. We found that where managers attend the complementary training offered, the workplace normally becomes a positive learning space. Mutual commitment to improving the quality of the relationships in the workplace can bring about a third space for reflection and behavioural change.

Notes

1. The Equality Act (2006) is an Act of the Parliament of the United Kingdom covering the United Kingdom, and covers the following areas: the creation of the Commission on Equality and Human Rights (CEHR); the outlawing of discrimination on goods and services on the grounds of religion and belief (subject to certain exemptions); to the introduction of regulations outlawing discrimination on the ground of sexual orientation in goods and services in both Great Britain and Northern Ireland (the Sexual Orientation Regulations

2006) and a provision relating to the creation of a public duty to promote equality on the ground of gender.

2. Medical anthropologists study cultural differences in health beliefs and the relationship between health practitioners and their patients across cultures. For an introduction see Helman (1990).

3. To standardise the initial language support for international nurses across the country in 2005, the UK government (through the Department of Education and Skills) provided teachers of Skills for Life with six modules of teaching materials for a course entitled Effective Communication for International Nurses. The module titles were Admitting Patients, Planning Patient Care, Implementing Care, Planning for Discharge, Communicating at Work and Making the Most of your Placement. This gives some idea of the scope of the taught curricula. A copy can be obtained from www.lsc.gov.uk quoting ISBN 184478469X.

4. For more details on the vocational requirements for nurse registration in the United Kingdom please refer to the Nursing and Midwifery council website http://www.nmc-uk.org/.

Acknowledgement

Thanks to Mark Bartram for first articulating and identifying these stages.

References

Agar, M. (1980) *The Professional Stranger*. New York: Academic Press.
Beck, A.T. (1975) *Cognitive Therapy and the Emotional Disorders*. Madison: International Universities Press Inc.
Bourdieu, P. (1977) The economics of linguistic exchanges. *Social Science Information* 16 (6), 645–648.
Bourdieu, P. (1982) *Language and Symbolic Power*. Cambridge: Polity Press.
Byram, M. (1997) *Teaching and Assessing Intercultural Communicative Competence*. Clevedon: Multilingual Matters.
Byram, M. and Fleming, M. (eds) (1998) *Language Learning in Intercultural Perspective: Approaches through Drama and Ethnography*. Cambridge: Cambridge University Press.
Byram, M., Nichols, A. and Stevens, D. (eds) (2001) *Developing Intercultural Competence in Practice*. Clevedon: Multilingual Matters.
D'Andrade, R. (1995) *The Development of Cognitive Anthropology*. Cambridge: Cambridge University Press.
Goffman, E. (1967) *Interaction Ritual: Essays on Face to Face Behaviour*. New York: Garden City.
Hammersley, M. and Atkinson, P. (1995) *Ethnography: Principles in Practice*. London: Routledge.
Helman, C.G. (1990) *Culture, Health and Illness: An Introduction for Health Professionals* (2nd edn). London: Wright, a division of Butterworth-Heinemann.
Holland, D. and Quinn, N. (eds) (1987) *Cultural Models in Language and Thought*. Cambridge: Cambridge University Press.

Norton, B. (2000) *Identity and Language Learning: Gender Ethnicity and Educational Change*. Harlow: Pearson Education Limited.
O'Grady, C. and Millen, M. (1994) *Finding Common Ground: Cross-cultural Communication Strategies for Job Seekers*. Sydney: Maquarie University.
Sarangi, S. and Roberts, C. (eds) (1999) *Talk, Work and Institutional Order: Discourse in Medical, Mediation and Management Settings*. New York: Mouton de Gruyter.
Woodward, T. (1991) *Models and Metaphors in Language Teacher Training*. Cambridge: Cambridge University Press.
Wringe, C. (1991) Education, schooling and the world of work. In D. Corson (ed.) *Education for Work: Background to Policy and Curriculum*. Clevedon: Multilingual Matters.

Appendix 1

Working Alongside International Staff: Intercultural Skills Short Course

Introduction to Working Alongside International Staff (Handbook 2005)

To manage today's diverse workforce you need a range of professional communication skills and management techniques which take into account the reality of dealing with people from a wide variety of backgrounds. The dynamics of people working together are influenced by factors including thier age, gender, ethnicity and educational background. Information and workplace processes can be subject to multiple interpretations through these cultural filters. So how can you motivate people to work as a team?

Someone's natural way of interacting with other people is determined by their personality, upbringing and beliefs – in other words, their culture. This perspective in turn determines whether decisions at work, such as in the course of recruitment, induction and appraisal, are culturally safe, that is, not based on ethnocentric beliefs. It is possible to learn strategies to modify your behaviour so you can become more flexible in your responses, better able to understand other ways of seeing the world and more adept at dealing with mis-communication in the workplace. You can learn how to maintain working relationships across cultural boundaries and how to counter (often unintentional) discrimination in order to develop a successful team.

At the heart of team-building is communication. Not the one way communication of instructions and orders but the reality of messy, negotiable communication with a feedback loop which means you can find out if what you said was in fact heard and whether you both understood what was intended. Without the feedback loop your intended message might be just whistling in the wind! Knowing how to deliver instructions which are understood is safer for you and your client, whilst managing relationships within your team is not just sociable but essential to the positive morale of the workforce, to enhanced productivity and to reducing absenteeism.

During the workshop you can focus on the realities of cultural diversity, raise your cultural awareness and identify more flexible and tolerant work practices and to boost the morale and performance of a multicultural workforce.

Working Alongside International Staff Outline Syllabus

Unit	Topic	Aim	Page	√
1	International recruitment – impact on the service	Explain why international recruitment fulfils organisational and departmental aims	5	
2	Roles: practice supervisor, mentor, manager	Explore the nature and extent of responsibilities of the team to the new member of staff	6	
3	Cultural maps and the construction of professional identity	Explain how the concept of a 'cultural map' can be used to describe patterns of expectations and communicate professional behaviour	7	
4	Cultural and linguistic filters to communication	Explain how experience is filtered through culture and language and engage in clarification strategies for positive relationships	8	
5	International staff in the workplace: patients	Reflect on and describe the impact of international staff on client expectations and rapport-building	10	
6	International staff in the workplace: teams	Reflect on and describe the impact of cultural diversity on team working in the workplace	14	
7	Stages of adaptation and acculturation	Engage with the psychological needs of international staff affected by culture shock and homesickness	19	

Unit	Topic	Aim	Page	√
8	The timescale and stages of cultural adaptation and learning needs	Demonstrate strategies for structuring the stages to independence and autonomy	21	
9	Effective feedback in practice	Demonstrate the use of the feedback loop in communication	22	
10	Productive feedback	Discriminate between observational and interpretative description	23	
11	Helping with pronunciation	Understand the concept of 'comfortable intelligibility'	27	
12	Helping with vocabulary building around colloquial language use	Learn about and demonstrate support for the tool: My Personal Lexicon	28	
13	Helping with English language learning in the workplace	Identify different types of language error and communication error and demonstrate correction techniques	30	
14	Problem solving through reflection	Learn about and demonstrate engagement with the tool: My Professional Identity Notebook	32	
15	I and T communication as performance indicators	Identify interactional and transactional communication to assess performance	34	
16	'Face' issues in the workplace	Demonstrate how the concepts of face impact on self-esteem and professional development	35	

Chapter 10

The Pragmatics of Intercultural Competence in Education and Training: A Cross-national Experiment on 'Diversity Management'

MANUELA GUILHERME, EVELYNE GLASER and
MARÍA DEL CARMEN MENDEZ GARCIA

Intercultural competence has been defined, in general terms, as 'the ability to interact effectively with people from cultures that we recognise as being different from our own' (Guilherme, 2000: 297). However, the qualifying term 'effectively' may point in very different directions, where the use of the term 'competence', the goal itself, is more controversial. The author attempts a general definition – 'interacting effectively across cultures means accomplishing a negotiation between people based on both culture-specific and culture-general features that is on the whole respectful and favourable to each'– that manages to avoid problems at the source, by embracing all possible moderate approaches, but it does not exclude potential conflict between colliding interests at the moment of application. Several authors have recently been focusing on the possible meanings of the notion 'competence', either attempting to narrow or to broaden its scope. Furthermore, 'it is wrong to assume that competence statements are objective, neutral and devoid of values but their value may well lie in bringing those considerations to the fore and render them open to debate', which does not necessarily hinder our work on it since 'the evolution of competence frameworks has the potential to pose questions about the purpose of knowledge and how it contributes to the good of society and the individual' (Fleming, 2007).

The term 'competence' was brought into education through vocational education and the emphasis on skills and behaviours rather than content knowledge was made a priority. However, the term, which initially focused on the pragmatics of professional training, has acquired a broader scope in international guidelines for school and professional education, coming to include 'a combination of knowledge, skills, attitudes, values and behaviours' (Council of Europe, 2005, CoE), along the same lines as the Programme for International Student Assessment (PISA) (OECD) and the Definition and Selection of Key Competences (DeSeCo) project (OECD), which singles out the 'ability to interact in heterogeneous groups' from its three key competencies. The latter, the DeSeCo Project, aimed to define and select 'individually based key competences in a lifelong learning perspective' (Rychen & Salganik, 2003: 2). While identifying some 'key competences', the project aimed to be a 'criticism of an overemphasis on knowledge in general education and specialization in vocational education' (Salganik & Stephens, 2003: 19). Furthermore, the DeSeCo Project underlines the need for respect and appreciation of the 'values, beliefs, cultures and histories of others', within the sub-category 'the ability to relate well to others' focuses on 'personal relationships', and reports that the recognition and valuing of diversity is also mentioned in the DeSeCo country reports (Rychen, 2003: 87). However, 'intercultural competence' is also understood here as principally and closely linked with a psychological readiness and preparation to be empathetic and to control one's emotions, that is, to be patient and tolerant with the other without, in our understanding, necessarily being prepared to work in ethnically heterogeneous groups and, therefore, to create a different work dynamics based on a new professional culture negotiated on equal terms within the multicultural group/team. Following Fleming's understanding of Wittgenstein, that 'we do not have to look inwards in order to find appropriate explanations of art, aesthetic experience and meaning but outwards into the cultural contexts in which we operate' (Fleming, 2003: 100), we look mainly into group dynamics and, therefore, at individuals in interaction, for appropriate explanations of the intercultural experience.

This was precisely the aim of the ICOPROMO project (2003–2006), which was funded by the Leonardo da Vinci Programme and supported by the European Centre of Modern Languages, Council of Europe (2004–2007). The project members attempted to define intercultural competence for professional mobility, firstly, by analysing existing models and by proposing their team models as well as a whole project model and, finally, by developing materials aimed at professional education in the field, while attempting to articulate the ideas collected and put forward with the target groups in each context (www.ces.uc.pt/icopromo). The project work plan moved beyond individually based competencies to focus on the interaction between individuals within a multicultural group who had a professional task to carry out through team-based communication and interaction. In addition to this, it aimed to explore the common ground between citizenship education and professional education.

The ICOPROMO project also targeted mobility as a key concept that was defined, both in real and symbolic terms, as the process of entering new ethnic cultures, either abroad or at home, in person or virtually. The project identified eight main thematic areas, with varying degrees of generality, namely 'Diversity Management', 'Intercultural Interaction', 'Biography', 'Ethnography', 'Emotion Management', 'Communicative Interaction', 'Intercultural Responsibility' and 'Working in Multicultural Teams'. Here we will only focus on a small number of activities developed within the first topic. Furthermore, mobility was not only understood as a physical geographical move, but also in the sense of 'competence as a guiding framework for career development and human resource management' (Salganik & Stephens, 2003: 24). This would reinforce the perception, developed in this project, of citizenship education as being linked to professional education since mobility, in its broadest sense, is not, in our understanding, meant to be exclusive to professional or social elites.

There is a need, in Europe, for a workforce that is prepared to identify and develop synergies that originate in the diversity of perspectives and types of interaction rooted in different cultural assumptions, values and attitudes. Furthermore, most models that are applied worldwide for the development of intercultural competencies in professional training refer, to a large extent, to North American contexts or to global business. There are, in fact, few studies in this area that focus on European cross-cultural professional relationships (e.g. Geoffroy, 2001). The ICOPROMO project aimed to contribute to the process of erecting a Europe of knowledge, but one whose knowledge is heterogeneous, interactive and promotes the validation of different intra- and international representations in the public arena. Our societies are going through a transformation process towards new forms of politics, social life and economy. This transformation includes a trend towards globalisation and internationalisation, as well as the development of network structures. This process can be characterised as a move from a more static-functional orientation of organisations and institutions towards a more dynamic procedural orientation (Castells, 2000). Employees are increasingly faced with inter*cultural* (not necessarily only inter*national*) encounters in their professional contexts. They have, therefore, to establish *active* communication with their colleagues, either at a higher level or at a subordinate level of the hierarchical ladder, or with their interlocutor in any professional situation. The ICOPROMO project brought together academics with different experiences of and perspectives on this subject (vocational education, academic approach, pre- and in-teacher training, pre- and in-service professional training, etc.) who built on their more promising and fruitful ideas and concepts in order to create comprehensive and integrated models in which they drew on their previous experiences, although they could be different and sometimes hard to reconcile. The ICOPROMO project also established a dialogue between academic institutions (universities, research centres/researchers, teachers and students) and professional training organisations, as well as communities of employers and employees, at the trans- and intranational level.

Diversity Management: Introduction

Within this topic, power relations arising, explicitly or implicitly, from different categories (pre-conceptions, prejudice, hierarchies, generalisations, stereotypes, etc.) were the main contribution to the whole framework of the project topics. Some of the themes dealt with in the activities could certainly be included in some of the other topics developed by the project members, but, the approach and perspective adopted here definitely had a greater focus on power relations.

In this chapter, we will illustrate the three main steps followed during the project, from the design to the evaluation of the activities: (1) conceptualisation and design by team members; (2) evaluation by consultants; (3) testing with target groups.

Selected Activities: Conceptualisation and Design

Diversity quiz

This activity attempts to promote discussion of the term 'diversity', to define this notion and its scope, as well as to identify the possible categories it may encompass by getting the target groups to reflect upon its meanings. The participants are given a 'Diversity Quiz' and are asked to answer the questions. Afterwards, these are discussed in groups and, finally, participants examine a flowchart and fill in a table. Moreover, the participants are encouraged to provide reasons for their opinions and choices and it is their task to find as many sub-categories of 'diversity' as possible. The Quiz includes questions of this sort: (1) What was your most memorable encounter with someone from another culture/race like? (4) Describe something about yourself that no-one can tell merely by looking at you. Some of the most provocative categories suggested for discussion were 'race', 'religion' and 'sexual orientation', bearing in mind that the project focused on intercultural interaction within multicultural teams in professional settings.

DIVERSITY QUIZ

1. What was your most memorable encounter with someone from another culture/race?
2. Describe a time when you experienced prejudice or discrimination.
3. Can you think of a commonly held stereotype you have of someone from a background other than your own with whom you have worked/often been in touch?
4. Describe something about yourself that no-one can tell merely by looking at you.
5. Does diversity exclude you?
6. How important do you think diversity management is in the workplace? Is it just another fad?
7. What specific aspects do you believe diversity affects?

Who is talking funny?

The focus of this activity is on the different status, often left implicit, given to different linguistic performances and it is meant to encourage participants to recognise and discuss prejudice that is often avoided because it causes social discomfort. The critical incident provided involves a situation where a German colleague, working in a European group, has an English accent that sounds a bit strange, even for a non-native speaker. After considering and discussing the spoken or unspoken responses of the other individuals before and after they are told that her accent is Kenyan, the discussion then focuses on prejudice against different accents and its consequences in the workplace and for public figures, for example politicians (activity published in Glaser *et al.*, 2007).

Culture and power

This activity tries to broach situations where events can take an unexpected course. Participants were again given a scenario and asked to consider which decisions to make and how best to be alert to less evident signs, which are more likely to occur in unknown settings where the cognitive logic or the rules of performance are not always easily perceived or, often, even out in the open. The given situation revolves around the new job taken up by an experienced CEO in a fictitious country and how she views the upcoming challenges, how the actual ensuing events catch her by surprise and how she manages to resolve the consequences and the power relations that emerge as the situation develops.

Strategies and Methodologies

Maria is a 50-year-old woman from *Polomo*, a country in the western corner of Europe which joined the European Union quite some time ago. She is very experienced in top management posts. She has just got a new job in *Ostopedia*, a country in the further end of south eastern Europe bordering on Asia not far from northern Africa which has just joined the European Union. Her company, a heavy metal compound producer named *Virola S.A.*, has bought a similar business there and Maria was appointed to run it. She has never been to Ostopedia. She is going to work in *Zotia*, its capital.

All the education and training activities developed in the course of the ICOPROMO project target adult learners who either already find themselves in professional settings or who are about to start a professional career. The overall intention of the training activities is to facilitate work in multicultural teams. Hence, it was important to take into account pedagogical considerations based on theories of learning that concern our specific target groups. As the term Diversity Management is used in many different contexts, we felt that it was necessary to start by creating a common understanding of this concept in the training group (which should ideally be a multicultural team). One activity designed for this purpose was the first of the three selected here, the *Diversity Quiz*. After a brief introduction to the topic, the facilitator encourages the participants, in a first step, to reflect on questions that are quite personal and specific, such as 'When you think about the term "diversity", do you only think about "other people", or do you include yourself'? The participants then share their reflections with a partner in the training group. The most interesting aspects of these discussions are then shared with the whole group. Reflection and dialogue therefore take the lead here and a combination of individual and group work is then the methodological option as far as training management strategies are concerned. The most relevant question here for achieving a common understanding of the complex issues related to diversity is 'What specific factors do you believe create diversity'? Which characteristics make a 'work environment "diverse"'? The ensuing discussion pertains to aspects such as age, ethnicity/culture, race, religion, sexual orientation and gender. In groups, the participants then consider how these aspects may influence relationships in the workplace and to what extent they may lead to conflicts. Diversity categories are singled out here, as well as their corresponding sub-categories, and the possible ways in which they can generate and be impacted by power relations are subsequently explored.

Although we did not purposefully build on any specific learning theory, the activities under review share a number of common features that may be traced back to concepts found in such theories. Thus, a basic principle reflected in the activities designed to deal with issues of 'Diversity Management' was first and foremost Freire's conviction that the teacher should not act on the students but rather that teachers and students should work with each other while sharing their own experiences and knowledge. According to Freire's maxim, all participants in the teaching/learning process are expected to both 'read the word and the world', adopting a critical approach to both (Freire, 1972). In this sense, the facilitators of our activities see themselves as a resource equal to the resources (knowledge and experience) contributed by the participants in the training. Ideally, the facilitator engages in a dialogue with the participants and thereby encourages them to reflect critically on their knowledge, experience and sociocultural context. Dialogue, in Freire's sense, is an important process that builds on mutual respect and results in informed action that fosters individual development and justice. Intercultural dialogue can therefore be engaged, but only from such a perspective. Freire is also deeply concerned with the idea of developing consciousness that has the power to transform reality. This aspect is particularly relevant for the issue of 'Diversity Management' that aims to reduce prejudice, discrimination and stereotyping in the workplace and, therefore, to change the current most frequent power relation framework.

The second activity selected above, *Who is talking funny*, deals with the status attributed to linguistic performance. Members of multinational/multicultural groups often unconsciously give a higher status to those whose linguistic performance corresponds to familiar and commonly accepted norms. In this activity, we try to make participants aware of the loaded aspects of pronunciation and of possible prejudice and negative stereotyping associated with linguistic performance that does not meet common or familiar standards. Participants read the description of a situation involving a speaker whose linguistic performance is different from that of the others. They are first requested to check their own response to such a situation and should then decide whether they feel that a different accent might possibly exclude someone from a (public) position of responsibility. The participants are then encouraged to take a mental step away from this fictitious situation to their own cultural/local environment and to consider the implications a local accent may have on a person's career. The main issue for them to consider is whether non-standard linguistic performance may give rise to public discrimination or whether this aspect of diversity is well tolerated in their own culture.

Our pedagogical approach in this activity is influenced by concepts of holistic and experiential learning. Holistic learning starts from the premise that the learner as an individual consists of many parts, specifically 'the intellect, emotions, the body impulse (or desire), intuition and imagination' (Laird, 1985: 121). All these elements must become active for learning to be effective. Experiential learning as opposed to cognitive learning (Rogers, 1969, 1983) addresses the needs of adult learners as it builds on the individual learners' previous experiences. As a result, the learners are personally involved in the learning process; they can make responsible contributions and are also able to evaluate their own learning. The effectiveness of activities, such as *Who's talking funny?* and *Diversity Quiz*, relies to a large extent on the participants' experience and on the reactions of people involved in such situations. The concept of experiential learning was further developed by Kolb (1984) who views learning as a cycle that includes four stages, that is, concrete experience, reflective observation, abstract conceptualisation and active experimentation. Kolb clearly points out that the learning cycle can begin at any of these stages and is also continuous in the sense that learners may repeat the learning cycle as many times as they need to. This also applies to our activities that, when used in different contexts and by different participants, may produce different results and hence different learning effects depending on the experiences or observations of the learners.

Finally, our pedagogical approach feeds on the ideas of transformative learning as defined by Mezirow. According to Mezirow (1991) adults learn by making sense of their experiences. Thus, 'disorienting dilemmas' are situations that do not fit our assumptions, become catalysts for critical reflection and can help us transform our behaviour, attitudes, opinions and beliefs. As a consequence, people become more aware, reflective, critical and open to the ideas of others by transforming their perspectives. The role of the educator is therefore to assist and support the learners in this reflection and transformation process. The activity *Culture and*

Power develops a scenario that can create such a 'disorienting dilemma' within the minds of the participants. By raising awareness of the hidden dimensions of power issues and their cultural specificities, learners are encouraged to challenge their own attitudes and to change their perspectives. In the scenario created for this activity, the participants have to put themselves in the position of an expatriate who has to select the members for a management team and who has to deal with the workers' representatives. In some business contexts, employees from wealthier parts of the world are often given more power in the company and more credit for their potential for high performance. This is particularly dangerous in an increasingly global environment where discrimination related to culture represents a major impediment to good and fruitful cooperation and will most likely result in conflict. The activity also encourages the participants to reflect on specific cultural habits, values and norms, with a particular focus on power relationships.

In all three activities discussed here, the role of the facilitator is merely that of a catalyst or a partner for dialogue. It is not our intention to make the facilitator come across as someone who has all the answers or all the solutions to the problems that may arise when dealing with diversity in the workplace. Instead, the facilitator should use a learner-centred approach and support cooperative learning and joint problem solving. It is of equally great importance to establish a learning environment that is conducive to open discussion and the sharing of experiences. Even though two of the activities begin with pair work and proceed with discussions in small groups of four, the overall size of the groups should not be larger than 25 to ensure that all participants have an opportunity to share their perspectives with the rest of the group. Likewise, it is essential that the participants are given enough time for the reflection and discussion processes, as learning can be severely hampered by cutting short discussions and dialogues. Finally, the learning atmosphere should foster trust among the participants, so that experiences and views can be shared freely during the training.

The Role of the Advisory Group: Evaluation of Selected Activities

The activities designed by the ICOPROMO Management and Development team were evaluated by an Advisory Group, made up of nine consultants recruited by our partners in Finland (International Management Education, IME), Austria (VAI-Siemens, Linz) and Portugal (CEFA, a national organisation for the in-service education of local council workers). These consultants were either professional educators who collaborated regularly with our partners or their own employees, who have a long experience of working with multicultural teams.

The data yielded by their very detailed reports showed that, as a whole, the consultants evaluated the activities designed for this topic, 'Diversity Management', quite favourably, acknowledging the importance of managing diversity in a multicultural work setting and giving credit to the material produced by the teams for exploring of this topic, particularly those activities that led trainees to reflect on real-life situations:

> To manage diversity individually or in a group is, perhaps, one of the most difficult tasks a professional working in a multicultural team has to face. Understanding and accepting 'the other' who is necessarily different from myself, and reaching compromise solutions (preferably avoiding conflicts) isn't an easy task and requires knowledge and skills. [...] The activities presented in this chapter are quite interesting, especially those that direct trainees towards real situations or those activities that involve situations that could happen to any member of a multicultural group.

However, regarding the presentation of the activities, one of the evaluators argued that the descriptions of how to implement the activities were too broad, leaving too much room for unplanned output. Therefore, suggestions for improvement included further guidelines and the specification of learning outcomes and conclusions.

Furthermore, and for purely pedagogical reasons, the predominant method used for the tasks was discussion. Therefore, on the one hand, two evaluators recommended a more experiential approach with, for example, additional activities involving role-playing, watching films or documentaries and brainstorming. On the other hand, a more substantial theoretical background was also requested by our consultants:

> More theoretical background would be helpful. More role-plays and experiential learning and exercises. The methodological approach needs to be reconsidered. Discussions predominate.

> In this case, pedagogic techniques like watching movies or documentaries, brainstorming or role-playing are particularly recommended.

Having produced a first module and having had it evaluated by our consultants, when we produced the second and final module on each topic, the teams took into consideration the comments and suggestions that had been provided. As a result, the general comments about the second set of activities produced under this topic was more positive as we managed to put into practice many of the suggestions put forward by the evaluators, for example, by adopting a more real-life approach, covering a wider variety of themes, paying greater attention to both written and spoken media and including recommended readings and links:

> Most themes are important. Some procedures appeal to life experiences or present real cases, which mobilizes the proposed competences and learning outcomes.

The weakest aspects of the activities produced under this topic seemed to be the stimulation of foreign language learning and, above all, the use of a variety of media. The strongest elements were the versatility of the activities (suitable for both monocultural and multicultural groups), their contribution to the project goals and to the development of intercultural responsibility and the incorporation of a multidimensional perspective on the topic.

Our Target Groups' Voices: Testing the Selected Activities

The activities singled out here, as well as the other activities produced during the project and selected to be tested, were included in the testing workshops carried out in three of the four countries involved, both by their authors and by other project members.

In **Portugal**, workshops were carried out at the (a) Research Centre, for a wide public including postgraduate students and professionals related to the field in one way or another, from all over the country; (b) CEFA – Centro de Estudos Autárquicos, for professionals working with the local councils and who voluntarily enrolled in the workshops; (c) AFMP – a local non-governmental organisation carrying out projects mainly with Romani groups; (d) ACIDI – the High Commission for Immigration and Intercultural Dialogue, where participants were attending an intensive course in order to become certified trainers for this governmental organisation.

In **Spain**, the workshops were carried out at the University of Jaén and meant to target Tourism undergraduates but ended up expanding their scope to include individuals in other fields and levels (e.g. postgraduate students, teachers) and were very popular among foreign and national Erasmus students, that is, students who had either just arrived in Spain or were about to leave their home country.

In **Austria**, activities were tested with undergraduate business students at the Johannes Kepler University in Linz who were taking special programmes dealing specifically with intercultural communication at the

Johannes Kepler University in Linz. Some of the activities were also discussed with small groups of professionals at the VAI-Siemens Linz headquarters.

The Finnish members of the Advisory Group also tested some of the activities with managers from **Russia** and the **Baltic countries**.

The second activity described above – *Who is talking funny?* – was also used in a workshop, organised in order to test a number of ICOPROMO project activities, at the premises of the **European Centre of Modern Languages**, Council of Europe, in Graz. This three-day workshop was attended by 21 participants from 20 countries who were mainly intercultural communication educators in Departments of Modern Languages at European universities.

Diversity quiz

In **Portugal**, most trainees had an academic background in the social sciences. All had a higher education degree (university or polytechnic). The most widely represented academic fields were Social Work, followed by International Relations and, in equal proportions, Sociology, Law and Educational Science. Except for two unemployed trainees, all of the participants were working in local government institutions, such as the city council, either in Coimbra or in the surrounding areas. Participants found the warm-up activity particularly interesting. This involved individually answering a number of questions and then sharing and discussing these answers and insights with three other trainees (groups of four). Participants found the last question of the quiz, 'What specific factors do you believe create diversity? Which characteristics make a (work) environment "diverse"?', particularly helpful. However, participants found the chart they were requested to fill in, in the following step, rather difficult to complete. One of the participants explained: '"Ranking" the factors (Age, Ethnicity/Culture, Race, Aspects of Diversity, Religion, Gender and Sexual Orientation) proved to be impossible, because they depend on contexts'. However, although it was difficult to fit the factors found into only one category, filling in the chart also proved to be helpful and stimulating since it generated a discussion about the grouping and categorisation of the various factors of diversity.

Educators/trainers who carried out the workshops where this activity was tested suggested that having a concrete example, such as a critical incident, would give participants some practical support and would make their task clearer and, therefore, more feasible. The categories provided under the heading of 'aspects of diversity' in the chart are age, religion, ethnicity/culture, race, gender and sexual orientation. The workshop participants then had to place the 'factors of diversity' they had previously uncovered in the 'Diversity Quiz' under these headings. The discussion raised issues of power emerging from the day-to-day practice of working in heterogeneous teams, more specifically when this was stimulated in the last step of this activity where the participants were requested to 'consider how they [factors of diversity] could affect relations at the workplace'. However, some trainers found that the power issue was not explicitly raised in this activity and might not be raised by the group if the trainer was not prepared to lead the discussion in that direction.

In **Austria**, participants were mostly Austrian students, studying international business at the University, who had taken part in a student exchange programme and were taking a mandatory cultural re-entry course. The level of trust among the students had substantially increased by the time this activity was tested and, therefore, participants were ready to share very personal experiences with the group. The activity was found suitable for participants who have some international experience; otherwise, it might be difficult for them to relate to the questions. The facilitator should also ask the participants how they 'managed diversity'. Furthermore, they should be encouraged to provide examples about how diversity is handled in the organisation. What are the major issues? What type of diversity do they have to cope with – and why is it difficult?

Who is talking funny?

In **Portugal** (CEFA), trainees responded very positively to this activity. The topic was appealing for several reasons, one of them being the fact that many had had difficulties when using foreign languages abroad. It became apparent that, even though many trainees had had those difficulties, the activity touched on some more subtle aspects that many of them had never thought about. Furthermore, by giving some more examples based on personal experience, the trainer expanded on this activity in a way that made the group more conscious of the actual discrimination that happens based on different levels of linguistic competence/performance. It became clear that most of the individuals in the group had not been aware of the seriousness of the issue. Another interesting aspect is the fact that the topic also allows for reflection upon one's home culture. Discrimination based on pronunciation occurs just as much in monocultural teams, when one or more members happen to have strong local accents.

However, trainees were expecting 'formulas' for intercultural interaction and this was not really the aim of most of the activities produced under the scope of the ICOPROMO project. Some trainees admitted that they had been expecting some sort of guidelines on how to deal with people from different nationalities. During the course, they realised that such an expectation was unrealistic, which in itself was already an achievement. They clearly recognised the value of reflecting upon and discussing the topics presented in the activities. Many of the trainees had experience of working in multicultural environments, and had come to the course seeking help with problems they had encountered. As much as they ended up enjoying the discussions and the exchange of points of view, and despite expecting more in the way of 'tips and guidelines', they concluded that the activities used in the training would probably help them with the problems they had encountered, but not in the direct, palpable way they had hoped for. This also has to do with their professional background, since many of them were working with the Roma and other disadvantaged communities. The aspects that received the highest score were 'help reflect upon teamwork dynamics in multicultural teams' (which achieved a perfect 4, i.e. the highest score), 'encourage change of behaviour' and 'encourage exchange of information, experience and ideas', which the teams took as an achievement in itself.

In **Spain** (2005), this activity worked extremely well with 43 learners (mostly students of Tourism, some of English, Philology, Business, Engineering, Social Work and Law). The students became highly involved and participative, as many of the questions affected them directly: Spanish and Portuguese (both nationalities in the course) have clear cases of non-European performances; strong local accents were a reality among the Spanish Andalucian students, the southern Italian participants and the German learners from Saxony; the question of diction among public figures was quite familiar to the students. All these issues were thus extremely thought provoking and fostered intense and heated debate. It was encouraging to talk about non-standard pronunciations in English. The fact that different English accents (not only American, South African and Australian, but also Portuguese, Spanish, Italian and German) are perfectly acceptable and that we are increasingly moving towards what is termed 'international English' greatly motivated the learners. Furthermore, they ended up feeling proud of speaking English with an accent.

In **Austria**, this activity was tested (for only 15 minutes) as part of a 'cultural sensitivity training' for students from, all study areas who were about to leave the country (no longer than 15 minutes). The trainers did not distribute the handout because they thought it would not be very meaningful to Austrian native speakers. In fact, most students stated they would not say anything about the accent. However, in the discussion students admitted that there were 'good' and 'bad' accents, depending on where the speaker came from, but they would not feel comfortable discussing this issue with someone with a 'bad' accent. Educators/trainers concluded that they should not have limited it to accents but should have extended it to grammatical correctness (and register). Furthermore, this activity was used to introduce the issue of stereotyping.

At the **European Centre of Modern Languages**, in Graz, this activity generated some controversy among the 21 multinational participants in this workshop who discussed the effects of a non-standard accent in a team setting. The prejudice that an accent can evoke was the main subject of the discussion. Some participants felt that an accent or other paralinguistic features were irrelevant, whereas others emphasised the importance of unconscious or unspoken reservations about to such issues.

Conclusion

Education and training have been formally separated ever since the educational systems began to take form. This gap has widened in higher education, with the former focusing increasingly on the 'education of the mind', whereas the latter has been more devoted to some kind of 'control of performance'. However, attempts to articulate both approaches have become more and more frequent and the intercultural field, quite understandably due to its nature and recent development, has been no exception. One obvious example in this same publication series *Language for Intercultural Communication and Education* was the work, entitled *Intercultural Experience and Education*, developed by the same research group, which explored the role of 'intercultural experience "in" and "as" education', mainly in connection with foreign language education and focusing on 'a more specific kind of experience than that of primary and secondary socialisation'. However, while recognising the importance of experience '"in" and "as" education', the ICOPROMO project also shared the principle that experience nevertheless 'is not a sufficient, even though a necessary, condition for interculturality. There must also be reflection, analysis and action' (Alred *et al.*, 2003: 1–5). To combine both experience and reflection, the design of these materials, in the form of 'activities' (of which we have given three examples above), was carefully developed keeping in mind the theory that the teams' participants had been acquiring and producing, as well as using examples of real situations they had experienced, heard about or invented. While the 'activities' were being tested, the 'critical incidents' used were complemented by the workshop participants' interpretations, suggestions, their previous experiences and their creative performances when role-playing them. It was curious to note that those 'activities' which were more closely connected with real-life experiences were more prone to be judged by academic colleagues as lacking in authenticity, confirming that reality can sometimes surpass imagination. The frequent use of discussion of 'critical incidents' in the design of the modules as well as, cumulatively or not, of the 'role-play' technique proved to be successful, thus corroborating the belief that 'the use of more crafted, stylised, theatrical devices which come closer to exploring human situations more realistically and in depth' can help us 'enter a world which is [therefore] objectified and subject to scrutiny' (Fleming, 2003: 98).

The materials produced within this project were not designed for a very specific target group, the only requirement being that participants should have some kind of social science academic background and some level of experience working in multicultural groups. Therefore, it was necessary to design very flexible, although situated, materials that focused on a particular context, but that had an elasticity that would enable them to be used with different groups. In so doing, it was our understanding that we were developing a 'general intercultural competence', perceived in terms of personal development, but we were not trying to 'generalise' a 'culture-specific competence', which must be situated in contextual and temporal terms, and therefore were not trying to 'enforce narrow categories of competence', which are generally translated into 'formulas' that are limited-in-scope (Rathje, 2007: 257–258). By giving examples that might stimulate reflection on the motives and the meanderings of intercultural interaction, team members aimed to lead target groups to be acquainted with different situations that were likely to occur in similar circumstances and to prepare them to handle such situations. We therefore endorsed the perception of intercultural competence as 'the ability to bring about the missing normality and therefore create cohesion in the situation' (Rathje, 2007: 262), that is, being able to, as a work group or team, create a new community of practice, even if temporary. The creation of new communities of practice in professional settings, whose members temporarily work with each other and may not be sitting together, entails the sudden development, negotiated or not, of a set of values, rules, forms of communication and interaction, which last as long as that task is being carried out. However, regardless of the turbulence this may cause, the urgency of the work to be carried out in a very competitive and global context requires that routines are established on the spot, that is,

> Global companies are looking for geographically, culturally, temporarily remote workers who, none the less, know how to *work together* to generate new knowledge and accomplish routine work in a volatile

work environment-they need creative workers. They are, however, looking for divergent, dispersed, innovative, flexible and creative workers over whom they can, nevertheless, exert enough control. (Farrell, 2004: 486)

As paradoxical as this description may sound, it refers to a reality that concerns the balance, or rather unbalance, between education and training. Despite the fact that, as the same author concedes, 'the standardisation of textual practice [like memos and minutes] is seen as a way of creating a global community of practice, where it is practice that links the community rather than values, experiences or shared stories' (p. 490), it is not possible to give up our goal since, as the author also admits, 'the issue of *power*, and the way it is so routinely embedded in every day knowledge that it becomes invisible' is a major instrument of pressure (pp. 401–492). Therefore, having such a combination of power, practice and participants who no longer have long-term shared experiences, principles and goals, diversity management competence becomes an important asset for multicultural teams. Byram adds to this perspective by calling for the need to raise awareness of multicultural, cross-cultural and intercultural issues and, therefore, for formal education that requires more than mere training, since 'acting interculturally involves a level of analytical awareness that does not necessarily follow from being bicultural' (Byram, 2003: 64–65). In sum, managing diversity goes beyond experiencing diversity to managing the power relations that diversity categories bring about.

Acknowledgements

The development of this topic, 'Diversity Management', and therefore the activities examined above, within the ICOPROMO project, also involved the participation of Clara Keating (Senior Researcher) and Daniel Hoppe (Junior Researcher), Centro de Estudos Sociais, University of Coimbra, as well as the contribution of Vivien Burrows, University of York, in the editing of the final texts.

References

Alred, G., Byram, M. and Fleming, M. (2003) Introduction. In G. Alred, M. Byram and M. Fleming (eds) *Intercultural Experience and Education* (pp. 1–13). Clevedon: Multilingual Matters.

Byram, M. (2003) On being 'bicultural' and 'intercultural'. In G. Alred, M. Byram and M. Fleming (eds) *Intercultural Experience and Education* (pp. 50–66). Clevedon: Multilingual Matters.

Castells, M. (2000) *The Rise of the Network Society*. Oxford: Blackwell.
Council of Europe (2005) *The Competency Workbook*. Mobility and Competence Project (2001–2004). On WWW at https://wcd.coe.int/com.instranet.Instra Servlet?Command=com.instranet.CmdBlobGet&DocId=1155136&Sec Mode=1&Admin=0&Usage=2&InstranetImage=124228.
Farrell, L. (2004) Workplace education and corporate control in global networks of interaction. *Journal of Education and Work* 17 (4), 479–493.
Fleming, M. (2003) Intercultural experience and drama. In G. Alred, M. Byram and M. Fleming (eds) *Intercultural Experience and Education* (pp. 87–100). Clevedon: Multilingual Matters.
Fleming, M. (2007) The use and misuse of competence statements with particular reference to the teaching of literature. In *Towards a Common European Framework of Reference for Language(s) of School Education: Proceedings of a Conference*. Waldmar Martyniuk, Poland.
Freire, P. (1972) *Pedagogy of the Oppressed*. Harmondsworth: Penguin.
Geoffroy, C. (2001) *La Mésentente Cordiale: Voyage au Coeur de l'Espace Interculturel Franco-Anglais*. Paris: Editions Bernard Grasset/Le Monde de l'Éducation.
Glaser, E., Guilherme, M., Mendez-Garcia, M.C. and Mughan, T. (2007) *ICOPROMO: Intercultural Competence for Professional Mobility*. Graz/Strasbourg: European Centre for Modern Languages.
Guilherme, M. (2000) Intercultural competence. In M. Byram (ed.) *Routledge Encyclopaedia of Language Teaching and Learning* (pp. 297–300). London: Routledge.
Kolb, D.A. (1984) *Experiential Learning*. Englewood Cliffs, NJ: Prentice-Hall.
Laird, D. (1985) *Approaches to Training and Development*. Reading, MA: Addison-Wesley.
Mezirow, J. (1991) *Transformative Dimensions of Adult Learning*. San Francisco, CA: Jossey Bass.
Rathje, S. (2007) Intercultural competence: The status and future of a controversial concept. *Language and Intercultural Communication* 7 (4), 254–266.
Rogers, C. (1969) *Freedom to Learn*. Columbus, OH: Merrill.
Rogers, C. (1983) *Freedom to Learn for the 80's*. Columbus, OH: Merrill.
Rychen, D.S. (2003) Key competencies. In D.S. Rychen and L.H. Salganik (eds) *Key Competencies for a Successful Life and Well-Functioning Society* (pp. 63–107). Toronto: Hogrefe & Huber Publishers.
Rychen, D.S. and Salganik, L.H. (2003) Introduction. In D.S. Rychen and L.H. Salganik (eds) *Key Competencies for a Successful Life and Well-Functioning Society* (pp. 1–12). Toronto: Hogrefe & Huber Publishers.
Salganik, L.H. and Stephens, M. (2003) Competence priorities in policy and practice. In D.S. Rychen and L.H. Salganik (eds) *Key Competencies for a Successful Life and Well-Functioning Society* (pp. 13–40). Toronto: Hogrefe & Huber Publishers.
Tennant, M. (1997) *Psychology and Adult Learning* (2nd edn). London: Routledge.

Afterword
Education, Training
and Becoming Critical

MIKE BYRAM

This is the fourth book on interculturality from Durham. The first was focused above all on the teaching of foreign languages and has the title *Developing Intercultural Competence in Practice* (Byram *et al.*, 2001). It collected accounts by teachers of how they had taken theoretical work on intercultural competence as a basis for planning their practice.

The second book, *Intercultural Experience and Education* (Alred *et al.*, 2003), extended the discussion and analysis of interculturality and explored other areas of the curriculum – formal, hidden, internal to schools and universities but also in informal learning beyond classroom walls – to argue that intercultural experience may be present in many locations where education takes place.

In the third book (Alred *et al.*, 2006), the concept of 'intercultural citizen ship' was introduced and used as a starting point for analysing how education systems develop or hinder a perspective on citizenship which extends beyond the nation-state. The subtitle 'Concepts and Comparisons' was as important as the title *Education for Intercultural Citizenship*.

Our argument in the second book was that experience of interculturality – an encounter with otherness – does not necessarily lead to someone 'being intercultural'. There must be reflection, analysis and action, and educators of all kinds have a role to play in ensuring this takes place. Simultaneously, educators who engage with this role should not be simply 'adding on' an intercultural dimension to their work. Their work will, we hope, be transformed by an intercultural perspective.

Our third book dared to become a little more prescriptive and defined in a series of axioms (Alred *et al.*, 2006: 233–234) a progression from 'intercultural experience' to 'intercultural citizenship education'.[1] The first point on the continuum is 'intercultural experience' which 'takes place when people from different social groups with different cultures (values, beliefs and behaviours) meet'. One becomes intercultural only when that experience is subject to analysis and reflection which lead to action. At a third point on the continuum, action becomes social and political activity and is designated as 'intercultural citizenship experience' which can be distinguished from a fourth point when that experience and activity takes place in democratic modes and addresses the significance of making judgements on the basis of explicit values.

The importance of making judgements is the point I wish to take up in this Afterword, by linking it to the notion of 'criticality'.

In his programmatic monograph on higher education, Barnett (1997) argues that higher education should lead students through four levels of criticality in three domains. Criticality takes three forms: critical reason, critical self-reflection and critical action. At the highest level of criticality students should critique the knowledge they are acquiring, become involved in a process of reflection on self, in a process of reconstruction of self, and become engaged through critique in action 'in a collective recon-struction of the world'.

These are extreme demands on higher education which he calls 'trans-formatory critique' and other kinds of criticality – acquiring critical skills, reflexivity for example – are perhaps more easily attainable.

What is important for us at this point is that 'criticality' can be defined and described, and has been found to be present in higher education in empirical studies (Soton website: www.critical.soton.ac.uk; Yamada, 2008). But it is not only in higher education that criticality can be found, as arti-cles in our first book show. For in those articles, in some cases deliberately based on a model of intercultural competence which includes the notion of 'critical cultural awareness' (Byram, 1997), teachers demonstrated how their learners in secondary schools can become reflexive and critique the knowledge and society by which they are surrounded.

Like Barnett's work, our third book on 'intercultural citizenship', had a programmatic character, whereas in this current book we have sought out authors who describe and analyse the teaching and learning they plan and experience irrespective of whether they call it 'education' or 'training'. In the introduction, Fleming has shown how both concepts are important in the characterisation of the processes our authors have described. Now, at the end, we need to ask whether the concept of 'criticality' is useful in the characterisation of the practices described, and this brings us back to the programmatic. It would be possible in principle to evaluate the teaching and learning – formal and informal – described in the preceding chapters according to criteria of acquisition of knowledge and skills, but by evaluating whether they have acquired an attitude of critique which leads them to challenge the knowledge and social practices in their environment, as well as reflecting critically on their own self-understanding.

However, external evaluation of these matters is likely to be difficult, and self-evaluation is more productive. Teachers/trainers can then ask themselves if and to what extent their purposes included the encouragement of some level of criticality in some domains of learning, and then analyse their success in realising their purposes. To take two examples, it is clear from Gavin Jack's chapter that his purposes included incitement to criticality in his students, whereas Barry Tomalin did not, and each would evaluate their success accordingly.

In fine, authors must be left to decide on their purposes – as must those who take inspiration from these pages in designing their own teaching and learning – but to complete the circle back to our earlier books, 'critical cultural awareness' and the critical stance of intercultural citizenship strongly suggest that criticality should be a crucial element of all intercultural training and education.

Note

1. Some of these ideas have also been taken up in Byram, 2008.

References

Alred, G., Byram, M. and Fleming, M. (eds) (2003) *Intercultural Experience and Education*. Clevedon: Multilingual Matters.
Alred, G., Byram, M. and Fleming, M. (eds) (2006) *Education for Intercultural Citizenship: Concepts and Comparisons*. Clevedon: Multilingual Matters.
Barnett, R. (1997) *Higher Education: A Critical Business*. Buckingham: Open University Press.
Byram, M. (2008) *From Foreign Language Education to Education for Intercultural Citizenship*. Clevedon: Multilingual Matters.
Byram, M., Nichols, A. and Stevens, D. (eds) (2001) *Developing Intercultural Competence in Practice*. Clevedon: Multilingual Matters.
Yamada, E. (2008) Fostering criticality in a beginners' Japanese language course. A case study in a UK Higher Education Modern Language Degree Programme. Unpublished PhD thesis, University of Durham.

Index